THE GOTHAM LIBRARY
OF THE NEW YORK UNIVERSITY PRESS

The Gotham Library is a series of original works and critical studies published in paperback primarily for student use. The Gotham hardcover edition is primarily for use by libraries and the general reader. Devoted to significant works and major authors and to literary topics of enduring importance, Gotham Library texts offer the best in literature and criticism.

Comparative and Foreign Language Literature:
Robert J. Clements, Editor
Comparative and English Language Literature:
James W. Tuttleton, Editor

Edward Dahlberg, 1969. (Courtesy of Bernard Gotfryd.)
"'The Heroic orbit' is closed to him because of the wild physical fact of his half-sight half vision."

John Cech

The Wages of Expectation:

A Biography of Edward Dahlberg

Charles DeFanti

New York · New York University Press · 1978

Copyright © 1978 by New York University

Library of Congress Cataloging in Publication Data

DeFanti, Charles, 1942-
  The wages of expectation.

  (The Gotham Library of the New York University Press)
  Includes bibliographical references and index.
  1. Dahlberg, Edward, 1900-1977—Bibliography. 2. Authors,
American—20th century—Biography. I. Title.
PS3507.A33Z63   818.5'2'09   [B]   77-94390
ISBN 0-8147-1763-2
ISBN 0-8147-1764-0 pbk.

Manufactured in the United States of America

PERMISSIONS

Quotations from *Alms For Oblivion,* © 1964, The University of Minnesota Press. Reprinted by permission of The University of Minnesota Press.

Quotations from *Because I Was Flesh,* © 1963, Edward Dahlberg. Reprinted by permission of New Directions Publishing Corporation.

Quotations from *Can These Bones Live,* © 1941, 1960, Edward Dahlberg. Reprinted by permission of the New Directions Publishing Corporation.

Quotations from *The Edward Dahlberg Reader,* © 1967 by New Directions Publishing Corporation. Reprinted by permission of the New Directions Publishing Corporation.

Quotations from *The Flea of Sodom,* All Rights Reserved by New Directions Publishing Corporation. Reprinted by permission of the New Directions Publishing Corporation.

Quotations from *Bottom Dogs,* © 1930, 1961 by Edward Dahlberg. Reprinted by permission of City Lights Books.

Excerpts from *The Sorrows of Priapus,* © 1956 by New Directions; copyright 1968, 1972 by Edward Dahlberg. Reprinted by permission of Harcourt Brace Jovanovich, Inc.

Quotations from *Truth is More Sacred,* by permission of the publisher, Horizon Press, © 1961 by Edward Dahlberg.

Quotations from *Reasons of the Heart,* by permission of the publisher, Horizon Press, © 1965 by Edward Dahlberg.

Quotations from *Epitaphs of Our Times,* © 1967 by Edward Dahlberg. Reprinted by permission of the publisher, George Braziller, Inc.

v

TO LENI
WHO SAW ME THROUGH

Contents

List of Illustrations

Preface

Never one of the world's most pliable personalities, Edward Dahlberg sensibly surrounded himself with a constellation of uncommonly generous and sensitive people, whose eagerness to assist me made this project possible.

Mrs. Julia Dahlberg deserves my deepest gratitude, not only for supplying me with priceless information about her husband's life, but for keeping him alive with her love and ministrations. I am sure that her support alone made it possible for me to know him.

Rlene Dahlberg graciously made available her recollections, her personal papers, and her vast circle of friends, thus making possible the very core of this book. Our summer at Ca'n Peretons on Mallorca stands as a high point in my life. I thank her especially for allowing me to meet Edward Dahlberg's brother, Michael Sands, his dear wife Minnie, and their sons. Their indispensable recollections are major ingredients in my story.

Coburn Britton deftly cleared away the debris of my first muddled encounter with Dahlberg and tutored me in the methods of weathering Edward's moods. Without Coburn's directions, I might never have survived as Edward's friend as long as I did.

Harold Billings, Edward's champion and bibliographer, was unfailingly generous with information he has painstakingly gathered. His beautiful letters encouraged me and his splendid assessments of Edward's character and work inform many passages in this work.

Professor Edwin H. Miller of New York University stood by me and advised me while I overcame awesome problems of style and organization in this project. His suggestions spirited me through in a fraction of the time I would otherwise have required.

John Cech and I became the closest of friends as we eagerly exchanged data and encouragement about our complementary projects. I am looking forward to the publication of his splendid study of the friendship between Charles Olson and Dahlberg.

To my old friend and colleague, Bernard Weinstein, I owe a lasting debt for having steered me to my earliest contacts with Dahlberg's circle. His many suggestions over the years added untold substance to this book. My friend, William O'Rourke, shared his brilliant insights into prose with me and accompanied Edward through some of his most tortured moments.

Professor James Tuttleton and John Kuehl spent many hours with my manuscript and offered much valuable advice, all of which I accepted. I am also grateful to Mr. Richard J. Schaubeck, Jr., of the Fales Library of New York University for permission to use material in the Division of Special Collections.

Other people, who gave unsparingly of their time and permitted me to interview them and correspond with them, included Wallace Anderson; Walter Arnold; Michael Blankfort; Warren Bower; Clara Breit; Dr. Isser Bobrove, Edward's most exceptional and poetic dentist; Garech Browne; Kenneth Burke; Terence Burns; George Butterick; Joseph A. Byrnes; my late teacher, Oscar Cargill; Mrs. Gladys Cargill; Eleanor Clark; Marvin Cohen; Max and Sarah Cohn; Mrs. Celia Conason; Robert Creeley; Gregório Durán-Tomas, who has traveled worldwide without leaving the island of Mallorca; Nick Ellison; James T. Farrell; Isabella Gardner; Lou Gilbert; Allen Ginsberg; Henry Goodman; Roger Goodman; Robert Goulet; Andrew Greenwald; Henry Hafer; Oscar Hechter; Granville Hicks; Sidney Hook; R. F. C. Hull; Anthony and Elaine Kerrigan; James Laughlin; Walter Lowenfels; Robert MacGregor; Jerre Mangione; Frank and Malachy Mc-

Court; Fred Martin; Paul and Nancy Metcalf; Herbert Miller; Professor Harry T. Moore; Professor Eric Mottram; Mrs. Kate Carla Nachtrieb; Emmanuel Navaretta; Alice Neel; Dorothy Norman; Joel Oppenheimer; Emil Palmer, whose charming and spirited recollections of the Jewish Orphan Home gave shape to much of my first chapter; Emmanuel P. Popolizio; Sylvia Porter; Benedict Read; Piers Paul Read; Kenneth Rexroth; Irving Rosenthal; Lorna Sacher; Dr. Arnold Schwab; Horace Schwartz; Edwin Seaver; Eleanor Siegel; Gilbert Sorrentino; Conrad S. Spohnholz; Dr. Joseph R. Starobin; Ruthven Todd; Lionel Trilling; John Unterrecker; Willis Wager; Theodore Wilentz; Jonathan Williams; and Professor George Woodcock.

My parents, Madeline and Charles DeFanti, deserve limitless praise for having encouraged and supported me and read my manuscripts. I delight in acknowledging also the many years of friendship and affection given me by Sylvia and Murray Fuhrman.

I wish this book to stand as a small memorial to my dearest friend, Willard Beecher, who provided me with the fortitude to complete this project and who taught me to celebrate the only life I'll ever have. The two grand old men in my life, Edward and Willard, could not have been further separated philosophically. I have felt profoundly alone since they both decided to leave me in the same year.

"The test of a man is his ability to remain my friend," Edward Dahlberg presumed, and all but a few had failed by the time I had met him. Since he was old during these years, my visits (which were often two a week) no longer turned into daylong marathons. Edward enjoyed frequent and lengthy telephone conversations, though. During the last evening we spent together, Edward had reluctantly agreed to address a City College graduate writing class in order to earn the money from one of his public service grants, which was taught by my friend Mark Mirsky. Familiar with Edward's acute sensitivity to even imaginary insults, I dreaded the one tactless or arrogant student question that could ruin the evening.

I had nothing to fear. To avoid the trappings of the "academic dump," we met in a student's apartment. All present had been carefully selected and coached and they were thrilled to be meeting the genius whom their teacher intensely admired. The students beamed as Mark rushed across the room and kissed Edward on both cheeks in the East European manner. Edward obviously needed this rush of adulation at this late point in his life. To my amazement, he accepted a glass of sangria and was soon holding forth to a group of admiring young women seated at his feet. As others were drawn into the group, their astonishment was palpable as Edward spun out the stinging archaic flourishes, conceits, and aphorisms that had become his trademark. There was no sign of the repetitiveness, fatigue, or irritability that I had come to expect in this man in his eighth decade. He even made a rare admission, as I brought him home by taxi—he had had a wonderful time. We embraced warmly, he thanked me repeatedly for my kindness in arranging the evening, and I left him feeling exhilarated. Three days later, my telephone rang at eight in the morning. Edward harangued me and cursed at me for one hour for not calling him, then slammed the receiver in my ear. I never heard from him again.

The Wages of Expectation

1.

Inceptions: 1900-1917

At the turn of the century on the Lower East Side of New York City, marital infidelity was perhaps the worst disaster that could befall a Jewish household. But when Elizabeth Simonowitz, née Dalberg, wronged her Polish immigrant husband, Harry, he brought more than traditional vengeance to bear upon her. He became convinced that she was pregnant by an itinerant barber named Saul Gottdank (as she indeed was), so he not only banished her from their household but announced that he would care only for the single son he was certain he had fathered. With the remaining two boys and the forthcoming bastard, she could do what she liked. And so, sometime in the winter of 1899-1900, Lizzie, herself an immigrant from Warsaw who spoke very poor English, deposited her two babies in orphanages. The older of these, named Michael, was then two-and-one-half years old. Now nearly eighty, he firmly retains his earliest memory: he is standing at a frosty window, with tears streaming down his face, probably at the Pleasantville Cottage Home for orphans at 150th Street and Broadway.[1]

Lizzie assumed her maiden name, made her way to Boston and,

on July 22, 1900, bore a son, Edward Dalberg, in a charity hospital. Gottdank was meanwhile occupied with his own family and his barbershop on Rivington Street, in the heart of the Jewish ghetto where he had met Lizzie. An immigrant from a small town in Austria, Gottdank had romantically pursued his migratory profession in Vienna during the reign of Franz Joseph. He had also spent much time in Berlin, and he never tired of repeating wondrous tales of bathing at Carlsbad, where waltzes were played until two in the morning. His passion for good food prompted him to become an excellent cook. But the lure of adventure and sumptuous living did not prevent him, while he was still a young and handsome man, from returning to his home town, marrying, and fathering three children. He seemed destined to be a respectable husband and father. Unfortunately, since no licenses were required at the time, anyone could work as a barber, so Gottdank soon found the trade overcrowded and the resulting poverty unbearable. To add to his misery, Austria's endless wars made it likely that he would be drafted at any moment. The Gottdanks made hasty plans to migrate to America, but Saul's wife lost her nerve and decided to wait until he had gotten situated. The poor woman discovered that she had made the worst mistake of her life by not accompanying him. By the time she arrived in America, her charming husband had evolved into a rake. At first she refused to live with him, but after a few months they were reconciled and another son was born. But the family could not be resuscitated: Gottdank continually craved, both then and later in life, numerous female companions. One of his mistresses was Lizzie Dalberg.[2]

The charms of this stumpy Polish peasant, who was no more than five feet tall,[3] are difficult to assess. Gottdank, like the many other men in her life, was never sufficiently taken with them to make them permanently his own, and even her son's idealized portrait of his mother in her prime is apologetic:

> A tintype taken of my mother in her early twenties showed a long oval face with burning brown eyes and hair of the same color. She did not have thick features, and her hands had the soul of the pentagram, which Plato considered the geometric

figure of goodness. There was much feeling in the appearance of her mouth, although most of her teeth had been removed by a quack dentist of Rivington Street in New York.[4]

Dahlberg intimates that Lizzie was always held in low esteem by men: her rich brother, Herman, in fact, brought her to New York after removing her from a convent where she had sought refuge from her mother, "to see whether he could peddle her flesh." Though only sixteen at the time, Lizzie resented her marriage of expediency with Simonowitz: She "would have preferred to make buttons than to lie in such an arid marriage bed."[5] She never succeeded in making a happy marriage, partly because of her notorious sloppiness, which grew worse as she grew older and which appalled everyone who knew her. Among the most distressed about her appearance was Dahlberg, who dwells on her poor hygiene in virtually every one of his six autobiographic works and in a letter to his brother, Michael Sands, in which he notes how frightening their mother was in her tatters.[6] In his second autobiographical novel, *From Flushing to Calvary*, Dahlberg described Lizzie somewhat advanced in years:

> Her thin dyed used-up carbonpaper hair was all tied up with petticoat rags. These curled her hair and gave it a dressy fluff which hid the barer parts. Her face, which she never washed till later, was thinly gauzed from a stale slept-in film.[7]

Thirty years later, in *Because I Was Flesh*, his sense of revulsion seemed equally strong:

> My mother's long nose sorely vexed me. I don't believe I ever forgave her for that, and when her hair grew perilously thin, showing the vulgar henna dye, I thought I was the unluckiest son in the world.[8]

Despite her frailties, Lizzie Dalberg was an aggressive, proud, and ambitious woman, who conveyed these qualities to her son. In many ways, she was the only person with whom he ever became intimate. With her smattering of "cultivated" German and her reverential, working-class (and, of course, Jewish) attitude toward learning, she instilled in him the idea that knowledge could be power:

> in some vague way she regarded a book as a demigod and she could not help having elevated emotions about a man who had both knowledge and money—a very weird and abnormal combination in this world.[9]

Although illegitimate, Dahlberg learned early to be proud of his surname, and the possible nobility attached to it.[11] There is a *Dalbergsstrasse* in Berlin, and numerous Dalberg families are to be found all over Europe.[10] Often Jews took the name of the province where they lived or of a local nobleman, but it was always tantalizing for Dahlberg to think that he might have been related to Lord Acton, two of whose four given names were Edward Dalberg.[12] Lizzie was also aware that she had numerous wealthy relatives in Europe, and on one occasion she tried to steer some of their riches toward herself.[13]

Early in 1901, before she had learned the barber's trade from Saul, Lizzie heard of the death of an extremely wealthy uncle in England. Although desperately poor, she somehow managed to get steerage fare for herself and her six-month-old son. But the trip was impetuous, and when they arrived in England Lizzie learned that all the uncle's money had been left to the church. She had no choice but to work as a parlor maid until she could afford the passage home.[14]

Back in New York, she found Saul on the verge of abandoning family life forever. He did so in 1903, when his oldest child was around five years old.[15] Utterly destitute, Lizzie seized the opportunity to join him in a flight to Dallas, but only after he had agreed to take little Edward. Saul opened a barbershop, the first one in Dallas to feature a lady "apprentice." Lizzie, who loved being the center of masculine attention, soon drew all the business: "A man would rather have her cut his throat than sit in Saul's chair." [16] Dahlberg was apparently not reluctant to share in his mother's newfound celebrity, since his first recollection was of "standing on a chair in my mother's barbershop in Dallas, Texas, singing to the cowboys." [17] He continued for the rest of his life to be fascinated by cowboys—by their superhuman manliness, their brutality, and their legendary freedom, which they seemingly enjoyed without responsibility. And Lizzie stood out poignantly in her son's earliest memory as the Delilah who cut the hair of these Samsons.

Lizzie and Saul were in no way equipped to sustain a cooperative business venture. She was far too susceptible to the blandishments of other men, while he craved variety and adventure which the drab Lizzie could hardly provide. When he began cheating on her, beating her, and robbing the till, she fled penniless to Memphis to earn a precarious living as a door-to-door peddler (always with her son in tow), a masseuse, and later as a quack physician who treated any and all ailments with a "violet ray lamp." She always seemed to gravitate toward shady activities, and among her most faithful clients were the myriad prostitutes in wide-open Memphis: "She learned that these ladies had a trade not too dissimilar from her own—they relieved the aches of men." [18]

The rapid turnover of men in Lizzie's life during these years encouraged her extremely perceptive and sensitive son to compare her with the "chippies" who constantly surrounded them. Moreover, at the turn of the century, lady barbers, like actresses, were viewed by the public as little more than prostitutes.[19] Dahlberg pointed out that the former, more often than not, supplemented their tonsorial incomes by servicing clients after hours.[20]

Lizzie was not destined to enjoy even this meager existence in peace. Saul, constantly penniless, relentlessly pursued her, fleeced her, and beat her until she fled, first to New Orleans; then to Louisville; and, finally, around 1905, to Kansas City, Missouri. There she and Edward settled on McGee Street and opened a shop, first on Walnut Street, and later at 16 East Eighth Street— the Star Lady Barbershop—under a railroad viaduct.[21] Lizzie quickly appraised the rough-hewn character of this cattle town and lost no time in routing her only competitor, another employer of lady barbers, by attracting both his trade and his employees away. This escapade necessitated her working eleven to twelve hours a day.[22]

Dahlberg gathered many impressions of Kansas City, which was still somewhat of a frontier town, and, while "not a senseless

Babel" like Memphis, it was far from genteel. Writing forty-five years later, he recalled:

> Dilapidated McGee was in the graveyard portion of the city, . . . but the latticed porches with the grass tangled around them were very pleasant on Indian summer nights, and men sat outdoors in their B.V.D.'s eating a half-pint of ice cream that cost five cents. . . . Kansas City was still an agrarian town which had little of the abstract and theoretical coldness that modern city-makers have who take the appelations of their avenues from the letters of the alphabet.[23]

Although Dahlberg later regarded Kansas City somewhat nostalgically, at five he had certainly come to regard his life and his surroundings as revolting. Having to share his mother's attention with countless men, he expressed his resentment by refusing to eat; by vomiting and by inexplicable neurasthenic attacks, depression, and talking to himself. She was simply perplexed by his behavior: "All that Lizzie could understand was that the child of her profligacy vomited and that he would grow up ugly." [24] Sometimes she beat him to stimulate his appetite, but this only compounded the problem and caused him to conjure up repellent fantasies: "Who can consider the carcasses he puts into his mouth? Filthy animals had wounded his childhood, and he would never be able to exorcise those abominable phantasms from his imagination." [25] Dahlberg rebelled against his mother in other ways. In one passage in *Bottom Dogs,* the author's earliest autobiographical work, the recalcitrant "Lorrie Lewis," who represents Dahlberg, manages to behave himself for a full week, "but after that he was worse than ever, and his mother shook her head, 'He's got one of his mean spells again!' " [26] Dahlberg, who forgot writing this episode, later contradicted it: "I don't think that's true. I was *never* good for a week. I came home often badly broken after brawls with Italian boys. They were all members of Mafia families." [27] Lizzie began to buckle under the pressure of her son's bad behavior. Perhaps impressed by Roman Catholic discipline which she had observed in the Polish convent, she decided to enroll her "adhesive child" [28] in a parochial school. This institution did not bring about the desired changes: "Lorry was very unhappy there; for the sisters who rustled through the halls were very aloof and distant, and the boys were bullies who belonged to gangs." [29]

In 1907, Lizzie apparently succumbed to the pressures of her son's delinquency, Saul's continuing harassment, the dishonesty of the wild lady barbers, and a quack abortion business she was running on the side. She suffered either a physical or an emotional breakdown. Dahlberg explained that, as the years wore on, surgery became "almost a pastime for her when she grew discouraged and felt that she had no future." [30] Again supposing that Catholicism might temper her son's nature, she sent him to a parish orphanage for the year it took her to recover.

Dahlberg's three poignant memories of his first stay in an orphanage confirmed his conviction of having had a "luckless" childhood. He was seven years old:

> [I remember] nothing, except a little boy and I were playing in a great pile of clinkers and we both stepped on a rusty nail. The nuns applied bacon to our wounds. But he, poor fellow, died of tetanus, and I, somehow or other, survived. I know this made a profound impression on me. I saw him in a casket. . . .
>
> All I know is that I was extremely lonely. . . . My mother finally came to see me I don't know how many months after I came there. . . . She brought peaches and I broke a tooth on the stone of a peach (fortunately, it was one of my first teeth). I wept: I wept because I was in the orphanage and I wept because I broke my tooth.
>
> [The Catholic orphans] beat me to pieces for being a Jew, [although] I was even more mortified than they were! [31]

Lizzie removed young Dahlberg from the orphanage in 1908, just as she was in the process of declining an army major's unexciting though secure proposal of marriage in order to marry an eccentric, vacillating character named Popkin. An aging and unsuccessful jeweler, Popkin managed to relieve Lizzie of all her savings, after which he abandoned her.[32] The marriage, which was probably illegal since Lizzie never divorced Simonowitz, lasted only a few months. Dahlberg seemed to understand his mother's inability (or unwillingness) to attract a trustworthy man: "Nobody can endure his own happiness. . . . Besides, what weakens human character so much as a long spasm of agreeable events?" [33]

When he returned to the streets of Kansas City, Dahlberg was a clumsy "momma's boy," as ill-equipped for the urban struggle for survival as when he left. The beatings by neighborhood Italian boys continued. At school he was baffled by arithmetic and manual tasks; and his handwriting, which remained unchanged throughout his life, never developed beyond a slow, palsied, backhanded form of printing. [34]

From 1909 to 1910, Lizzie was an ambitious if not a very successful mother. Although she still had to divide her leisure hours between her son and several of her admirers, she seemed determined to keep the boy under her roof. She sought desperately for ways to keep him from running the streets,[35] and from herding with "lower class youths," including (ironically) the sons of the "dago" fruit dealer, the only ones "who never tormented or hurt me." [36] Culture, which Lizzie had always coveted for herself, occurred to her as a possible antidote to the boy's waywardness. Dahlberg was given piano lessons and sent to Hebrew School, where, at age ten, he had his first real encounter with Judaism.

There were few Jews in Kansas City at the time, and their habits were far from Orthodox. Many of them were not purely of Jewish background, having had ancestors from colonial Christian families who married Jews around 1800. Dahlberg's Sunday school teacher, Sara Barth, was from the only Jewish family in the town of Rocheport, Missouri. Much later, she told her son, Henry Hafer, that she had taught Dahlberg Hebrew, although, according to Hafer, his mother never knew the language: she recited Hebrew prayers by rote.[37]

Miss Barth virtually adopted the rather pathetic Dahlberg, who had at the time large piles of black, curly hair. She attempted to teach him to play the piano, but his fingers stumbled on the keys and she came to regard him as tone deaf. Dahlberg responded warmly to the affection she lavished upon him. She introduced Dahlberg to Harry Myers, the rabbi of the small Kansas City congregation, and to her circle of friends, mostly unmarried Jewish women like herself, who also seemed more than eager to help this boy from such an obviously disadvantaged background. Laura

Neubauer, Katy Wollman (a scion of the famous New York Wollman family), and Ethel Feinerman were among his strongest advocates. In their company, Dahlberg learned he could speak easily on virtually any subject. The ladies, in turn, were charmed by his precocity and became determined to rescue him from his squalid background. They, too, were privy to the rumor that lady barbers were also prostitutes.[38] Dahlberg found himself developing a certain charisma based on his ability to arouse pity and compassion in women.

Dahlberg's halcyon days as the pet of these many Jewish mothers were not to last, for his natural mother was grooming another, very selfish beau. Lizzie met, and tried to inveigle into marriage, Capt. Henry Smith,[39] an ex-vaudeville entertainer and aging riverboat pilot at the end of a career which had once earned him the phenomenal wage of $280 per month. A short, squat man who weighed 250 pounds, his craft had been a Chester excursion boat—first a cargo plying from New Orleans to Kansas City and St. Louis, until trains replaced the steamboats.[40] Smith sensed the desperation of Lizzie, to whom every suitor always seemed to be the last. She was an easy victim of his wiles, and he saw no reason to share her with her demanding and squeamish child.

Smith, on the other hand, was not entirely repugnant to the young Edward. Callous as he was, the captain became the first man to occupy a steady role in Dahlberg's life, and although he later blamed Smith for having destroyed his mother's hopes, it is clear that as a child, Dahlberg considered him a father surrogate: "I used to lean on this obese man who perspired copiously. He just didn't want a little boy leaning against him." [41] Dahlberg assumed that the price of Smith's attention came high: "Had he not used Henry Smith's fleshy, perspiring shoulders as a bastion, the boy's whole life would have been different." [42] Given the option of subsidizing either a jolly (Smith had been in vaudeville) if useless man or her increasingly wayward child, Lizzie characteristically made the wrong choice. She took Smith and again sent her son to an orphanage. Although he was a clever mechanic, easily capable of supporting himself and perhaps a wife as well, Smith found it more convenient to live off Lizzie for seven years. Dahlberg, who, like his mother was charmed by the jovial captain, maintained that Smith wasn't a parasite, but, rather, "suffered from a lack of moral sensibilities." [43] But he never came to terms with Smith. In *From Flushing to Calvary,* for instance, Smith is held responsible for Lizzie's death: "Oh, Henry Smith, where was Henry Smith? Probably laying around with some skirt or chippy in St. Louis." [44]

Dahlberg's ambivalence also extended to his mother, for whom he offered excuses defending her actions: "I loved my mother very dearly, but she was deceived. There were trustees [of the orphanage] in Kansas City who said there would be carousels and scenic railways there. So my poor mother was beguiled." [45] Lizzie might have been told about annual picnics and field days, when the orphans were sometimes taken to amusement parks.[46] Even though she visited the asylum only twice during the five years her son was there, she could hardly have imagined carousels in the grisly orphanages of the time. The best excuse which she probably offered her bewildered son was that she was trying to protect him from Saul,[47] who actually did appear in 1915 looking for his son.[48] Lizzie refused to reveal Edward's whereabouts, and the boy lost his last chance to meet his natural father, who died before 1920.[49]

The eleven-year-old child shrank at the sight of the grim, dungeonlike Jewish Orphan Asylum at Woodland and Sawtell Avenues,[50] in a run-down, partly black section of Cleveland, where he was placed in April 1912. The foreground of the complex was dominated by an ornate but inactive fountain,[51] while most of the buildings were constructed as crude, redbrick imitations of Dutch architecture. Some of the open areas were grassy, but in Dahlberg's time much of the surfacing was cinder compound, which could scrape orphans' knees and elbows. "Newcumbers," as all recent arrivals were dubbed, could easily be appalled by what lay hidden from public view: the fetid "pond," actually a flood excavation filled with refuse, and the orphans' quarters: the dining hall; two infirmaries; the basement playroom; and the immense dormitories, which were uniformly barren, chilly, and illuminated by newly installed bare lightbulbs.[52]

Most orphans, who arrived as "little pissers," that is, while still at the bedwetting stage, often came to have fierce loyalty to the home. It had been founded in 1868, mainly by Districts 2 and 6 of B'nai B'rith, to take care of midwestern Jewish orphans of the Civil War.[53] Though all Jewish holidays were observed, and attendance at Sabbath ceremonies was mandatory, it was not difficult for an

"Das Weisenhaus." The Jewish Orphan Home. (Courtesy Lorna Sacher)

The Playroom. (Courtesy Lorna Sacher)

orphan to leave the asylum with a limited sense of Jewish culture and tradition. At a time when many jobs were closed to Jewish applicants, many of them altered their names. Dahlberg, who spent much less time in the home than the average orphan, tended to be anti-Semitic:

> How much of the Jew there is in me, I don't entirely know; but I assure you I've always been bludgeoned by the Jews. They have mistreated me more than any other people and I haven't really much use for them. I wouldn't like to see them decimated or anything like that; I just have no use for them.[54]

The orphanage in Dahlberg's time was populated by five hundred children, averaging about three hundred boys and two hundred girls, who were strictly segregated from each other, except in school. Dahlberg's claim that he never spoke to a girl for five years,[55] however, is questionable. The school, up to the eighth grade, was on the grounds of the orphanage, but if the institution could afford to keep them after grammar school the orphans were sent to a Cleveland high school. More often, as in the case of Dahlberg's friend, Emil Gottlieb, they were released at fifteen or sixteen,[56] so Dahlberg was considered fortunate in that he was allowed to graduate from high school.

The austere institution was run by the stern, gray-bearded "Doc" Samuel Wolfenstein ("no orphan would have doubted he

"Doctor" Wolfenstein. (Courtesy of Lorna Sacher.)

> His children love Doctor. Call their love
> a myth, call on them to explain it—and they answer:
>   'Foolish! We love Doctor.
>   *50 Book,* J. O. H. Alumni Association

was God—had he not picked his nose").[57] Rabbi Wolfenstein had been superintendent since 1877, and in his annual report for 1893, the twenty-fifth anniversary of the JOA, he recorded callously that it cost $700 a year to keep an orphan, and the children had all the water they wanted.[58]

Certainly, poor diet could be a problem. Eggs were served once a year, on Passover, and green-pea hash was the most common dish. Five potato chips were doled out on festive occasions.[59] The orphans seldom grew very tall: Dahlberg, who had been fairly well nourished for the first twelve years of his life, wrote a haunting, if hyperbolic, description of his playmates: "They were a separate race of stunted children who were clad in famine. Swollen heads lay on top of ashy uniformed students. Some had oval or oblong skulls; others gigantic watery occiputs that resembled the Cynecephali described by Hesiod and Pliny." [60] Dietary hardships produced some compensations. If they were denied milk, the orphans also had no sweets, which possibly accounts for the fact that, like Dahlberg, they had sound teeth even into old age.[61] If they somehow obtained candy, they would stick it with a pin and then suck the pin to make their treat last indefinitely.[62]

Although Dahlberg reached the towering height of six feet while he was at the home, he somehow avoided one of the grotesque nicknames imposed upon many orphans. The name "Hitchie" or "Hookie" was given to boys with hooknoses, recalled Lou Gilbert, an alumnus who is now a well-known actor. Since Gilbert grew fond of his sobriquet, he is still called "Giggie," because he giggled as a child.[63] Max Cohn, who was an especially diminutive orphan, acquired the name "Shrimp," which Dahlberg bestowed on an orphan who resembles Cohn in *Bottom Dogs*. Cohn is also represented as both "Pinkie" and "Shrimp" in *Because I Was Flesh*. Dahlberg's "Watermelonhead" was a real person who had an elongated, oversized head, as was "Mushmelonhead," the unfortunate owner of a "round, rather softish head which suggested a mushmelon." [64] Dahlberg commented that orphans, like Homer's warriors, were identified by stock epithets. He was especially fond of "Bonehead," the most able warrior in the JOA, since his skull was as resilient as a helmet.[65]

Young Dahlberg felt that he had witnessed nothing in the rugged streets of Kansas City that could match the fury of these indestructible orphans. Frustration which they were unable to vent on the institution they leveled at each other. Dahlberg never forgot being beaten senseless on numerous occasions: "Brutality was an orphanage fetish." [66]

Emil Palmer, who was Emil Gottlieb in the home, was a very tough orphan who also recalls the terror:

What I remember is that there were two fellows who were very strong in the home. They were in their last year—that would have made them fifteen or sixteen years of age—and one of them was the home bully. Every morning—you could count on it—you'd get up and you'd run into what they called the Big Playroom there and there was this bully ready to start having a fight with this other fellow. And they really used to have terrific fights.[67]

Lou Gilbert acted out a fistfight as he related a similar anecdote:

What I remember in the home: the rats running around, the smell of fumigation, the taste of the food that I used to put into my pocket because I couldn't eat it, my bullshitting my way through, my fighting, the development of my voice because I had to yell, against kids, "Knock it off my shoulder!"—hoping they wouldn't. The whole thing was survival and I survived.[68]

Internecine wars were less ferocious, perhaps, than the merciless battles waged by the orphans against the "micks" from nearby Irish slums. A simple snowball fight could cost an orphan an eye: "as soon as they got warmed up, [the micks] started to put rocks inside the snowballs making out they were icy-like." [69] Better fed, better clothed, and somewhat bigger than the orphans, the Irish carried knives;[70] but they were no match for JOA strategy, as one orphan recalled:

Joe Michaels conceived the idea of going at them in an organized way. So he formed three platoons, commanding the main one himself and appointing captains of the other two. One platoon approached the "micks" down the hill as the other two proceeded along the two sides. The "micks," believing they had the center platoon outnumbered, approached with daring, when the two side platoons with a flank movement, closed in on them, and it was then the "micks" got their worst drubbing. In my time they bothered us no more.[71]

Though Dahlberg became a veritable chronicler of the brutal life at the orphanage (few alumni have found his accounts unreliable), he never felt comfortable in his orphan community which most of the children regarded as home. Unlike most of the

Younger orphans as they looked in Dahlberg's day. (Courtesy of Lorna Sacher.)

others, who had no strong recollections of family life,[72] Dahlberg continually brooded on his earlier existence. Lou Gilbert remembers him as an aloof, ominous figure, who appeared highly scornful of the other orphans. He developed a peculiar twitch in his left eye, and this, together with his supercilious attitude, earned him more than his share of trouble.[73] Max Cohn recalled that Dahlberg's eccentricities, combined with his tendency to be a "loner," brought frequent hazing down upon his head. One incident entered into orphan folklore:

> In the dormitories, one of the windows looked out on a little porch. One night the orphans took him in his blanket and left him out on the porch. . . . He was completely unconscious, totally unaware of what was going on until the next morning.[74]

Dahlberg had unusual competence in certain areas. In spite of his general ungainliness, he excelled in tag, high jumping, and Ping-Pong,[75] though he recoiled from most organized, competitive athletics (which had been introduced into the JOA in 1914),[76] partly because of his self-consciousness, but mainly because his exact contemporaries, the members of the class of 1917, were a notoriously rowdy bunch.[77] Thus, his playmates included boys several years younger than himself: Max Cohn was his playmate, as was Lou Gilbert, who remembered Dahlberg rolling marbles with younger children: he was so tall, and his arms were so long, that he could stretch halfway across the playroom floor before releasing the aggies. The smaller orphans were simultaneously amazed and resentful of the advantage Dahlberg found in one activity where he could never lose.[78]

He quickly found another such activity, though it was in the academic area. During his many solitary moments, Dahlberg satisfied the intellectual hunger bequeathed to him by his semi-literate mother. He fed his fantasies with Oscar Wilde's *De Profundis*, Tolstoy's *Autobiography*, and the newly translated *Jean-Christophe* by Romain Rolland. Normally reticent, he would astonish the less bookish orphans by reciting, in a voice which had changed very early into a rich baritone, line after line from these romantic works.[79] Dahlberg had stiff and often very vocal competition from many other highly motivated orphans. An extraordinary number of future intellectuals, scholars, and scientists were being spawned among his contemporaries at the JOA, including Adolph Brown, later a world-renowned plastic surgeon; Andrew Meikle-john, first president of Amherst College and founder of the *Encyclopedia of The Social Sciences;* Sam Kutnick (also known as "Peter Pen"), who was a close friend of Robinson Jeffers; and George Silver, George Robbins, and Ben Goldman, prominent communist intellectuals whom Dahlberg came to know again in the 1930s. Achievement seemed always to have been of a positive nature: the alumni director of the JOA was unaware of any orphan who ever turned to crime or committed suicide.[80]

Dahlberg's most formidable competitor may have been Jack Girick, the darling of the orphanage and especially of Doc Wolfenstein. A sterling scholar, whom the school later sent to Hebrew Union College to become a rabbi, Girick had started the literary society at the home. The first person to dare to talk openly about sex, he later became the first alumnus on record to be psychoanalyzed. Lou Gilbert remembered first being introduced to the ideas of Bertrand Russell by the beloved "Jake," as he was known to the younger orphans.[81] He was described by one alumnus as "the personification of 'The Home,' . . . the number one alumnus of the Home, first in the hearts of all who love and honor him." [82]

Later in life, Girick came to detest Dahlberg. Like Dahlberg, he had yearned to be a writer and to chronicle life at the JOA, though his later career as a "director" of the home left him no time for such work. Dahlberg's nightmarish account of the place (in *Bottom Dogs,* which first appeared in 1929) brought the JOA the last type of celebrity that Girick would have wished. By that time, he had become perhaps the most enlightened administrator the home had ever known and, like many former orphans who became trustees and active alumni, he was outraged that potential benefactors often withheld donations after reading Dahlberg's Zolaesque account of the place.[83]

Both Girick and Doc Wolfenstein left the JOA in 1913, within a year after Dahlberg's arrival. The administrative change was so dramatic that the ensuing years came to be referred to whimsically as "A.D." ("After Doctor").[84] The *Weisenhaus* (orphan asylum) fell

Simon Peiser, Dahlberg's hated "Simon Wolkes." (Courtesy of Lorna Sacher.)

"To him religion was life, and he its servant."
50 Book, J. O. H. Alumni Association

under the rule of a harsh disciplinarian named Simon Peiser. An exceedingly stern-looking, rabbinical individual who was never known to smile,[85] he inspired both awe and fear in his charges. He is represented as the hateful "Simon Wolkes" in *Bottom Dogs, From Flushing to Calvary,* and *Because I Was Flesh.* Despite Dahlberg's opprobrium toward him, Peiser received nearly as much attention as Henry Smith and Saul Gottdank in the autobiographies, for a strange relationship seems to have developed between the man and the boy. Peiser quickly recognized an outstanding scholar in Dahlberg and apparently encouraged him in subtle ways, even though Dahlberg never failed to speak of the superintendent as a monster and denied ever receiving anything but abuse.

The boy, in turn, sought affection from Peiser and regarded him as a kind of father, although Dahlberg was inevitably disappointed by what he regarded as the superintendent's callousness and unwillingness to serve as a surrogate. Sadly, it would not have been permitted in an institution such as the JOA for Peiser to extend the intimacy that Dahlberg demanded.[86] His seeming "rejection" by this man was far more painful to Dahlberg than was Henry

Smith's failure to become his father. Dahlberg at times seemed to have felt the same degree of ambivalence toward Peiser as toward his mother.[87] In *From Flushing to Calvary,* both Simon Wolkes and Lizzie, like many other irresoluble characters in Dahlberg's fiction, are sent to untimely deaths. In a passage from this book, written mostly in 1930, Lorrie Lewis laments the death of Wolkes as intensely as if this man were his natural father:

> and now wolkes was dead and now that he returned to him seeking the warm wine and wafer in the dream-blood of his living brain, he wept because he could not transubstantiate the wafer and wine which he had drunk and eaten in his sleep and out of which wolkes had risen a beautiful jehovah substance, he wept because all the king's horses . . .[88]

Although Dahlberg fashioned for himself several other father figures, none has undergone such agonizing reappraisal as Peiser. In *Because I Was Flesh* (1964), Wolkes becomes an austere, scarcely human tyrant, eager to punish orphans in the harshest manner possible—by expelling them without "confirmation." A Catholic deprived of the Eucharist was no more bereft than an orphan banished without the blessing of the home. Even his masculinity was imperiled: "No girl would marry one who had been expelled. He would always be in disgrace with Gizella, Mary Brown from North Yakima, Washington, Ida Lewis from Detroit." [89] Unlike two of Dahlberg's characters, Harry Kato and the rebellious Herman Mushtate, the author never succeeded in being thrown out; in fact, he never got into much trouble.

In later years, however, Dahlberg came to believe that Peiser singled him out for persecution:

> Though Number 92 [Dahlberg] called on the Lord for help, he could not stop retching. After he had vomited on the school desk, Simon Wolkes, showing an underlip upon which the scrolls of the Torah had soured, told him to control himself. And how he did want to control himself—so that he could

J. O. H. Class of 1917. Dahlberg is at the top, center. Peiser is directly below, with legs crossed. (Courtesy of Lorna Sacher.)

walk by the side of Wolkes and touch his bony, Jehovah fingers which smelled of Cashmere Bouquet Soap.[90]

The rather tiny, beady-eyed Peiser developed in Dahlberg's imagination into a scourge of godlike proportions. Dahlberg's needs to compete with this man and remain the center of his attention are apparent in two of the author's orphanage memories. In one, Dahlberg wins a debate from the most brilliant girl in the orphanage. Although more startled than anyone else by this feat, Peiser simply stalks away and fails to praise or encourage him. In the second, Dahlberg remembered having some trifling difficulty with Peiser, "and it was in considerable proportion due to him":

I said, "You have immensely underestimated me." I later wrote him a letter when I had left the orphanage, saying that there is no reason for either of us to assume that there is a basis for friendly feelings. And he asked why. But I think I was too incoherent, being a boy of eighteen, in telling him how cruel and crafty he was.[91]

Homeless, unskilled, and with his left eye beginning to go blind, Dahlberg was graduated in June 1917. The class picture shows him lean, smiling, and quite handsome, standing at the apex of a pyramid formed by forty-four orphan heads. Sitting directly below him, scowling and cross-legged, is Simon Peiser.[92] Though in later life he refused to look at the photograph, Dahlberg would have enjoyed the symbolism.

NOTES

1. Interview: Michael Sands, April 18, 1972. Neither Sands, nor another brother, Morris, was ever mentioned in Dahlberg's works. Numerous letters from Lizzie to Sands survive.
2. Letter: Eleanor Siegel, April 25, 1973. Miss Siegel is the daughter of the late Bertha Siegel, one of Gottdank's daughters.
3. *Because I Was Flesh*, p. 3.
4. Ibid. The portrait to which Dahlberg alluded is lost. A striking resemblance between him and surviving portraits of Saul is quite apparent.

5. Ibid., p. 7.
6. Letter: Harold Billings, August 5, 1973. Interviews: Minnie (Mrs. Michael) Sands, April 18, 1972; Sarah Cohn, February 13, 1973.
7. (New York: Harcourt, Brace, 1932), p. 17.
8. *Because I Was Flesh,* p. 3.
9. Ibid., p. 177.
10. Interview: E. D., Feb. 11, 1973.
11. The name, of course, means "Valley-Mountain."
12. Louis Zukofsky, *Bottom on Shakespeare,* I (Austin: The Ark Press, 1963), p. 348.
13. Michael Sands remembers visiting one of Lizzie's wealthy brothers at the Continental Hotel sometime in the 1920s. Dahlberg had taken Sands to visit this man, who may have been Herman Dalberg, in order to ask him for money.
14. Interview: E. D., Nov. 12, 1972. *Because I Was Flesh,* p. 8.
15. Letter: Eleanor Siegel, April 25, 1973.
16. *Because I Was Flesh,* p. 9.
17. Interview: E. D., May 5, 1972. Cf. Sands's first recollection (p. 1).
18. *Because I Was Flesh,* pp. 10-12.
19. Interview: Alice Neel, February 8, 1973. It is significant that Dahlberg casts his mother in the role of Mary Magdalene in *Because I Was Flesh.*
20. *Because I Was Flesh,* p. 13.
21. "Kansas City Revisited," *The Leafless American,* ed. Harold Billings (New York: Roger Beacham, 1967), p. 26.
22. *From Flushing to Calvary,* pp. 46-59.
23. "Kansas City Revisited," p. 20.
24. *Because I Was Flesh,* p. 41.
25. Ibid., p. 49. Dahlberg remained phobic about roaches and rodents throughout his life.
26. (1930; rpt. San Francisco: City Lights Books, 1961), p. 27.
27. Interview: E. D., Dec. 5, 1972.
28. *Because I Was Flesh,* p. 61.
29. *Bottom Dogs,* p. 5.
30. Dahlberg admitted that most of her "operations," of which there were seven, were unnecessary. She may have been ashamed to admit her emotional instability to her son.
31. *Because I Was Flesh,* p. 60.
32. Ibid., p. 60.
33. Ibid., p. 39.
34. According to Mrs. Marguerite Beecher, a psychologist who has studied handwriting analysis, the leftward slant indicates egotism (a turning toward the self), while printing (as opposed to script) reveals the tendency of the author to write in a persona.
35. Interview: E. D., Feb. 27, 1973.
36. "Kansas City Revisited," p. 22.
37. Interview: Henry Hafer, Mar. 9, 1973.
38. Interview: Mar. 9, 1973. Sara Barth married Hafer's father, a wealthy

businessman, and lived on Riverside Drive while Dahlberg was at Columbia. She apparently helped Dahlberg financially throughout her life, although she always kept her financial affairs secret (see Ch. II).

39. He became "Kentucky Blue Grass Henry Smith" in two of Dahlberg's books.
40. Interview: E. D., Feb. 27, 1973.
41. Interview: E. D., Feb. 27, 1973.
42. *Because I Was Flesh*, p. 64.
43. Interview: E. D., Feb. 27, 1973.
44. *From Flushing to Calvary*, p. 280. Lizzie Dahlberg was very much alive in 1932, when this book was published. E. D. was not present at her actual death in 1946 (see Ch. V).
45. Interview: E. D., Dec. 5, 1972.
46. Simon Peiser, "Second Picnic," *50 Book*, ed. Lou Schreiber, Jack Girick, Lorna Sacher et al. (Cleveland: JOH Alumni Association, 1938), n.p.
47. Interview: E. D., Jan. 29, 1973.
48. Interview: E. D., April 2, 1973. Letter: Eleanor Siegel, April 25, 1973. Saul was traveling with his seventeen-year-old daughter, Bertha, to whom he wanted to introduce Edward. No meeting ever came about.
49. Saul dropped out of Dahlberg's life forever, but he turned up many times in attempts to exploit Bertha.
50. Letter: Horace Schwartz, Feb. 28, 1973. Schwartz came to the orphanage about ten years after Dahlberg.
51. A photograph, taken around 1916, shows Dahlberg, his best friend, Albert Gottlieb, and Gottlieb's brother, Emil—later Palmer—in front of this fountain.
52. Founded in 1868, the JOA became the JOH—Jewish Orphan Home, in 1919. Bellefaire, an organization which cares for emotionally disturbed children rather than orphans, supplanted the JOH in 1929, although the JOH Alumni Association has retained its original name. Lorna Sacher was the secretary of this association for forty-three years.
53. Interview: Lorna Sacher, May 31, 1973.
54. Interview: E. D., Jan. 14, 1973. Dahlberg provokes the ire of many Jewish readers, and especially of ex-orphans, like Horace Schwartz: "Dahlberg, from my small contact with him and from my reading of his work seems a certain, almost classic type of American Jew. He has left the religion, if he ever really belonged to it. He therefore hates Jews, hates himself, and hates America. A Jew without an identity is a poisoned creature. Every line of his writing is informed with venom and a deep sense of self-loathing. He is sort of an American Celine. . . . He regards himself as totally rejected, and writes accordingly, then makes a career out of it." (Letter: Feb. 28, 1973.)
55. *Bottom Dogs*, p. 105.
56. Interview: Emil Palmer, Feb. 1, 1973.
57. *Because I Was Flesh*, p. 69.
58. Interview: Lorna Sacher, May 31, 1973.

59. Interview: Max Cohn, Feb. 13, 1973. Mr. Cohn was a fellow inmate of Dahlberg's and for many years his friend in New York City.
60. *Because I Was Flesh*, p. 76.
61. Interview: Lorna Sacher, May 31, 1973.
62. Interview: Lorna Sacher, May 31, 1973.
63. Interview: Lou Gilbert, Feb. 3, 1973.
64. Interview: Max Cohn, Feb. 13, 1973.
65. *Bottom Dogs*, p. 42; *Because I Was Flesh*, p. 69.
66. *Because I Was Flesh*, p. 69.
67. Interview: Emil Palmer, Feb. 3, 1973.
68. Interview: Lou Gilbert, Feb. 1, 1973.
69. *Bottom Dogs*, p. 73.
70. *Because I Was Flesh*, p. 77.
71. H[enry] S[eligman], "The Micks," *50 Book*, n.p. Mr. Seligman arrived at the orphanage in 1908 and would have been a contemporary of Dahlberg.
72. Interview: Lorna Sacher, May 31, 1973.
73. Though Dahlberg became blind in his left eye, no one I interviewed had any knowledge of the exact nature of his eye affliction.
74. Interview: Max Cohn, Feb. 13, 1973.
75. Interview: Max Cohn, Feb. 13, 1973.
76. *50 Book*, n.p.
77. Interview: Max Cohn, Feb. 13, 1973.
78. Interview: Lou Gilbert, Feb. 3, 1973.
79. Interviews: E. D., Jan. 31, 1973; Max Cohn, Feb. 13, 1973.
80. Interviews: Max Cohn, Feb. 13, 1973; Lou Gilbert, Feb. 3, 1973; Lorna Sacher, May 31, 1973.
81. Interview: Lou Gilbert, Feb. 3, 1973; *50 Book*, n.p.
82. *50 Book*, n.p.
83. Girick, who is now in his eighties and in poor health, would not speak of Dahlberg, nor will he read the latter's books.
84. *50 Book*, n.p.
85. Ibid.
86. Interview: Lorna Sacher, May 31, 1973.
87. Peiser, like Lizzie, lived on in real life. Dahlberg corresponded with Peiser's nephew, Ernest E. Peiser, until the latter died in 1971.
88. *From Flushing to Calvary*, p. 251.
89. *Because I Was Flesh*, pp., 74-75.
90. Ibid., p. 97.
91. Interview: E. D., Feb. 4, 1973.
92. *50 Book*, n.p.

2.

Vagabond to Expatriate: 1917-1926

The sidewalks of Cleveland were to Dahlberg an even less hospitable environment than the Jewish Orphan Asylum. Another orphan, speaking of both his own and Dahlberg's rough transitions, commented:

> A Jewish upbringing in an orphanage is certainly not a preparation for the brute realities of American life, particularly for an orphan with no money and no prospects. I can attest that ... when a young Jewish boy is released from an orphanage [and] goes out into the big ugly world, he is thrown into a considerable funk.[1]

Although Dahlberg had maintained an irregular correspondence with his mother, Lizzie had managed to visit her son only twice during his five-year stay in the grisly asylum. He had, then, little reason to imagine that he would be welcome at her home in Kansas City from which he had been ejected five years before.

The summer of 1917 found him drifting joylessly from one unskilled job to another until, it seems, his restlessness, born of desperation and loneliness, suddenly surfaced: the wandering Ishmael in him emerged. When, twelve years later, he composed an autobiographical sketch for the first American edition of his first novel, *Bottom Dogs,* he offered this abbreviated account of his postorphanage wanderings:

> The next five years were spent in a kaleidoscopic succession of occupations, which took him all over the country. He has been a Western Union messenger boy in Cleveland, trucker for the American express, driver of a laundry wagon, cattle drover in the Kansas City Stockyards, dishwasher in Portland, Oregon, potato peeler in Sacramento, bus-boy in San Francisco, longshoreman in San Pedro, clerk in a clinic, and vagabond everywhere.[2]

This blurb, written at a time when Dahlberg was offering himself to the public as a new voice of the proletariat, is not a chronological account of his activities, some of which are probably imaginary. He remembered later that none of these jobs lasted more than a few weeks; far more time was spent on the road.[3] On one occasion, he was collared by a brakeman on a freight train and turned over to a "gorbellied Sheriff" who jailed him overnight in Hannibal, Missouri, on charges ranging from vagrancy to suspected draft-dodging.[4] He was able to convince the authorities that, at age seventeen, he was still too young to be conscripted.

Dahlberg's vision was worsening, especially in his left eye, and his health was generally deteriorating. He finally fell back upon his mother, who was still plying her trade in the Star Lady Barbershop, which seemed to her grown son even more squalid and dingy than he had remembered it.[5] The reader of *Because I Was Flesh* will learn that Capt. Henry Smith, whose one achievement in later life was the invention of a streetcar bell which he never patented, had by this time grown entirely useless and lived by bleeding Lizzie. Dahlberg explained that Smith was included in this part of the book to heighten the pathos of Lizzie's dilemma; in real life, the wily captain had run off with "some little chippie" several years earlier.[6] In his absence, the ragtag stream of pitiful men, similar to the ones Dahlberg had remembered with disgust from his childhood, continued their parade through Lizzie's doors.[7]

Unhappy memories combined with growing disgust with his surroundings made Dahlberg's stay in Kansas City brief. Certainly, he could imagine neither a future nor a home for himself there: "I had no idea what I wanted to do or be. The plain truth is that I had no conceptions worth the remembrance." While staying at his mother's home, he worked briefly in the Kansas City stockyards;[8] indulged in lustful fantasies about the eight-year-old daughter of a lady barber;[9] and, he tells us, unburdened himself of his virginity with the aid of one of the readily available prostitutes in the neighborhood.[10] But his mother's ever growing sloppiness, combined with her sordid personal life, her needling, and her oppressive tendency to treat him like an infant pushed him to the point where he felt he would prefer vagabondage to what dubious stability his mother could offer.[11]

The summer of 1918 saw Dahlberg launched on a cross-country jaunt which would be fictionized in *Bottom Dogs* and in *Because I Was Flesh* in 1964. These adventures were greatly admired by Jack Kerouac and many other would-be sons of Walt Whitman.[12] A brief stopover at the Cleveland orphanage was far less melodramatic than Lorrie Lewis's traumatic encounter with his past in *From Flushing to Calvary*,[13] but Dahlberg did hear tales of one of his classmates, the daring Max Harris, who became the first alumnus to join the Communist party. Harris had returned to the home to regale the orphans with stories about Bolshevism and the workers' paradise in Soviet Russia.[14] Dahlberg pretended to ignore these tales; although like many of the orphans he found communism attractive, he quickly dismissed Harris as "crude and rather lumpish." [15] Obviously, he was not willing to share the stage with another, more celebrated ex-orphan; nor was he ready, as he would be in the 1920s and 1930s, to embrace the idealism of Marxist revolution. At this time, he was soaking himself in the dandyism of Wilde, the agrarianism of Tolstoy, and the aloof urbanity of Shaw to soothe his feelings of abandonment and inadequacy.

Dahlberg's involvement with Shaw's prose (mainly the introductions to the plays) led him to read W. H. Davies's *Autobiography of a Supertramp*, to which Shaw had contributed a glowing introduction.[16] Dahlberg could see in Davies a hobo who invested the vagabond's life-style with sophistication, respectability, and British candor—all qualities which the young writer preeminently admired. But Davies's writing was lacking in the sense of tragedy which Dahlberg felt lay at the core of his own life. Knut Hamsen's novel, *Hunger*, first published in 1890, gave Dahlberg his model for the talented yet alienated, impulsive, and self-destructive young hero.[17] Like Dahlberg, the unnamed narrator of Hamsun's masterpiece projects his anxiety onto everything around him; he relates poorly to people; he sees everyone else as "strange";[18] he is hopelessly awkward with women and pitifully vain.[19] So impressed was Dahlberg by this book that he seems to have lifted one of the most moving episodes of *Hunger:* upon awakening one morning, Hamsun's young hero supposes that his slow starvation has caused him to lose his hair: "To warm my hands, I pushed my fingers through my hair, back and forth, crossways and sideways; small handfulls came loose, tufts came away between my fingers and spread over the pillow." [20] Forty years later, Dahlberg heightened this effect in a passage that fairly echoes the one above:

> Nineteen years old, I was more ashamed of my ravaged pate than I was of my rancid drawers. Already an old child, I studied my hairline every day. One evening I attended a spiritualistic seánce and instead of handing the medium a note asking her to speak to the dead in my behalf I told her to beg Esau to give me his hair.
>
> The medium replied, "Do not be despondent, my infant; take heed, and eat only wild locusts and honey, and you shall be as hirsute as St. John the Baptist."
>
> For a whole hour I was jubilant, and that night I saw the hairy saint in the wilderness; when I awakened I found a sheaf of locks on the pillow.[21]

By far the most perilous aspect of Dahlberg's new migratory existence was "ridin' the blinds," [22] or jumping freight trains. The ever present fear of railroad goons who would maim, kill, or jail freeloaders haunted the young tramp:

> I remember when I was in Ogden, Utah, there were twenty-five or more vagabonds either on the locomotive or in the boxcars. And word got to us that the trainyard detectives were waiting for us. I was so terrified because I could not bear to be

locked up again. The food was vile, and the whole experience was implacably monotonous, so I jumped off the train. Sometimes I jumped off at forty-five miles per hour and it was only a miracle that I did not lose my life or limbs.

Often a freight train would come to a halt, only to recoup with other cars and go in the opposite direction: "You would wake up and find yourself in some deserted part of the continent. I remember when I first left Cleveland, I got on a freight train and almost went back to Cleveland after a whole day and night's travel. How this ever occurred, I don't know." [23]

Dahlberg spent the last few months of the summer of 1918 zigzagging westward through such places as Omaha, Nebraska; Green River, Wyoming; and Salt Lake City, Utah. At one point, the freight train he was riding came to a sudden halt. He jumped off, not knowing where he was, only to find himself lost in the Mojave Desert.[24] Nearly dead, he wandered until he came to "an abandoned hovel. . . . I saw an iron keg filled with water. I leaned upon the barrel, thrusting my head into it—and drank kerosene!" [25] Intoning like Jeremiah, Dahlberg later proclaimed: "I resolved that if I could endure this I could be a soothsayer." [26]

Six feet tall, withered to a mere 110 pounds, Dahlberg was forced to abandon his role as a "supertramp." His wallet had been stolen and his clothing was completely frayed and caked with dirt. His only alternative to starvation was to wire his mother for train fare back to Kansas City. He arrived during the last weeks of World War I, probably in late September 1918. In his weakened condition, unskilled labor (which was all he was suited for) was out of the question, so he enrolled at a small junior college on the outskirts of town.[27] He apparently remained there only a few weeks, during which he joined a small ROTC unit as a way of defraying some of his expenses.[28]

Since the demands of the ROTC program had been moderate, Dahlberg decided to enlist in the regular army when he left the college. On October 26, 1918, he became number 5-288-970, a private in the Armed Forces of the United States.[29] Ungainly, nearly blind in one eye, and prone to temper tantrums, Dahlberg failed to realize that he would probably make the worst soldier imaginable, since he had no notion of the hard realities of military life: "I had no guidance at all. Nor had I seen a good book in my life." [30] The Great War was nearly over: the Hindenburg line had already been broken on September 27, and Austria was about to surrender; but Dahlberg recalled Lizzie's near-hysteria: "My poor mother was aghast. She wrote to me, 'You know, you're going to be killed, my son.' " [31] But Lizzie's son was disillusioned not so much by the rigors of army life as by its absurdity:

> I was in officer's training after which I would have become a second lieutenant [32] and thus the first to be killed. They were sending over green soldiers. I was never told how to discharge a bullet. We simply paraded eight hours a day— squads right and squads left. That's all we ever did! [33]

Either Dahlberg's clumsiness or a brawl with a fellow recruit abruptly ended his soldiering. Throughout the rest of his life, his vanity prevented him from discussing the accident which finally destroyed the sight in his left eye. He either slipped during drill practice and gouged his eye with his rifle butt,[34] or he angered one of his comrades who hit him in the face with a rifle or some other blunt instrument.[35] Pain and fear drove Dahlberg to panic and go AWOL. He fled immediately to his mother's home in Kansas City, where he found that his troublesome eye had now become permanently blinded.

Lizzie was able to prevail upon some of her more influential patrons to get the army to accept her son back without pressing charges—he had been AWOL for two weeks. Because of his newly acquired "disability," he was honorably discharged on December 14, 1918—after less than two months in the service.

With his prospects in Kansas City as poor as ever, Dahlberg decided to hitchhike, with a few dollars borrowed from Lizzie, to the West Coast. He spent two weeks in Needles, California, on the Arizona border, where he had little luck as a cattle drover. He then made his way to the coast, and finally, in January or early February 1919, he rolled into Los Angeles with only three or four dollars in his pocket.[36] Again ragged and exhausted, the young tramp found that "Nobody cares to keep company with grief, indigence, and mishap." [37] For a few days he slept in vacant lots and lived by "moulting" his honesty "in a far shorter period than

the serpent needs to slough his coat." [38] Begging and petty thievery
sustained him for awhile. Fortunately for Dahlberg, Los Angeles
was still a city of only a million people which had but one YMCA
residence hall, for it was there, at Seventh and Hope streets, that
he met Max Lewis, the man who would become the prime influence in his life. Dahlberg was having difficulty gaining membership at the Y, since he looked like a derelict and had almost no
money. Suddenly, he was astonished to see a familiar face:

> [Max] had actually been in the orphanage with me. He was
> about three and one-half years older than I, and as a much
> older boy he would not be bothered with someone younger.
>
> He was very scrawny, about my height, and quite hand-
> some, but he had acne. Once [in the orphanage] I teased him.
> I said, "Max, you must have syphilis!" [39]

Lewis was destined to appear in most of Dahlberg's autobiographical writings, as Maurice Lewes in *Mimes,* as Max
Maxwell in *Bottom Dogs* and *From Flushing to Calvary,* as Lao-Tsu
Ben in *Because I Was Flesh,* and as Anonymous in *The Confessions of
Edward Dahlberg.* Dahlberg recognized in his friend some of his own
character traits: "[Max] didn't want any part of other inmates of
the orphanage because they were so stupid.[40] They were deformed
and had stunted intelligence [while] he was clever, but he took
great interest in me." [41] But Max combined his snobbishness with
competence in just those areas where Dahlberg felt deficient: in the
ease with which he handled people (especially women); in his
ability to read with instant comprehension. Dahlberg was overwhelmed by this figure who was willing to give him the paternal
support which he desperately needed.

For awhile both men lived on the fifteen dollars a week Lizzie
began sending from Kansas City, while Dahlberg sat at his
newfound master's knee absorbing comments on Shakespeare,
Tolstoy, Romain Rolland, Gorki, Chekhov, and Hardy.[42] He also
learned that their backgrounds were exceedingly similar: Max, like
Dahlberg, was not literally an orphan, since his ne'er-do-well
father had deposited him at age ten in the orphan asylum. Lewis,
however, was not given by nature to sedentary discourse; like his
father, Jeremy, he was a speculator and a schemer.[43] By the time

Dahlberg met him, Lewis had already become "a Y.M.C.A. member, a Mason, had founded the American Legion Post in Los Angeles, gone to David Starr Jordan's peace lectures, and read Samuel Butler with considerable conviction." [44]

Lewis was not reluctant to share the shadier aspects of his career. Before Dahlberg had met him, Lewis had saved several thousand dollars by working as the merchandising manager at Meyers Siegel Department Store in Los Angeles, but he had been forced to quit the job after having an affair with one of the owners' daughters. Almost immediately he lost his money in a poker game in Mexico, and he had to resort to elaborate schemes to recoup his losses. First, he tried to relieve the cultural poverty of the people of Los Angeles by organizing a musical academy. But the public showed little interest, and since Lewis was unable to attract Jascha Heifetz, Edward MacDowell, and other musical luminaries as he had hoped, this venture proved a disaster.[45] Next, speculating that new home wireless sets would catch on sooner than they actually did, Lewis arranged an exhibition to demonstrate the latest models, but nobody bought them. Attempts to find gold in Lake Tahoe and in the Mojave Desert were likewise doomed to failure.

Max's "clandestine" business sense was most acute in times of economic peril.[46] When Dahlberg began squandering much of his allowance on books, Lewis, remembering that his friend was an army veteran, advised him to apply for disability benefits for the loss of his eyesight.[47] By Lewis's standards, however, even with Dahlberg's stipend, the finances of the two men were constricting.

At this time, Max learned that an acquaintance, the owner of a shop which sold women's apparel, had been imprisoned for seducing an adolescent boy. Lewis immediately visited the man in prison and offered to manage the boutique until his release could be arranged. Max also extracted a verbal promise that he would be given half the business if he could somehow get the charges dismissed. The man agreed and signed over his checking account to Lewis, who gave the detective on the case a fifteen-hundred-dollar bribe. Numerous other gratuities were dispensed to magistrates, law clerks, and others of Lewis's acquaintances. He also learned (or doctored evidence to prove) that the "victimized" boy was a notorious homosexual whose jealous lover had gone to the police and pressed morals charges against the shopkeeper. Charges against this man, which might have brought him a fifteen-year jail sentence, were dropped, but to Lewis's chagrin, he expressed his gratitude by offering only a complete and stylish wardrobe for Lewis's mistress: the promise of business partnership had been forgotten.[48]

Lewis's disappointment was short-lived. His talents were numerous, but none impressed Dahlberg more than his superhuman sexual prowess. Lewis was as generous as he was reckless with the objects of his desire:

> Once, when he tired of a mistress, he said "Edward, you take her. I'm tired of this woman living with me." Mind you, I would never touch a friend's mistress, so I was absolutely a corpse. She tried to make advances, but to me she was like a sister. The three of us had been friends—we used to eat together, talk together. . . . I couldn't do it.[49]

Lewis could easily spare a mistress, since he reputedly had eight of them in eight different towns on the outskirts of Los Angeles. His adroitness with women was accompanied by callousness and even brutality. Dahlberg records with obvious satisfaction his friend's fondness for exploiting and degrading women:

> a scholar of female flesh, . . . he mused upon the worth of carnal entertainments, considering whether it would not be more sagacious to muzzle his secret parts. . . .
> After Tsu Ben seduced a woman, he would rummage through his mind for a subterfuge whereby he could escape from her. He had graved well over a hundred maidenheads; abhorring injustice, he believed that only a scoundrel would allow a virgin to grow musty.

But Lewis's strongest preference was for married women, since he found it "more convenient for the [husband] to provision for her than for him to keep her. Also, he believed that ground grubbed up by another would prove more arable for him." [50]

Dahlberg remained in the background, wallowing "in the paradoxes of Oscar Wilde," [51] and assuming the role of a dandy, while Max continued in his active role of Lothario until his health began to decline. With caressing words, Dahlberg diagnosed his friend's disease as tuberculosis brought on by his combined amorous and commercial excesses: Dahlberg recalled Lewis growing bald like himself: "He had lost considerable weight and precious tufts of his silken hair. Of late he had not fornicated at all and could not understand why he had not been compensated for his recent abstemious habits and had his health restored to him." [52]

Not until death appeared imminent did Lewis follow his doctor's advice and move to the Mojave Desert. There, about thirteen miles from Victorville, California, he bought a grocery store and a few acres of land on credit. He was also able to acquire a half-ton truck from a dealer who guaranteed him twenty miles per gallon. When the vehicle actually delivered less than seventeen, Lewis stopped making payments and simply kept the machine. [53]

Lewis used his truck to transport goods and sell them on his cornered market at grossly inflated prices. Malted milks cost 75 cents, while a single avocado was $1.50. He also expanded his capital by winning in a poker game half a dozen cottages which had been used in the set of a Hollywood movie. These he removed to his land where they formed the core of a motor lodge which in a few years became Apple Valley, a luxurious resort which survives to the present day. [54] Lewis added the Cactus Cafe and alongside that built a garage for which he hired mechanics to service the motor vehicles of his rapidly increasing clientele. [55]

Dahlberg often vacationed in the Mojave Desert with his friend and alter ego, whose initiative and independence never failed to astound him: "[Max] would rather have been the sole maker of his own evil than be under obligation to another for a single benefit." [56] But while it was Lewis who first inspired Dahlberg to begin writing, [57] the younger man could not stand in the shadow of Lewis's imposing accomplishments without feeling diminished: "Whenever I encountered a person capable of making a paradox I became his vassal. I was now the slave of Oscar Wilde and the wit of Anonymous." [58]

Envious competition grew between the two men. Dahlberg, convinced that he was the only one Max had met who was his superior, wanted to surpass him. He accused his mentor of having a "coarse strain" in his nature. [59] Soon a rupture which would never heal developed in the relationship. In 1932, Dahlberg dedicated *From Flushing to Calvary* to Lewis, and though he included a portrait of him in every one of his autobiographical works, the two never met or corresponded after 1942. Lewis, as seemed inevitable, became a millionaire and bought a mansion in Altadena which was surrounded by dogs and an electrified fence. He remained in touch with the outside world only through a secretary and, like Howard Hughes, refused all personal interviews.[60] Dahlberg paradoxically both blamed and absolved himself for losing his dearest friend—the only one of his many friends he openly regretted having alienated: "He wanted money and he wanted tranquillity—pecuniary tranquillity, and he felt that I would somehow trouble him. Well, I would trouble him! Because he wasn't employing his fine mind!" [61]

As Dahlberg admitted repeatedly, however, his own mind was sparked by Lewis's power. While Lewis acknowledged his own limits as a preceptor, he was aware of the free higher education available in California. But Dahlberg did not immediately follow his friend's advice to enroll at the Berkeley campus. Perhaps taking his cue from Lewis, Dahlberg imagined he could easily turn his wit and booklearning to immediate profit. At the time, the most obvious outlet for the talents of a young writer of genius seemed to be in writing scenarios for the silent films. He enrolled in a correspondence course to study this new art and tried his hand at acting as an extra in *Beverly of Graustark,* starring Wallace Reid.[62] According to Dahlberg, he fell off several horses and his face eventually stayed on the cutting-room floor; but the most poignant (and chilling) memory of his acting career is of his being tormented by envy while watching the character actor, Theodore Roberts, eat a watermelon:

> He . . . was the proprietor of a Rolls Royce. He had snowy hair, a terra-cotta complexion, and a usurious mouth. In a little while, he took a pearl-handled knife out of his pocket and, placing a watermelon on his obese lap, cut dainty rectangles from it. Not once did he glance at me. Each swallow he took was a stone thrown at me. Now, as he rots somewhere in the ground, with an expensive sculptured saint guarding his vault, I cannot expel my hatred of him. Actors

have no conscience because they are always acting, are continually somebody else.[63]

Dahlberg's scenarios were no more successful than his acting; his ideas were bizarre and imaginative but unmarketable. The aesthetics of the infant movie industry were not sufficiently developed to appreciate "The Ballad of Reading Gaol" adapted as a western.[64] A screen version of "The Private Papers of Henry Ryecroft" was simply too esoteric for an audience that doted on Mae Murray and the adventures of Tom Mix. Dahlberg recalled: "All my manuscripts were dispatched to me forthwith. They were terrible. . . . If you were to read them, you'd be bedridden for days!"[65] Alone in Hollywood with no prospect of earning his living, he sank into a depression deeper than any he had ever known. His days were empty, since "savage work was hebenon for me."[66] For the first time he seriously considered taking his own life:

> A suicidal feeling came over me as regularly as the four seasons. I do not remember how many times I have killed myself. Anyway, I said farewell to Eohippus and Tom Mix's horse; both are buried and the world ought to be the better for it.[67]

Dahlberg sought the advice of Max Lewis, who thought that he might ripen his talents at the University of California at Berkeley. Dahlberg's career at "Rabble University," as he called it,[68] extended from 1922 to 1923, the only segment of his life which he chose to remember as "happy."[69] Although accompanied as usual by chronic loneliness and "priapic woes,"[70] he found pleasure in cycling the distance from Berkeley to Oakland, "before it was a black den of thieves."[71] Another of his favorite pastimes was riding the ferryboat plying back and forth past Goat's Island to San Francisco while he indulged his fantasies and searched for women: "one day I met rather briefly one delightful girl, but I didn't see her again. I didn't know where she lived or anything about her. Then another—she wanted marriage, I didn't."[72]

His coursework irritated him thoroughly and brought to the surface the antagonism toward academia which would remain with him throughout his life and which he burlesqued in the most stilted "academic prose": "What need had I of the sour pedants of human syntax, or of courses in pedagogy, canonized illiteracy? I saw that anybody who has read twelve good books knew more than a doctor of philosophy." [73] Dahlberg, who regarded himself as an autodidact, strenuously resisted academic discipline. He endured the normal college curriculum, although the impact of his coursework seemed to have been very slight. His most acid satire was reserved for formal educators:

> I espied a band of youths flogging a professor . . . until he pleaded, "Sirs, please leave off," but exhorting him never to be gentlemanly with them again, they kicked him.
> I objected. "You'll kill him," I said.
> The wide-shouldered student retorted: "We murder him once a week, but he insists he's alive. That's a pedant for you. He says it's his point of view against ours. We're destitute. Who'll listen to us?" [74]

Dahlberg's isolation became somewhat relieved late in 1922 when several left-wing organizations, attracted by his articulateness and his strident intellectuality, welcomed him at their meetings.[75] He gained additional attention by publishing two excerpts from his early writing in the college magazine. The earlier of these, entitled "The Sick, The Pessimist, and the Philosopher," employs a narrator who is almost a replica of Raskolnikov in *Crime and Punishment,* which Dahlberg and Max Lewis had read together at the YMCA. So totally did Dahlberg identify with Dostoevski's egomaniacal student that, throughout his career, he continued to employ similar morbid and introspective personas:

> He [an unnamed "philosopher"] had no friends; he did not seek out people, and those who infrequently saw this idiosyncratic and apparently austere person strolling in the sunlight, without hat, talking to himself, did not go out of their way to meet him. They stared at him, though not brazenly; but that in itself was an intrusion; he felt their eyes upon him.[76]

Through the device of this paranoiac individual, Dahlberg (also like Raskolnikov) seemed to be steeling himself against the death of his mother—Lizzie was destined to survive for another twenty-four years. Like Dahlberg and Raskolnikov, the "philosopher" feels immobilized by hopelessly ambiguous feelings toward his mother:

> His mother died. He was much more moved by her death than he expected; it severed his last bond with the world; it hurt him, though it was that he secretly desired. Though he had always felt a sort of dutiful affection, even at moments a genuine love for his mother, he experienced in her existence a restraint, though, in truth, she never did restrain him—could not hold him back in his comings or goings. But in those moments, when man disregards the means, the averages, the petty commonalities that stifle and make life a wry and dried up thing, love would go out from him to his mother, even to the herd he despised. . . . Alone he could be with all mankind.[77]

Dahlberg lived out much of his imagined hero's eccentricity, especially his misanthropy. Supposedly to conceal his receding hairline, the Berkeley Raskolnikov completely shaved his head.[78] He emerged briefly from his total isolation to live with a girl, but soon he ran back to hermitic ways which saved him any involvement with the college community. Self-mockingly, he recalled: "Why should a burgeoning Heinrich Heine run after women? Since not one came to kneel at my learned feet, I had no other course but to resume my literary work." [79]

One who became a warm friend was an "older" student named Kate Carla. Dahlberg's constant illnesses stood out in her mind as, fifty years later, she recalled first meeting him as a tall, bushy-haired young man who asked if he might borrow her notes, saying he had been ill and missed several days of class.[80] Since the attractive young woman did not recognize Dahlberg's very tentative proposition, the two avoided the pitfalls of romance by keeping their relationship a "virgin" one:[81] "All I received from Kate was the worst part of her body, her mind, and I longed for the song of the dolphins and to hymn praises to the olive yards by the river Alpheus." [82] Despite frequent wry comments about their relationship, the young Dahlberg considered her mature and knowledgeable; she believed that she introduced him to the classical approach, "the attitude of relating to others rather than self-identification and preoccupation." [83] But whether or not her influence brought him to Hellenic wisdom, the relationship as a whole was the warmest Dahlberg had ever known. The two took long walks in the hills and were delighted that they could laugh together over anything, especially foolish puns. She was the only person who could tease him with impunity about his peculiar appearance and mannerisms, which were, she felt, accurately depicted in his novels:[84] "His sense of inferiority shows itself in his determined aggressiveness: this has always been a characteristic. He can't tolerate imperfection or opposition: he can pour it on, but he can't take it. That's why I teased him a lot!" [85]

Kate Carla appeared twice in Dahlberg's works as a delectable but unyielding object of his desire—as Portia Kewling in *Because I Was Flesh* and as Kate Carla in the *Confessions*. She roared with laughter as she recalled Dahlberg's farcical reminiscences of his heated discussions with her and his halfhearted attempts to seduce her: "It's fond in a way, because Edward is fond . . . and he's still oppressed with the whole preoccupation with sex which Edward explored long before it became a fashionable thing in the Sunday newspaper and in that dreadful book, *Portnoy's Complaint.*" [86]

The robust Kate Carla may have been the first person to dare accuse Dahlberg of being a misogynist. While he protested the opposite, he justified his avoidance and condemnation of women by regarding them as *belles dames sans merci*.[87] The books he read both before and during his university days redoubled his feelings of trepidation. He doted on Hazlitt, whose *Liber Amoris* seemed to echo his own frustrations:

> Very few women have ever loved men of letters. . . . Hazlitt's *Liber Amoris* is about a tart decoying a man of letters who had a refrigerated wife. . . . It is the naked, honest portrayal of an unfortunate attempt to gain a few kisses and embraces. This was terrible for a man of Hazlitt's stature, a genius who suffered from hunger, penury! [88]

Little time existed for Dahlberg's courses, since he preferred doing his own reading and working on three novels. One of these was modeled upon Dostoevsky's *Poor People:* "That manuscript, fortunately, was lost," [89] Dahlberg remarked. Another was an imitation of Cervantes. The third, possibly reflecting the influence of Romain Rolland, was based upon the life of Beethoven. He was also beginning another manuscript, entitled *Mimes,* which foreshadowed most of his later work. Probably completed around 1925, it was donated to the University of Texas in 1968 by Kate Carla (by then Mrs. Harold T. Nachtrieb), who had no notion of how she came to possess it.[90]

Mimes is definitely the most important of Dahlberg's three apprenticeship pieces. Only a few years removed from the orphanage, Dahlberg wrote of his bumming through the West, his stay at the YMCA, and the sufferings of a Russian-Jewish boy named "Leonid Gottinger" (born of the gods) with his barber-mother in Kansas City. Saul Gottdank busily seduces Lizzie at his Rivington Street barbershop, while hopelessly sensitive young Leonid, deposited in an orphanage, crumbles under cruel regimentation. The manuscript was probably written over several years—it includes autobiographical episodes from later in his life, though the prose remained creaky and pretentious at best: "With what joy he would throw open the casement and catch in his tiny palms the fluffy particles of snow that fell from the poetic heavens, that realm of beauty and of change of the inward eye." [91] Appalling as much of the writing may have been, it demonstrates the remarkable fixity of Dahlberg's thematic material. And the brooding, self-pitying, and self-mocking narrator of all Dahlberg's fictional works was already firmly outlined.

He published a second piece, a didactic story entitled "The March of the New Generations," in the college magazine in April 1923. Lengthy and tedious, this piece betrays amateurish attempts to imitate Nietzsche, Dostoevski, and Wilde:

> With the dawn he rose and walked till noon. Before him he saw a walled city; he approached it and then knocked at the gate, which was opened, and the guards, after examining his fingernails, permitted him to enter.... Though he had traversed the city a dozen times, he could not even learn the geographical name of the place. He tried to inquire of the pedestrians; some seemed amazed, others indignant and affronted.... "Where am I?" [92]

The allegory pompously concludes with these admonitions:

> Do not, my friend, confine yourself to any one of the Schools.
> Do you reverence the cosmic unity and majestic formality of
> the classicists, and take wing with the romanticists, but be you
> neither of these.[93]

A brief, italicized postscript acknowledges the author's debt to Leo
Tolstoy and Romain Rolland, "who has been my guiding light for
the past three years." [94]

Dahlberg felt his impassioned publications would bring him the
campus celebrity he coveted, but his social ineptitude excluded
him as before. Soon, bitterness overtook and soured every aspect of
his life at Berkeley: "Every cafeteria was an ulcer food station," he
recalled. "The beds were lymphatic. . . . I did not find one professor
who was intelligent." [95] In a desperate bid for attention, he began
disrupting activities:

> I was in the English Club at the University, which was
> considered a great honor. Hildegaard Flanner, who had a love
> affair with Robinson Jeffers, was reading her poetry. It was all
> rhymed doggerel about women's breasts. Throughout the
> reading, I persisted in laughing uproariously, for which I was
> expelled at once.[96]

Dahlberg left Berkeley, "the most refrigerated university in the
world," [97] with less than two years of college credit and far more
uncertain about his future plans than he indicates in *Because I Was
Flesh*. Although both Columbia University and its cosmopolitan
locale seemed fertile ground for the cultivation of his literary
talent, his allowance from his mother and his army pension did not
begin to cover his expenses. The summer of 1923 found Dahlberg,
at twenty-three, confused, homeless, without friends, and back in
Kansas City:

> My life was a heavy affliction to me at this time; the chasm
> between my mother and me had widened. I blamed her for
> everything; whom else could I find fault with except my sole

protector? Why had she not provided me with a family? . . .
Why had not my mother given up that common trade? Was I
to stumble in the winds too? [98]

Tired and faded, Lizzie would most certainly have welcomed
her handsome and educated son as the male protector of her
declining years, for she was still desperately encouraging "suitors,"
all of whom were even more pitiful than the ones Dahlberg had
remembered from his childhood:

> There was not much variety to the sort of beaus who came
> into Lizzie's parlor; they were stubby, with round, par-
> simonious necks, and wore serge suits and vests with a pocket
> for a watch that was as large as a silver dollar.[99]

Not surprisingly, Dahlberg's visit to Kansas City was more
embarrassing than comforting to him, but it may have caused him
to confront one fact about himself to which he had been
deliberately blind: his father was Saul Gottdank. While she had
not seen Saul since Edward had been in the Jewish orphanage, and
she had not heard from him in half a decade, Lizzie was given to
ceaseless complaining about the scoundrel who had ruined her life.
Certainly the violence of her feelings toward Gottdank must have
suggested to Edward that there had been a very strong bond
between them.

As it happened, Lizzie never openly admitted to her son that
Saul Gottdank was his parent. But Dahlberg later claimed that one
day, at his mother's house, he discovered a photograph of
Gottdank, whom he recognized immediately as his father. In a fury
he later regretted, Dahlberg destroyed the picture, but he remembered the face as a handsome one: "Saul was a real dandy." [100]
Half a century later, he was still certain that the photograph might
have passed as his own.[101] Confronted with such evidence, Lizzie
could not deny that *"verdammter Saul,"* whom Dahlberg had been
taught to loathe from his earliest childhood, was indeed his father.
Although he did not publicly announce the fact of his paternity
until the publication of *Because I Was Flesh* in 1964 (even Michael

"Verdammter Saul" Gottdank, Dahlberg's father. (Courtesy of Eleanor Siegel.)

Sands was not certain of the fact), this horrifying revelation opened a rift between Dahlberg and Lizzie which never healed.

His visit to Kansas City also provided Dahlberg with two less dramatic but quite useful bits of information. Lizzie somehow knew that another of her children, a half brother to Edward, was living and studying somewhere in New York. In addition, Dahlberg was delighted to learn that his childhood Sunday school teacher, the affectionate Sara Barth, had married a wealthy man named Hafer and was living in an elegant apartment on Riverside Drive.[102]

With a stipend from his mother, Dahlberg moved into Livingston Residence Hall at Columbia University after being enrolled as a "special student." As such, he was permitted to take numerous graduate courses while fulfilling his course requirements for a bachelor in science degree in philosophy.[103] In one of his first courses he discovered Milton Goldstein, another alumnus of the Jewish Orphan Asylum, who, while studying part-time, was serving as a governor at the Pleasantville orphan home.[104] Goldstein reunited Dahlberg with Max ("Shrimp") Cohn, who was now pursuing a successful career as a commercial artist and painter. While their interests differed greatly, the three men caroused in Manhattan, ogled women on Broadway and in Morningside Heights, and played touch football in Central Park during their leisure hours. On one of his visits to Dahlberg's room in Livingston Hall, Cohn was surprised to notice a small framed photograph of Romain Rolland.[105] Although Dahlberg at the time easily succumbed to Rolland's sentimental romanticism and his identification (like Raskolnikov) with the sensitive and demoniac Napoleon,[106] he later denounced the French writer as a "twentieth-century Werther" and a "worm-eaten Romantic": "At twenty, I would have imagined he was a demigod; nevertheless, he was a very bad writer." [107]

But it was just this sort of "mawkish" romanticism which young Dahlberg craved in formulating his self-image. He also identified with Rolland's not-too-radical "humanist" socialism; his futile attempts to sustain the "old traditions" in art and literature; and his horror, very similar to that of Matthew Arnold, at the cultivated man's destruction by the philistines. Rolland was surely the writer Dahlberg hoped to be: outspoken and courageous, he had defended Alfred Dreyfus in 1895: "He owed allegiance to no government." [108]

Despite his joy in reading and the happy times spent with his few friends, the emptiness of Dahlberg's life soon began to overpower him. He remembered the first year of his career at Columbia as "the most refrigerated era I've ever gone through. . . . You couldn't find anybody worth talking to." [109] Nearly twenty-four, he had not yet learned to charm women, who seemed inaccessible since Columbia was still very much a men's college with classes separate from those at Barnard.

Some relief was granted by Mrs. Hafer, who proved to be most eager in offering her former star pupil both emotional and perhaps financial support. He was pleased to learn that Mrs. Hafer moved in a fashionable circle which included such wealthy and well-known people as Katy Wollman and Milton Goodman, who also may have aided him.[110] Mrs. Hafer's son, who is now in his fifties, remembers Dahlberg appearing at parties, often uninvited, tall, thin, very elegant, and dressed always in a smart salt-and-pepper suit with a matching vest. Seemingly playing the role of Oscar Wilde, whose decadence he continued to admire, Dahlberg would sprawl in an easy chair and monopolize the conversation with esoteric subjects which perplexed most of the other guests. One evening, young Hafer was foolhardy enough to challenge Dahlberg on a fine point in Shakespeare, whom he had been studying at Horace Mann School for Boys. The Columbia dandy exploded at the boy's "insolence" and denounced him as an upstart and a spoiled brat.[111]

The task of finding his brother was approached by Dahlberg with considerable hesitation, since the prospect of establishing firm family ties made him uneasy. Lizzie had encouraged him to make the contact, but he probably balked at the idea of sharing her attention (and her stipends) with someone whom he had never met. But several months of searching produced Michael Sands, who was living in Bensonhurst and studying engineering at The Cooper Union. Dahlberg made one visit to his brother's rooming-house, but found him not at home. Since no message had been left, Sands learned only that he had had a visitor, but when Dahlberg came again, Sands, for reasons he has never understood, sensed the kinship. He startled Dahlberg by inquiring mildly, "Are you my brother?" [112]

Their first meeting was strained, since it became clear that neither of these very different men would have had anything to do with the other had they not been brothers. Sands, who was very short, lean, meek, and nonliterary, and Dahlberg, who was tall, rawboned, nervous, and highly articulate, spoke primarily of their mother, of whom Michael had no recollection. Dahlberg made numerous unexpected demands, including one that Sands assume the name "Dalberg," but the latter would agree only to help support Lizzie when she became too old to work.[113]

With his private life growing more complicated, Dahlberg approached his studies frenetically and impatiently—just as he dealt with people. A friend recalled something of Dahlberg's reading and writing habits:

> He really had no discipline. He would read, say, Sir Thomas Browne, and memorize whole paragraphs. He would do this with several other writers, then he would sit down to write with their sentences going through his head.
>
> His method of writing was circular. It would go on as long as his energy would last—writing a circular set of impressions. Then he would transfer that to a more linear process.
>
> He always took extensive notes. Finally, they would all be juggled into manuscripts.[114]

He chose the most difficult courses, which included Philosophy 144, Irwin Edman's course in the Philosophy of Art, and John Dewey's practicum in the historical relations of philosophy and education.[115]

Anathon Aall, Visiting Professor of Philosophy from the University of Christiania in Oslo, gave a seminar in the doctrine of the Logos,[116] which introduced Dahlberg to the anti-Nicene Fathers—Tatian, Clement of Alexandria, and Tertullian. Aall recognized that he had an outstanding student in Dahlberg, who both admired and envied his teacher; but the younger man discovered that he had a hopeless block against learning foreign languages, especially dead ones. Without Greek and Latin, he had to rely on the Loeb Classics editions of the ancients, which include page-by-page translations.

Dahlberg resented sharing Professor Aall's brilliance with his classmates, whom he recalled with loathing:

> The class began at eight o'clock in the morning; the students, wild asses, chewed the thistles of knowledge. All lubbers, they slouched in their filthy trousers rolled up to their thighs, so that Anathon Aall was ashamed to lift his eyes. While he spoke about the origin of the Logos, going back to Heraclitus, the Nous of Anaxagoras, Philo, John, Clement of Alexandria, and Tatian, they snored, belched, and ate cracknel.[117]

One of the students in the class, Sidney Hook, suggested how Dahlberg may have appeared to these students whom he satirized so bitterly:

> He was a very confused and unhappy person who thought with his guts. I tried not without sympathy for his perplexity in the face of rational argument to help clarify his ideas but he seemed more interested in saying something startling than in making sense. It was clear to everyone but him that he wasn't cut out to be a philosopher. I tried to encourage him to work on aesthetics, at that time a field cultivated by people with more sensibility than analytic rigor. His own sensibility seemed highly developed for the noisome and the smelly.[118]

The tone of Professor Hook's letter suggests one reason why his friendship with Dahlberg was ill-fated: since the latter resented most of his professors it is not likely that he would welcome another student, even one of Hook's caliber, as his preceptor.[119]

Dahlberg quite naturally selected John Dewey, the most prestigious member of Columbia University's philosophy department, as the target of his most withering scorn. As a self-styled "romantic," Dahlberg had little patience with the champion of "that cutpurse philosophy,"[120] pragmatism. Dewey, then in his sixty-fifth year, had never been a colorful lecturer (Irwin Edman recalls his first lecture as "a shock of dullness and confusion" [121]), and certainly he was never given a chance by the intolerant Dahlberg, who recalled him as "an unbearable bore": "He mumbled; you couldn't understand a word. Even his prose was nasal. What's more, he's responsible for 'progressive education' and the decline of learning in this country." [122] But "Dr. However Pointless" (as Dewey is caricatured in the *Confessions*) ranged further in his discussions than Dahlberg ever suspected. Edman emphasized the necessity of having to get used to "the long sentences, with their string of qualifying clauses, to the sobriety, to the lack of image and colour" in Dewey's speech before one could realize that" "here was a man actually *thinking* in the presence of a class. To attend a lecture of John Dewey was to participate in the actual business of thought." [123] Sidney Hook added that:

> If anyone kept notes and then reread them, he would discover that there was a remarkable coherence in the positions developed by Dewey—thinking aloud with hardly a note before him. . . . You may quote me as saying that Dahlberg in the course of the lectures he attended never understood a word that Dewey was saying because he had no grasp of the problems Dewey was trying to clarify. . . . Dahlberg didn't know enough to ask questions or make objections.[124]

With his character still largely unformed at age twenty-four, Dahlberg was moved more to hero worship than to rational inquiry. The target for his idolatry became a nonresident lecturer in philosophy, Father Cornelius Clifford, a Jesuit who divided his time between his parish in Whippany, New Jersey, and his courses in the early Church Fathers and the philosophy of Thomas Aquinas.[125] He also found time to listen sympathetically to Dahlberg's innumerable problems and offer the young man both the encouragement he desperately needed and an example of continence which both attracted and repelled Dahlberg. The author's highly idealized descriptions of the priest indicate that Dahlberg felt he had finally found the father for whom he had been searching. Clifford's calm, ascetic temperament fascinated the young man, as did his appearance:

> He had a glorious nimbus of snowy hair . . . [126] [and] Celtic eyes, the hue of an Iberian sky, his head was covered with albic down and his rosy cheeks were washed in the blood of the paschal lamb.[127]
>
> Had not celibacy been imposed upon him, he would have loved some beautiful woman.[128]

Photographs of Clifford confirm Dahlberg's impressions of the priest, who, thirty years after his death, remains part of Whippany's folklore. Sometimes the young writer would travel by ferryboat and train to Whippany, just for the privilege of being seen with this eminent priest who, Dahlberg claimed, had once confided to him "that there was no advancement in the Church for a learned man." [129]

Father Clifford's tutelage actually did little to fill the inner void of his disciple, who had still to resolve his difficulties in associating with other people—especially women: "For well-nigh a year I lived by myself in a womanless world desolate as the northern regions of Hudson Bay and its surrounding snow ponds. I had no luck with the damsels on campus." [130] During his senior year at Columbia, Dahlberg met two young coeds in quick succession, Ruth Gross and Fanya Fass, who was serving as the librarian in Philosophy Hall. Much to the consternation of their fellow students and Fanya's parents, Dahlberg's affections oscillated rapidly between Fanya and Ruth.[131] Rumor circulated that the three were living in a menage; Father Clifford stopped seeing Dahlberg, who experienced once again the pangs of "parental" rejection. Fanya appeared in a section of *Mimes:* "Her fine, aquiline nose, a knowing nose which betrayed her Semitic origin, was given to wrinkles of twinkling perversity, was ever sniffing in the academic dust which lay in thick clouds about the books." He does not write of Ruth's devastation about the scandal in which she found herself. Michael Sands recalled walking with her on a bridge over the Harlem River: "The girl was so miserable. . . . She leaned over the rail and said, 'It looks so black down there.' I was afraid for her life." [132]

With Father Clifford gone and his love life beset with seemingly insuperable difficulties, Dahlberg was forced to endure yet one more repudiation. Mrs. Hafer's small-town Victorian sensibilities were outraged, and she immediately disowned him. Her son explained: "The fact that he was moving toward communism didn't bother my mother. It was only when he transcended *her* moral code by living with women before he married them that she rejected him." [133]

On June 3, 1925, Dahlberg received his bachelor of science degree in philosophy, just at the time when he learned that his mother, who had sold her barbershop, was raising chickens on a small farm in Northmoor, a suburb of Kansas City. Though his contact with Lizzie had been sporadic at best while he was at Columbia, at this juncture she seemed the most stable person (and perhaps the only person) he could turn to. He invited her to live with him New York City, and, while she was settling her affairs in Missouri, he filled his time by enrolling in a summer graduate course [134] and searching for a job and an apartment. The only suitable quarters he could find were in Astoria, Queens, "a cheap German borough with grum and gritty delicatessens and hardware stores and the dead bricks of tenements." [135] The barrenness of Astoria contrasted so violently with Morningside Heights that in a few weeks Dahlberg impulsively moved to Bensonhurst in Brooklyn, "then a rheumy marshland," [136] which was no improvement. Unfortunately, financial problems had trapped him there, so he brought his mother to live with him in the three-room apartment at 357 Midwood Street.[137] Michael Sands joined them to help meet the expenses.

Times were hard. His engineering degree notwithstanding, Sands could find work only as a handyman, while Lizzie had only a small (if stable) income from three cottages she rented in Kansas City. By September, Dahlberg had found a job teaching English at James Madison High School in Brooklyn, but he quickly ran afoul of the school administration: "After one semester I was not asked to return because I suggested that pupils read the tales of Chekhov, Tolstoi, Gorki, and the novels of George Gissing and Gogol instead of the prescribed rubbish by Zane Grey, Dickens, Thackeray, and Jack London." [138]

One of his students was Sylvia Porter, now a nationally known economist and newspaper columnist. As a very bright and ambitious thirteen-year-old, she felt "extremely receptive" to this unusual and imposing teacher, who seemed old beyond his years and had a strange eye which both attracted and repulsed the students. Miss Porter was soon "completely under his spell," as she discovered that Dahlberg blankly refused either to follow the usual boring curriculum or to give examinations. It was also known that he was shunned by the rest of the faculty—rumor had it that he was a communist. The students were titillated, as Miss Porter recalled:

> He stood out. He was unforgettable. He didn't belong. He always dressed in Harris tweeds, not the way the other teachers dressed. He didn't act the way they acted, he didn't teach the way the other teachers taught. He was completely out of it. . . . He was completely on his own in a rigid school system; before there was *any* permissiveness, he would have made Summerhill look silly.[139]

Dahlberg responded to the girl's warmth and adulation by giving her and another female student the unique privilege of visiting him at his home. This trip to a remote part of Brooklyn, to which Miss Porter had never been, left an indelible impression upon her. Dahlberg's apartment had no furniture—he used his larger books as chairs! This idea struck her as remarkably efficient. Sometime in the afternoon, he invited the girls to pose for "portrait studies," as he called them; the two were asked to pose while he photographed them wearing furs and other feminine garments which he lent them.

Unfortunately, his small coterie of admirers could do little to prevent his being transferred to Thomas Jefferson High School, where he immediately repeated his indiscretions, and he was not rehired at the end of the school year. Henry Goodman, who taught in the English department during Dahlberg's tenure, recalled the latter's solitariness and absolute avoidance of the rest of the faculty: "I would think that I shared what seemed to be the general impression of him—that he looked down on the other members of the department and that he had a very superior attitude toward other people in general." [140] Mr. Goodman's son, Roger, added that an exceptionally familylike atmosphere prevailed in the English department at "Jeff": "When I was growing up, they became part of the household. Dahlberg simply couldn't fit in." [141] Dahlberg was quick to agree with this appraisal: "My recollections of the high school are very nebulous. I had nothing to do with the faculty, so I guess my contempt was a touchstone for my perceptions." [142]

Though Dahlberg was hardly perturbed by the sudden end of his high school teaching career, he ended up in an equally unstimulating job as a social worker and married Ruth Gross in January 1926.[143] The marriage was a rash one, since Fanya Fass was still very much a part of Dahlberg's life, and within two months he was separated from Ruth and courting Fanya, who was still employed as a librarian at Philosophy Hall. Fanya's parents, Esther and Nathan Fass, thoroughly disapproved of her consorting with a married man. On February 28, the elder Fasses surprised Dahlberg and Fanya while they were discussing plans for elopement after Dahlberg had secured an out-of-state divorce. A furious argument ensued, during which Dahlberg punched Mrs. Fass in the mouth and dislodged two of her teeth. The police were summoned, and Dahlberg was arrested and held without bail until Mrs. Fass preferred assault and disorderly conduct charges against him.[144] On March 4 he was convicted; he received a ninety-day suspended sentence and was ordered to make bond for $500 and to keep the peace for six months.[145]

The scandal, which broke in all the major newspapers in the city, disgraced Fanya and cost Dahlberg his civil service job; it also caused him to change the spelling of his name. Fanya defended the man she wanted to marry, even against the magistrate, named Gordon, who sought to conciliate her parents. He asked the defendant and the young woman if she and her "fiancé" had studied much philosophy together:

"Yes, we have," replied Miss Fass.
"You are believers in the new freedom aren't you?"
"Well, I believe that is rather a personal question," replied the witness.
When the Magistrate said he found Dalberg guilty and remanded him without bail Miss Fass turned abruptly and asked:

"Can I prefer assault charges against my parents?"

"Young woman," returned the Magistrate, "don't try to add insult to injury in this case, by asking [sic] such a sugges- tion!" [146]

The Dahlberg affair was bruited in and around Columbia University, especially after he and Fanya were finally married.[147] The young couple despised their unwanted celebrity, and the new bride was known to be uncomfortable in the marriage itself. Sidney Hook and his wife had the Dahlbergs over to dinner several times and noted Fanya's frightened behavior: "She used to echo his ideas. When I once mildly expressed surprise she told me that whenever she disagreed with him in public he would beat her up when they got home. Whether this was actually true I had no way of knowing but they separated or divorced not long after." [148]

To support both herself and Dahlberg, who was now unem- ployed, Fanya opened a small pottery and antique shop on fifty- first Street and Madison Avenue.[149] She proved to have an excellent business sense: trade became so brisk that soon she needed an assistant. An advertisement she ran in the *New York Times* was answered by a young and penniless artist named Alice Neel—now one of America's most distinguished painters.[150] She remembered that Dahlberg mainly loitered about the shop and left business matters to his wife, "although, because I was a very good looking girl, he would send me up on the ladders to look up my skirts." [151] It seems that Fanya, a talented musician, was frequently absent from the shop, since she was busy giving piano lessons at the apartment in Bensonhurst.[152]

With Fanya heavily occupied, Dahlberg was left to deal with his boredom and his mother's growing unhappiness with life in New York. Lizzie pathetically began, as she had years before, to try to sell herself through poorly worded matrimonial ads in the news- papers. She succeeded in submerging Dahlberg in her problems: "Since I was useless, I began to sleep late; I craved to be the four- footed beasts in the darkness, for the sun confused and punished me. . . . I already began to doubt that my mother lived, though I dreaded that she would die, and I would lose her image." [153] What little tranquility may have existed in the small apartment, now housing four, was soon shattered by quarrels between the women

Fanya, painted by Alice Neel, 1930. (Courtesy of Alice Neel.)

of the house. Faded Lizzie resented the scrupulous and dynamic manner of the young, attractive Fanya, with whom she now had to share her son and who, in the heat of an argument, once accused her of being a "madam." [154]

Dahlberg was not entirely sorry to see his petulant mother, exasperated with the living arrangements her son had provided, return to her chicken farm in Northmoor, Kansas. The shop was prospering, and Fanya had convinced one her her wealthy clients to invest heavily in it.[155] Dahlberg inveigled Fanya into entrusting him with a considerable portion of the funds, to buy ceramics and other artifacts in Europe.

On Saturday, July 3, 1926, Dahlberg embarked third-class on the S.S. *Rotterdam* for Paris and London. The fare was only $98, the food was good, the ship was filled with students, and Dahlberg found himself having a very fine time: "I was stupid enough not to mind."[156] He found himself quite bedazzled by Europe, and, since the attractions of the literary world there completely eclipsed his interest in objects d'art, he hired an agency to handle the buying.[157] Fanya soon became aware that Edward would never return.

NOTES

1. Letter: Horace Schwartz, Feb. 28, 1973.
2. New York: Simon & Schuster, 1930.
3. Interview: E. D., Nov. 24, 1972.
4. Interview: E.D., Nov. 24, 1972. Conscription had been instituted on May 18, 1917.
5. *Because I Was Flesh,* pp. 92-93.
6. Interview: E. D., Feb 27, 1973.
7. *Because I Was Flesh,* p. 97.
8. Ibid., p. 102
9. Ibid., p. 99.
10. Ibid., p. 103.
11. In *Bottom Dogs,* Lorrie Lewis at age eighteen is given a "licking" as punishment for getting his overcoat dirty (p. 142).
12. Laurence Ferlinghetti wrote that he reissued *Bottom Dogs* in 1961 because he saw the book as "a pre-Beat *On the Road* with its journey through American back streets, orphan's homes, barbershops, dancehalls & YMCA's, etc." (Letter: August 15, 1972.)
13. Lou Gilbert recalled several of Dahlberg's brief visits to the home.

14. Interview: Lou Gilbert, Feb. 3, 1973.
15. Interview: E. D., Feb 11, 1973.
16. (1908; rpt. London: Jonathan Cape, 1968.)
17. Dahlberg often claimed he was never influenced by Dostoevski.
18. Knut Hamsen, *Hunger,* trans. Isaac B. Singer (New York: Noonday, 1967), pp. 134-335.
19. Ibid., p. 171.
20. Ibid., p. 129.
21. *Because I Was Flesh,* p. 126. A photograph taken in 1932 shows Dahlberg with a receding hairline, but far from bald.
22. See *Bottom Dogs,* Ch. X.
23. Interview: E. D., April 2, 1973.
24. Interview: E.D., April 2, 1973.
25. *Because I Was Flesh,* p. 119.
26. *The Confessions of Edward Dahlberg,* p. 39.
27. Dahlberg could not remember the name of the school.
28. Henry Hafer owns a "Missouri ROTC" insignia given him by Dahlberg.
29. United Stated of America, Certification of Military Service, form GSA 6954.
30. Interview: E.D., Sept. 16, 1973.
31. Interview: E. D., Sept. 16, 1973.
32. Obviously one of Dahlberg's fantasies, since he remained a private throughout his brief military career.
33. Interview: E. D., Nov. 24, 1972.
34. Interview: Frank McCourt, May 5, 1973. Mr. McCourt is an old friend of Dahlberg's.
35. Kevin O'Carroll, Dahlberg's younger son, and many other relatives believe this account.
36. Interview: E. D., Dec. 12, 1972.
37. *Because I Was Flesh,* P. 115.
38. Ibid., P. 125.
39. Interviews: E. D., April 2, 1973; Nov. 16, 1972.
40. Interview: E. D., April 2, 1973.
41. Interview: E. D., Nov. 16, 1972.
42. *Because I Was Flesh,* P. 128.
43. Interview: E. D., April 2, 1973.
44. *Bottom Dogs,* pp. 220-321.
45. Interview: E. D., Nov. 16, 1972.
46. *Because I Was Flesh,* p. 129.
47. Interview: Michael Sands, April 19, 1972.
48. Interview: E. D., Nov. 16, 1972. Michael Sands knew Lewis well and worked for him during the 1930s.
49. Interview: E. D., Nov. 16, 1972.
50. *Because I Was Flesh,* pp. 135-336.
51. *Confessions,* p. 61.
52. *Because I Was Flesh,* p. 137.
53. Interview: Michael Sands, Feb. 20, 1973.

54. Interview: Michael Sands, Feb. 20, 1973.
55. Interview: E. D., Nov. 16, 1972.
56. *Because I Was Flesh,* p. 138.
57. Interview: E. D., Dec 29, 1972.
58. *Confessions,* p. 43.
59. Interviews: E. D., May 22, 1972; Nov. 16, 1972.
60. Interview: Rlene Dahlberg, Mar. 12, 1973. Dahlberg and Rlene (sic), who was then married to him, tried unsuccessfully in 1952 to see Lewis.
61. Interview: E. D., Aug. 15, 1972.
62. *Confessions,* p. 105.
63. Ibid., p. 106. Robert died in 1928.
64. *From Flushing to Calvary,* p. 79.
65. Interview: E. D., Jan. 29, 1973.
66. *Confessions,* p. 109.
67. Ibid., p. 115.
68. Ibid., p. 109.
69. Interview: E. D., Feb. 27, 1973.
70. *Because I Was Flesh,* p. 144.
71. Interview: E. D., Feb. 27, 1973.
72. Interview: E. D., Feb. 27, 1973.
73. *Because I Was Flesh,* p.143.
74. *Confessions,* pp. 119-20.
75. Interview: Kate C. Nachtrieb, Feb 11, 1973.
76. *Occident,* 80 (November, 1922), 141.
77. Ibid.
78. Interviews: E. D., Nov. 24, 1972; Kate Carla Nachtrieb, Feb. 11, 1973.
79. *Because I Was Flesh,* p. 146.
80. Harold Billings, interview: Kate Carla Nachtrieb, Dec. 8, 1968.
81. Interview: Kate C. Nachtrieb, Feb 11, 1973.
82. *Confessions,* p. 137.
83. Harold Billings, interview: Kate C. Nachtrieb, Dec. 8, 1968.
84. Interview: Kate C. Nachtrieb, Feb. 11, 1973; Harold Billings, interview: Kate C. Nachtrieb, Dec. 8, 1968.
85. Interview: Kate Carla Nachtrieb, Feb. 11, 1973. She was referring to *The Sorrows of Priapus* (New York: New Directions, 1957).
86. Interview: Kate Carla Nachtrieb, Feb. 11, 1973.
87. Harold Billings, interview: Kate Carla Nachtrieb, Dec. 8, 1968.
88. Interview: E. D., May 22, 1972.
89. Interview: E. D., Feb. 11, 1973.
90. Letter: Harold Billings, Aug. 5, 1973.
91. "Mimes," *Bottom Dogs, From Flushing to Calvary, Those Who Perish* and hitherto unpublished and uncollected works, ed. Harold Billings (New York: Minerva Press), p. 19.
92. *Occident,* 81 (April 1923), 465-66.
93. Ibid., p. 479.
94. Ibid., p. 480.

95. Interview: E. D., Nov. 24, 1972.

96. Interview: E. D., July 1, 1973.

97. Interview: E. D., Nov. 24, 1972.

98. *Because I Was Flesh,* pp. 163-64.

99. Ibid., p. 157.

100. Interview: E. D., April 2, 1973.

101. Eleanor Siegel (Gottdank's granddaughter) supplied a similar photograph of Saul.

102. Interview: Henry Hafer, Mar. 10, 1973.

103. Letter: Andrew Greenwald (Assistant Manager of the Records Division of the Registrar of Columbia University): April 3, 1973. The middle initial is a mystery.

104. Coincidentally, Michael Sands, Dahlberg's yet undiscovered brother, had been raised at Pleasantville (see Ch. I).

105. Interview: Max Cohn, Feb. 13, 1973.

106. See *Jean-Christophe,* trans. Gilbert Cannon, esp. Vol. X (Chicago: Open Court Publishing Co., 1912), p. 504.

107. Interview: E. D., Feb. 23, 1973.

108. Interview: E. D., Feb. 23, 1973.

109. Interview: E. D., Feb. 27, 1973.

110. Interview: Henry Hafer, Mar. 9, 1973.

111. Mr. Hafer related that his only brief meeting with Dahlberg since the 1930s ended abruptly when Dahlberg denounced him as a "Park Avenue Tartuffe."

112. Interview: Michael Sands, Feb. 20, 1973,

113. Sands did eventually use the name Michael Dalberg, but he changed it back to Sands after falling out with his brother in the 1940s.

114. Interview: Feb. 12, 1973.

115. *Bulletin of Information: Philosophy, Psychology, and Anthropology* (New York: Columbia University, June 21, 1924), pp. 14-16.

116. P. 16; Interview: E. D., Dec. 5, 1972. The course was entitled "The Influence of Hellenism on Christianity."

117. *Confessions,* p. 160.

118. Letter: Sept. 11, 1972.

119. Hook and Dahlberg became bitter enemies in the 1930s while both were members of the Communist party.

120. *Alms for Oblivion* (Minneapolis: University of Minnesota Press, 1964), p. 77.

121. *Philosopher's Holiday* (New York: Viking Press, 1938), pp. 138-39.

122. Interview: E. D., Dec. 28, 1973.

123. Edman, *Philosopher's Holiday* (New York: Viking Press, 1938), pp. 139-141.

124. Letter: Sidney Hook, May 8, 1973.

125. *Columbia University Bulletin,* June 21, 1924, p. 14.

126. Interview: E. D., Feb. 27, 1973.

127. *Confessions,* p. 181.

128. Interview: E. D., Feb. 27, 1973.

129. Interview: E. D., Feb. 27, 1973.

130. *Confessions,* p. 137.
131. Interview: Max Cohn, Feb. 1, 1973. Letter: Sidney Hook, Sept. 11, 1972.
132. Interview: Michael Sands, Dec. 9, 1972; *Mimes,* p. 69.
133. Interview: Henry Hafer, Mar. 9, 1973.
134. Letter: Andrew N. Greenwald, April 3, 1973.
135. *Because I Was Flesh,* p.208.
136. Ibid., p. 205.
137. *New York Times,* March 5, 1926, p. 9.
138. *Because I Was Flesh,* p. 226.
139. Interview: Sylvia Porter, Aug. 30, 1973.
140. Interview: Jan 7, 1973.
141. Interview: Jan 8, 1973.
142. Interview: Jan. 11, 1973.
143. *New York Times,* March 5, 1926, p. 9.
144. *New York Journal,* Mar. 2, 1926, p. 1.
145. *New York Times,* Mar. 5, 1926, p. 9.
146. *New York Journal,* Mar. 2, 1926, p. 2.
147. Interview: Max Cohn, Feb. 1, 1973.
148. Letter: Sidney Hook, Sept. 11, 1972.
149. Interview: Michael Sands, Feb. 20, 1973.
150. Interview: Alice Neel, Feb. 8, 1973.
151. Interview: Alice Neel, Feb. 8, 1973.
152. Interview: Michael Sands, Feb. 20, 1973.
153. *Because I Was Flesh,* p. 226.
154. Interview: Alice Neel, Feb. 8, 1973.
155. Interviews: Alice Neel, Feb 8, 1973; Michael Sands, Mar. 8, 1973.
156. Interview: E. D., April 14, 1973. *New York Times,* June 28, 1926, p. 35.
157. Interview: Michael Sands, Feb. 20, 1973.

3.

Expatriate Years: 1926-1929

Dahlberg found he could live most flamboyantly on slightly more than fifty dollars a month in the Paris of 1926. He found a dilapidated but attractive studio which opened on a lush, walled garden, in the Atelier Autueil in the northern outskirts of the city. From there, he could range anywhere in the expatriate mecca for less than ten francs in carfare.[1] (These were old francs, about the equivalent of two cents.) He equipped himself with the cape and soft, wide-brimmed hat of a bohemian gentleman (his trademarks for years to come), and had no need to work, thanks to his army pension, his few savings, the money left over from his antique buying, and two dollars a week Michael Sands was able to send him.[2]

He had shipped with him a great deal of manuscript material, including some poetry, essays, and a group of autobiographical fragments, some of which he presented to Eugene Jolas, who was preparing the first issue of *transition* magazine.[3] Jolas had broken away from the leisurely but extremely prestigious journal, *This Quarter,* which had been publishing in its first two numbers both American, British, and Irish expatriates, including Ernest Heming-

61

way, Ezra Pound, James Joyce, Kay Boyle, Robert McAlmon, Ernest Walsh, and Jolas himself.[4]

Though Jolas held the manuscripts for several weeks and then rejected them, Dahlberg was relatively unperturbed, for he had found his way to La Coupole, "a cafe famous for having persons such as Kiki the courtesan,[5] Kay Boyle,[6] and McAlmon. Joyce also went there, and, of course, Hart Crane, and the notorious drunken doctor in *Nightwood* with his patron, Djuna Barnes." [7]

Dahlberg found it easy to devalue the majority of his fellow expatriates: "While they drank, I read. You cannot write anything while you are carousing." [8] He made an exception, however, in the case of the acerbic Robert McAlmon, whose personality he found compelling: "He was a tubercular bantam with sharp, querulous hair, and a thin, exasperated mouth. Everything about him was scant except his prodigal heart and his vocabulary of four-letter words. He was the most obscene man I had ever met." [9] Dahlberg warmed not only to McAlmon's studied artistic manner and appearance but also to his sentiments: "He was the epitome of the self-appointed exile who hated the antiseptic, epicene American town and took the greatest yea-saying joy in depicting it." McAlmon had "resolved to be outrageous," and, like Dahlberg, "he had insulted everyone." [10] He was able to relate exciting and romantic tales of two other writers suffering from artists' ailments— Emanuel Carnevali, an Italian writer who was the secretary of Joel Spingarn,[11] and the flamboyant Irish writer, Ernest Walsh. Carnevali wrote in English, which he had learned virtually by osmosis, while Walsh "had been a pilot in the First World War, had fallen in a plane in a Texas airfield, and been discharged from the military hospital as an incurable invalid. He looked so ill that strangers often avoided him." [12] Walsh, who "endeavored to compose Chaucerian verse in the American vernacular,"[13] according to Dahlberg, coedited the first two numbers of *This Quarter* with the Scottish painter and writer, Ethel Moorhead. But by October 16, 1926, when Dahlberg journeyed to Roquebrune, a small village about fifteen miles from Montecarlo where Moorhead had been staying, he found that Walsh had already succumbed to tuberculosis. *This Quarter* number 3 became his memorial issue.[14]

Though she had just buried her warm friend and collaborator,

Miss Moorhead received Dahlberg graciously. He, however, was put off by her spirited and extroverted manner, and especially by her feminist activities, described by Kay Boyle: "Before the war, Ethel Moorhead had been active in the woman's suffrage movement in England. She had smashed plate-glass windows with a hammer, trembling with nervousness as she struck; she had set fire to churches, and been forcibly fed." [15] Filtered through Dahlberg's memory, Miss Moorhead emerges as something less than a plucky standard-bearer of women's rights:

> [She] had been a lean, stiff figure, with a long theoretical nose, an acrimonious mouth, and wore thick lenses over which she darted her suspicious glances. . . . She was a dogmatic feminist, had marched to Whitehall with a battalion of suffragettes, and whenever this procession of Irish and London Furies came upon a man they cried out, "Shame." [16]

Dahlberg, however, admired the obvious literary talents of this "highly intelligent she-bigot,"[17] since "she despised the Calibans of the bookish world: Arnold Bennett, Chesterton, Van Wyck Brooks, Gorham B. Munson, and Ernest Hemingway" [18] and published his own work.[19]

The Dahlberg items accepted for publication in *This Quarter* number 4 were a strange assortment, although they filled nearly a fourth of the magazine. His first contribution, a mawkish story about a suicidal and fantasy-laden Irish girl, "The Dream Life of Mary Moody," found Dahlberg far out of his element. In a narrative which would have been handled easier by a hard-core naturalist such as Farrell, Dahlberg related the inevitable decline of an ill-starred, Irish-American proletarian child. Her father, a drunken "bottle picker," dies of his vice, while the mother lapses into catatonia. Mary suffers a breakdown after preparing her father's corpse for burial. She comes to inhabit a world of sexual and romantic fantasies which may often have been Dahlberg's own. Though the story is graced with a few promising descriptive passages, Mary is hurried to a hasty and predictable death after absentmindedly stepping into the path of a milk wagon. Her squalid funeral rites are narrated in a stilted "Irish" dialect considerably inferior to that in Stephen Crane's "Maggie." [20]

Miss Moorhead also included selections from *Bottom Dogs,* then a "work in progress" entitled "Beginnings and Continuation of Lorry Gilchrist," [21] some vers libre poems which contained, in montage form, much of the "Bensonhurst" material later to be included in *From Flushing to Calvary* (1932) [22] and, most important, a statement entitled "Ariel in Caliban," in which the author expounded literary priciples that would dominate his writing for the next decade.

Dahlberg began his essay by announcing ceremoniously that he was, philosophically, abandoning the flamboyant Oscar Wilde because "though extraordinarily elastic in his appreciation of form, Wilde was still a little too eclectic. Too many things disgusted him. He, who lived fully in his dream world, did not realize the lyric possibilities of the commonplace" (p. 260). In disowning Wilde, Dahlberg was simultaneously embracing the primitivism and proletarian naturalism—the "bottom-dog" style—which gained him his earliest attention. In the same essay he espoused a theme which would persist in all of his future writing—his detestation of the machine: "Nothing has contributed so much to the aesthetic of modern diablerie as modern industrialism" (p. 258).

In the most revealing portion of this rather premature apologia, Dahlberg proclaimed that he would henceforth turn to a new and more dynamic preceptor than Wilde:

> James Joyce has done with ordinary Dublin what no artist has done with the subway and surface cars of New York. He has found Ariel in Caliban. Joyce is the poet of smell, color and sound. He has a better stomach than Zola and a finer feeling for subtle analogies than Flaubert had. He has mingled perception and audition more sensuously than any of his Parisian predecessors. He is the most virile of all the neurotics. (p. 260) [23]

Evidence that Dahlberg was grooming himself as the American James Joyce was not long in coming. He wrote a story (not published until the summer of 1931) entitled "Coney Island

Angelus Bells," which proved to be a stark imitation of *Ulysses*. Dahlberg's honkytonk *Walpurgisnacht* is textbook stream of consciousness:

> Sideshow circusbarkers were calling
> "Try the whip!
>   "Show your sweetie"
> "swirling . . .
>   whirling . . .
>   tickling . . ."
> The handtruck racket of sightseeing tired-businessmen's wheelingchairs rollercoasting down the boardwalk.
> "Win a kewpie doll"
>   "Try the hammer"
> barranging clanging, auctioneering, barranging coney island angelus bells.[24]

Dahlberg claimed he turned down an opportunity to meet Joyce,[25] as in later years he would entirely repudiate Joyce as well as his own early writing as "a dull litany of revulsions—sick ink." [26] In fact, he became uncomfortable with his Joycean imitations soon after his arrival in Paris: a number of these early works were published simply because they were the manuscripts he had available. Kenneth Rexroth explained Dahlberg's uneasy flirtation with Joyce in this way:

> At the time [1924-25] that Joyce had started *Finnegans Wake* (it was then called "Work in Progress") and it was just being published in *transatlantic review*, a rumor, spread largely by Robert McAlmon, who was doing some of the typing for Joyce, went around the Left Bank that Joyce was writing an epic in the style of Thomas Nashe. This created quite a little flurry; and Djuna Barnes wrote a book, really one of her best, which is sort of a lesbian *Tom Jones*, a satire on masculinity called *Ryder*. . . . And then there's the pamphlet, *Ladies Almanack*. . . .[27]

I'm sure this whole Baroque style started off with Djuna
Barnes—I don't have any doubt about that at all.[28]

Theoretically, Dahlberg may have been rehearsing for his later
style of writing, but Ethel Moorhead had already paid him for his
contributions to *This Quarter* and she encouraged him to expand his
"Lorry Gilchrist" (soon to be "Lorrie Lewis") material into a
naturalistic novel. Friction was growing between the two, however,
since she resented Dahlberg's attempts to usurp editorial authority
and impose his taste upon the magazine. He blamed their
arguments on Miss Moorhead's supposed "anti-Semitism" [29] and
the fact that "She really wanted me to go to bed with her,
[although] she was an extremely homely woman. Why should I go
to bed with a crone when I had a lovely minion?" [30] The "minion"
in question was Winifred Eaton Webb, the niece of the wealthy
Cleveland industrialist, Cyrus Eaton. In 1927, she and Dahlberg
moved together to Brussels,[31] where he was able to complete the
manuscript of his novel for which he had neither title nor
publisher. Since Winifred did not have access to the spectacular
wealth of her family (she had, in fact, been temporarily disowned
by her father for having left her husband, a young physician),
poverty began to threaten the young couple. Nevertheless,
Dahlberg, though once again terrified by "the depths of penury,"
was awed by the opulence of his mistress's background, which was
not limited to material wealth. Her beauty, her quick wit, and her
patrician education were peerless attractions: "She had gone to
Mount Holyoke and done her work with Tucker Brooke in
Marlowe. She was by no means an insipid person." [32]

Dahlberg's blissful interlude with Winifred was interrupted by
several short periods of estrangement before she was finally
"reclaimed" by a delegation consisting of her husband, Cyrus
Eaton's two sisters, and a friend of the husband, all of whom
escorted the young lady back to America. Her return, Dahlberg
thought, was not entirely involuntary:

> She was under the impression, quite erroneous, that I was
> hankering for her fortune. She was to inherit a million dollars,
> but actually *she* made all the overtures to me. . . . I don't know

whether I'd want to be hanging on to the pecuniary petticoats of a woman.[33]

After the humiliating conclusion of his "amorous dalliance" with Winifred, Dahlberg was again broken by solitude.[34] Deciding upon a "geographic" cure for his loneliness, he set out to meet Carnevali, who was suffering from what some doctors thought were advanced symptoms of syphilis; he had returned to Italy to recuperate.[35] After exchanging a few letters with the Italian, Dahlberg journeyed from Brussels to Bazzano, "a hilly medieval town, two and a half hours by steam train from Bologana, to visit him." [36] In Italy, Carnevali's affliction had been rediagonosed as "encephalitis lethargica," a form of sleeping sickness. Dahlberg located him in a sanitarium,[37] where it took Carnevali several hours to muster the strength to see his visitor. But Dahlberg was far from disappointed at the only meeting he would ever enjoy with the fiery Florentine: "We had a very convivial supper; I brought him the most marvelous pastries I've ever had, and cigarettes, and the eighty dollars which had been the payment for my contribution to *This Quarter*. I gave that to Carnevali, although I had no money myself." [38]

Dahlberg's enthusiasm for Carnevali was reciprocated. Here were two kindred spirits, violently disappointed men, famished for recognition, and self-styled decadent romantics. Dahlberg strongly identified with a passage in Carnevali's autobiography (then still a manuscript) [39] in which the author complained:

> There was no help for me, no cure, because of the major sin I had committed: that of loving success. Above all, I was an envious man, madly jealous of all the writers who had got out more than one book. (I am jealous now, yes jealous even of Shakespeare. I am frantically in need of praise, I am crazy about being considered a major poet, and the fact that there may be other poets greater than I am makes my heart sick.) [40]

Carnevali's physical condition barred a long visit, so Dahlberg returned for a time to Paris. There he filled many of his empty hours with the poet Walter Lowenfels and his wife Lillian,[41] who had introduced him to Hart Crane at La Coupole, together with "the man who was the homosexual alcoholic in *Nightwood.*" After accompanying Crane and his friends through a number of all-night parties,[42] he shifted his attention to Arabella York, then separated from her husband, Richard Aldington: [43] "They had been living on the Island of Bandol, and were neighbors of Lawrence and his wife Frieda." [44] Still badly bruised by the loss of Winifred, Dahlberg agreed to accompany Arabella to London, where he arrived with only twelve dollars in his pocket. There, however, Arabella proved to be the most fortunate acquaintance made by him during his expatriate years. Through her he met most of his important literary connections, most of whom clustered at the Chelsea Pub:

> She introduced me to F. S. Flint, who was the founder of the Imagist movement, and who was responsible for the publication of *Bottom Dogs.* . . . Through Flint I met Eliot. T. M. Ragby became an ardent admirer of mine, and Herbert Read was there. I only learned years later that he was a great admirer of mine—not until 1941 when he began *Politics of the Unpolitical* with an excerpt from *Can These Bones Live.*[45]

In "diggings" in Chelsea, Dahlberg took the cheapest quarters he could find but soon he moved to a Quaker house in Sydenham Hill.[46] Meanwhile, Flint, after encouraging Dahlberg to organize his manuscript into presentable form, set about arranging to have the book published by Constance Huntington of G. P. Putnam's Sons. D. H. Lawrence was offered a small fee to write an introduction.

Dahlberg was impressed, probably even overawed, by Lawrence's reputation, but the two men were not destined to meet until Dahlberg was about to return to America in 1929—and then only by accident—in Sylvia Beach's famous Shakespeare & Co. Bookshop. Dahlberg, in fact, avoided an encounter, preferring to let Flint and Huntington approach Lawrence for his help. With uncharacteristic humility, Dahlberg commented: "How could a nobody, who had never published anything, prevail upon Lawrence, who had a tremendous reputation at the time (although he wasn't making much money), to write an introduction?" [47]

It is a sad fact that people saved all of Lawrence's letters, "but he saved no one's." [48] Obviously Dahlberg was a pestiferous correspondent, as we can tell from Lawrence's lengthy and increasingly exasperated replies to his letters, in which the younger man seemed to be writing as if to a parent. The earliest Lawrence letter is encouraging, if somewhat condescending: the master didn't like Dahlberg's "old-fashioned wart of sordid realism" at first, but he thinks he reaches his stride when he moves on to the orphanage. Dahlberg's apprehension of the "blindness" of the American consciousness, "the curious street-arab, down-and-out stoicism, something very dreary and yet impressive, denuded like those brown and horrid rocks in Central Park, seems to be the real theme." Here was the strongest encouragement Dahlberg had ever received, offered by a "Titan" of modern literature. Lawrence added some paternal advice in a postscript: "Best stick to your guns—don't weaken and get sentimental or hopeful or despairing— that bony stoicism is the thing." [49] He pressed on about this "stoicism" in his next letter: "What I like about your novel is that it does not whine and doesn't look to other people for help. The individuals remain on their own and that is so much the best." But Lawrence also sensed the weakness that plagued even the best of Dahlberg's works—his self-pitying sentimentality: "don't get so vague and wishy-washy about your private affairs—it's so weakening." [50]

Lawrence quickly grew impatient with Dahlberg's attempts to involve the older writer in his private life. Moreover, the American's petulance and his obsession with money strained the tenuous relationship. In one letter, Lawrence is piqued that Dahlberg has fussed about the cost of postage stamps, while in another he offers wry advice, which Dahlberg himself became fond of quoting: "for HEAVEN'S SAKE LEAVE OFF BEING UNLUCKY—you seem to ask for it." In this same letter, Lawrence begins, somewhat facetiously, to rummage for a title for Dahlberg's forthcoming novel: "[Putnam's] say you think of *Hot-dogs!* for a title, but surely it's too cheap. Better *Cold Feet*—They've [i.e., the orphans] all got cold feet all the time. Or else a proper phrase: *It's cold on the Bed Rock!* I think the second is better." [51]

Lawrence was fatally ill while writing the introduction and certainly resented being involved with a manipulative young

American author whose work he in fact did not like. He fulfilled his obligation by supplying one of the least inviting prefaces ever to launch an author's career:

> It is a genuine book, as far as it goes, even if it is an objectionable one. It is, in psychic disintegration, a good many stages ahead of *Point Counter Point.* . . . It is, let us hope, a *ne plus ultra.* The next step is legal insanity, or just crime. The book is perfectly sane: yet two more strides and it is criminal insanity. The style seems to me excellent, fitting the matter. It is sheer bottom-dog style, the bottom-dog mind expressing itself direct, almost as if it barked. . . . I don't want to read any more books like this. But I am glad to have read this one, just to know what is the last word in repulsive consciousness, consciousness in a state of repulsion.[52]

Walter Lowenfels, who had encouraged Lawrence to write the introduction, recalled Dahlberg's furious reaction:

> He wrote to Lawrence telling him how violently he disagreed with what Lawrence had written. . . .
> Lawrence was ill at the time and I wrote him how sorry I was to have gotten him involved in such a dispute after all he had done to help the book.[53]

Lawrence had not actually been eager to damage Dahlberg's career—he even suggested that Dahlberg remove the introduction from the American edition if he hated it so violently. And he offered consolation: "It won't hurt *English* sales, as Putnam knows, even if it is a bad sales-letter in America. I can't help it anyhow—I had to write what I felt." [54] Not only was this advice not taken; Dahlberg nurtured his hatred by including the introduction in every edition of *Bottom Dogs:*

> Lawrence was really a glut of malice. He took a young man and utterly decimated him.[55]
> Lawrence considered the waifs in that Jewish Lazarhouse, the orphan home in Cleveland, almost unborn. Those gray

puking gnomes, their necks covered with impostumes and
their heads pestered with ringworm, were all belly and no
feeling, so hungry were they for a plate of porridge they could
eat, or for that other sop they were never given, affection.
What did Lawrence, the son of a poor drunken Derbyshire
collier, expect? [56]

Dahlberg exploded at the notion, set forth by a critic, that *Sons
and Lovers* had influenced him in writing *Bottom Dogs*.[57] Throughout
his life, Dahlberg was irked by Lawrence's success in fictionalizing
his feelings for his mother:

> I wasn't influenced by Lawrence at *all!* Not at all! That's a
> small, wanton, niggardly conjecture! *Sons and Lovers* the
> prototype of *Bottom Dogs?* He's crazy. . . .
> I did not know Lawrence, I had never read his work. After
> Lawrence agreed to read my manuscript, he sent me the first
> edition of *Lady Chatterley's Lover*—that's what happened. But
> before writing *Bottom Dogs* I hadn't read a thing of
> Lawrence.[58]

Although Dahlberg was later to be strongly influenced by *Studies in
American Literature,* there is little evidence that he was seriously
reading much contemporary literature early in his career, except
for Joyce and Dos Passos. Thus, the many resemblances between
the two books may well be coincidental.

Dahlberg lapsed into gloom as the fate of his book became more
uncertain. Constance Huntington, chief editor at Putnam's, decided to inaugurate *Bottom Dogs* as a numbered edition limited to
520 copies, since he thought the book might be considered obscene.
Dahlberg recalled, "Censorship was very austere at the time, and I
feared that the book might have been banned—which would have
been a glory." [59] To ease his friend's disquiet, Walter Lowenfels
sent Dahlberg to visit Hart Crane, who was living at Villa Street
with the artist Eugene McCown.

> Both Hart and Gene read Dahlberg's book and were im-
> pressed with it. Gene did an imaginative drawing we all liked.

Hart said it got the quality of the book exactly. If you looked carefully at the design you could see that it was a man's mouth talking through his asshole.

Dahlberg took the picture and sent it off to the London publisher. A few days later, he showed me their response: "We thought your book was dirty. But we didn't think you did!" [60]

While Dahlberg probably did not appreciate this clever slap at the censors (intended for the dustjacket of his book [61]), he respected Crane's literary judgment, especially in the light of the praise he had given the manuscript.[62] In addition, Dahlberg was intrigued by the remarkable biographical parallels between himself and the self-destructive poet: "Hart Crane was born July 21, 1899, and I on July 22, 1900. When he was a soda fountain clerk in his father's fancy ice cream parlor in Cleveland, I was then an inmate of an orphanage in the same city. For a short space of time Crane was a navvy in a munitions plant in Cleveland, and so was I." [63] Nightmarish stories of Crane's being "the brunt of the bestial, Faustian altercations between his parents" fascinated Dahlberg. By the time the two men met, Crane's drinking was out of control and he had been the victim of near-fatal beatings in Paris bars and elsewhere: "I got him out of one scrape. *Gendarmes* took all of his money—I had to give him money, otherwise he would have starved." [64] The story of this rescue may have been no more genuine than Dahlberg's insistence that he did not suspect Crane's homosexuality: "Of course, I had *heard* about pathics, but had not the scantiest suspicion that Hart Crane was a pederast. Crane was a stocky, virile man with a Jovean square face, mizzling, foggy eyes, gun-metal gray hair, and a smouldering, amorous mouth." [65] Apparently forgetting the innocence which he proclaimed publicly, Dahlberg later contradicted himself: "I knew [that Crane was a homosexual] shortly after coming to Villa Seurat, because a number of times he asked me to go and see him at McCown's. And then he told me." [66]

Dahlberg's attention became riveted on Crane's relationship with his mother, Grace Crane, "against whom," John Unterrecker writes, "Harold had no defenses." [67] Perhaps Lizzie was a model of motherhood by comparison with this wheedling, vicious, and insensitive woman. Only in 1932, after Crane had died, did

Dahlberg seek her out. His dislike of Grace was instantaneous when he met her at the Midtown Hotel, where she was a wardrobe mistress:

> She was a monument of stupidity! She was a foot-soldier! She should have been a palace guard at Buckingham. . . . She was telling me [of] the day when she and Hart went dancing in California, and that Hart was the secretary to some very rich man who was homosexual, and that she virtually fell through the floor when she heard that Hart was homosexual. Then we went through the family album of Hart at different ages.
>
> Of course, you could see that with a manufacturer of confections who was a sensual businessman, married to a Christian Scientist,[68] that the consequence would almost inevitably be homosexuality, because there was an enormous feud between his mother and father. I guess the son felt, "Well, if marriage is like this, I don't want any part of it." . . . I'm only conjecturing what must have been in Hart's head, for I never asked him. I never discussed homosexuality with him— that was his own private life.[69]

Without question Dahlberg's interest in the poetry of Hart Crane was overshadowed by his preoccupation with the latter's personal background. He felt that Hart's talent was wasted, his poetry a "compost" of "turbid, amorphous doggerel . . . glutted with neologies, solecisms, and jazz dada locutions." Only Crane's first few poems, those in *White Buildings,* have any merit, the rest of his work being "the slag of Acheron." [70] Was his "failure" as a writer the outcome of his devastated childhood? Dahlberg replied: "Everyone completes his life when he quenches his appetite. After that, he resumed his life as an ambulatory cadaver. . . . The wound may be there, but that doesn't hinder you from ripening. Weak people nourish their wounds; others employ them to be better men." [71]

Having arranged the final details for the publication of *Bottom Dogs,* Dahlberg found that he had few interests and fewer friends left in Paris. Even Hart Crane seemed to be making preparations to return to America (though he actually didn't leave until late in

1929 [72]). F. S. Flint attempted to draw Dahlberg into the circle of Edith Sitwell; T. S. Eliot (whose mild anti-Semitism, Dahlberg claims, offended him [73]); and Frank Morely, an editor at Harcourt, Brace. But Dahlberg would not be enticed. With his advance from Putnam's, which came to under a thousand dollars,[74] he embarked, in April 1929, for New York. *Bottom Dogs* was not actually published in England until November. It bore a dedication to Winifred Eaton Webb, but when Simon and Schuster brought out the American edition in February 1930 the book had no dedication.

To readers familiar with later "bottom-dog" fiction, Lawrence's introduction, which named the genre, will seem squeamish if not somewhat petulant. Dahlberg was justifiably annoyed that although Lawrence used the word "repulsive" eight times in two consecutive paragraphs, he never mentioned the author's name, only that Dahlberg seems to have reached a level of human consciousness "lower than the savage, lower than the African Bushman. . . . Lorry Lewis is in too deep a state of revulsion to dramatize himself." [75] Though Dahlberg himself repudiated *Bottom Dogs,* he consistently defended his first novel against Lawrence's charges of insensitivity and vulgarity:

> I wanted to show what an impoverished American was denied: earth, sky, food. So I expunged these things. They're not mentioned in the book since I simply depicted an impoverished pauper in America who is too hungry to look at the sky and the flowers—so there *are* no flowers and no sky, simply this pusillanimous jargon, which I now so deeply regret.[76]

Bottom Dogs itself seems rather more lusty, even humorous at times, than Lawrence's remarks indicate. Lizzie Lewis (named after Max Lewis) is neither an immigrant nor Jewish, as she becomes in Dahlberg's later autobiographical fiction. Burdened with an ill-behaved, clumsy, and illegitimate son named Lorry, she must drag him along with her while she works as a peddler and, later, as a lady barber. Since Lizzie was still alive at the time, no mention of her shady dealings—her abortion racket, her quack medical practice, and her violet-ray treatments—appears in *Bottom*

Dogs as in *Because I Was Flesh.* [77] Instinctively repulsed by his squalid surroundings, symbolized by the flushing of the toilet in the barbershop, Lorry vomits with the slightest provocation. Just as she is the center of his attention, Lizzie lies at the core of his revulsion.[78] Due to his total preoccupation with her sloppiness, her "blues," and her perpetual whining about her bad luck, Lorry is helpless with other children. One of them hits him in the head with a brick because he is "cockeyed." [79]

In language that smacks of incestuous longings, Lorry attempts with increasing futility to win her attention away from her many suitors and the personal problems of her sluttish employees. Finally, she succumbs to the blandishments of a short, fat riverboat captain named Henry (he is here represented as thirty-six years old) who finds the boy "too forward" and easily convinces Lizzie to send Lorry to an orphan home. Thoroughly traumatized by this callous rejection, the boy, like his creator, frees Lizzie of all blame for her actions.

In an idiom which skillfully suggests without imitating midwestern speech, Dahlberg carefully sketches the spartan orphanage—the kitchen of Christine, the "lousy cook," who withholds her filthy food from the children; the drab brick of most of the buildings, which stands in grotesque contrast to "marble hall . . . where they had slabs of marble that had streaks of blue in them that looked like varicose veins. They were memorials for dead trustees and rich merchants, who had their names chiseled in gold on them, and who had donated for the upkeep of the asylum anywhere from a hundred bucks up" (p. 43).

"Doc," the superintendent based on Wolfenstein, is universally regarded by the orphans as "God in disguise." [80] The role of Jehovah suits this sadistic man, whose corporal vengeance is quick and unrelenting: "His many ways were awfully hard on kids who almost did it in their pants waiting; they just couldn't stand the pause; no one ever knew who would be next; not even the eighth grader who said the morning prayers" (p. 50). After his peculiar mannerisms cause him to become the orphanage "fall-guy," Lorry lapses into near-catatonia. His mother, though "very much upset" by his reports of starvation and torture, is easily dissuaded from rescuing him: "Henry said the kid was just lonesome, and that it would do him good to get a few hard knocks" (pp. 62-63).

Herman Mush Tate, a confirmed coward and human garbage pail as well as Lorry's closest friend, emerges (at least in Lorry's fantasy-laden mind) as the symbol of smoldering orphan rebellion against the monstrous institution. After listening to a stirring sermon, one of Doc's best, on David and Goliath, Mush Tate assumes the role of David and shatters all the chapel's stained-glass windows with his slingshot. For his misdirected heroism, he suffers expulsion, the worst infamy an orphan can endure. Dahlberg renders the outcast's last days at the home in one of the most moving passages he ever wrote. Poor Mush is a celebrity in spite of himself:

> he walked down to the playroom, and all the boys circled around him, the big and the small, and each one approached him, half-timidly, like a shopkeeper asking his alderman for a political favor, and shook his hand. Mush looked downcast and deeply affected. Slowly he gathered the papers, the ball bearings from several roller skates, a bag full of agates, which Shrimp scrutinized very closely, three horseshoes which had fallen off the gardener's nag on different occasions—all this from his playroom box, number 13, his entire estate. Then lingeringly he took from his jacket pocket his notebook and fingered its pages as a Hindoo would the Bhagavad-Gita. Finally he turned about face, with a military gesture, on the boys, looked each one in the eye, and willed his notebook and all the contents therein to Bonehead-Star-Wolfe, who wore nearsighted glasses and stuttered. That was his last ironical gesture. (p. 87)

After the orphanage chapters, the novel moves at a slower pace as Lorry tries, with little commitment, to find his intellectual and sexual identities. Though obsessed with the idea of catching a venereal disease, he finally summons the courage to solicit a prostitute, from whom he immediately flees "with a sense of one who had just gotten absolution from a cardinal sin" (p. 125). In the solitary confinement of his private world, Lorry's thoughts can only wander back to his mother who, although she abandoned him and hasn't visited him for years, represents the only illusion of security he can conjure.

With considerable trepidation, Lorry makes his way back to Kansas City and the Star Lady Barber Shop. His mother's first comment is a perfunctory: "Lorry, how awful thin you got." He responds, in the highly affected speech he has now adopted: "Yes, I suppose, mother. Shall we sit down? You must be tired" (p. 131). He immediately recoils from this strange woman, whom he finds more slovenly than he ever imagined she could be. Lizzie, though intent on controlling every aspect of her son's life, as always subordinates his concerns to her continuing search for a husband. She succeeds, as before, only in being bilked of her funds.

In disgust, Lorry flees his mother and launches himself on a cross-country pilgrimage identical to the one Dahlberg took himself. By the time he reaches Portland, Oregon, he is so devastated that he vomits constantly, all the while envying "those college dudes" who have "nothing to do but study books and sit on their rumps in the classrooms" (pp. 206-7).

Lorry's spirits revive as he moves on to San Francisco, where he promptly makes plans to settle. He studies Market Street, the jazz parlors, and the many sailors' hangouts. But his joy is suddenly soured when he naively accepts a night's lodging from a homosexual Swedish dockhand. Lorry has never encountered homosexuality before. Although he feels uncomfortable when the man's hands stray over his body, he does not decline to sleep in the same bed with him. The initiation which follows is one of the most unsavory experiences of Lorry's life:

> Suddenly, he started up, the feel of something against him, his body in a sluice of sweat; the dockhand was whining after him as he jumped into a pair of pants, got into his shoes without tying the shoestrings, and went out through the door, and down the hall steps like a streak. (p. 217)

His panicky flight takes him all the way to Los Angeles, where, penniless, he seeks lodging at the YMCA. Since he looks like a vagrant and cannot pay the five-dollar membership fee, the officials almost throw him into the street, but "a rather tallish fellow, who was as slim as a camel, tapped Lorry on the shoulder and gave him one of those strong-character handshakes" (p. 220). This deus ex machina is, of course, the godlike "Max Maxwell"

(Max Lewis), who at this critical point single-handedly reverses the fortunes of the hapless Lorry Lewis. Although Maxwell is partly a comic hero, he is basically the quintessential gentleman—everything Lorry wishes to be. In addition to Lewis's manifold achievements in real life, Maxwell "had been a tree surgeon somewhere in Maine; he had beat it out of New York for various personal and subtle legal reasons, sold land precariously near the Pacific and below sea level."

Dahlberg carefully detailed the rise and fall of Maxwell's fortunes (see Chapter II); the prose in this section moves with the quickness and spontaneity that characterize Lewis's "enviable" love life:

> Once [Max] went in hiding [from a woman he had abandoned] and stayed with a Y.M.C.A. chambermaid whose breasts he thought weren't bad, although she was almost forty. The chambermaid was kindhearted: she let him sleep with her fifteen-year-old daughter who had fine calves and limped a bit: but Max Maxwell stroked her hair and felt that she was too young to be carnally disturbed. (p. 226)

Dahlberg had not even begun to come to terms with his alter ego, Max Lewis, in 1929, so in *Bottom Dogs,* the further development of Max Maxwell's character is simply left for future novels. As Lorry's boredom increases, his sojourn at the Y comes to an abrupt halt after Maxwell, a tireless prankster, chases him down the hall with a toilet plunger. When two chambermaids complain about his "indecent exposure," Lorry is instantly expelled (p 256).

"Solomon's Dance Palace," the final chapter of *Bottom Dogs,* written later than the rest of the novel, incorporates elements of surrealism and disjointed narrative which would characterize Dahlberg's second novel, *From Flushing to Calvary.* Los Angeles now seems garish and overpoweringly impersonal as Lorry wanders aimlessly, finally drifting into a popular dancehall where a jazz wedding is about to occur. Although he thoroughly enjoys the popular melodies, which flood his consciousness while he gathers his impressions of the place, he is quickly overcome by his fear of strangers. Though he tries to tell himself that he is oppressed by the tinsel and the "jaundiced electric lights," it soon becomes obvious that he is a hopeless wallflower. His clumsiness and anxiety cause him to bump into everyone on the dance floor and to mash the toes of his partner, who suddenly becomes masculine and overbearing to him (p. 262). Lorry retreats to the soda fountain, then leaves with a cheap but seductive young woman who succumbs to his hilariously awkward advances. Lorry sabotages this small triumph by succumbing to his obsession with venereal disease, which he projects onto all of nature:

> The winter leaves were rolled up; they hung on the branches impotently. They appeared diseased, perhaps, he ruminated, a foreboding to him. "Ninety-eight out of every hundred get it from whores, the other two from toilet stools, and they're liars," he remembered, repeating a line out of some sex pamphlet distributed by the U.S. public health service. Perhaps he would go through some sort of clinical conversion; it might make a change in him; convalescents had visions, he had heard. Some kind of hospital calamity might push him out of the monotonous dead level he had been in for months. (p. 268)

The novel peters out on this tired note, with no forecast of relief for Lorry's ennui. He wanders off, uncertain what to do next, but certain that external forces will be solely responsible for his fate: "Something had to happen to him, and he knew nothing would" (p. 269).

Although Dahlberg's experiments in re-creating turn-of-the-century midwestern speech were fairly successful, he was quite uncomfortable with the idiom. It had been nearly two decades since he had lived with people who spoke in the Kansas City street dialect, and he had tried very deliberately, in California, at college, and in Paris and London to acquire the language and manner of a dandy and then of an expatriate gentleman. Although he would continue to employ regional speech in his second novel, his misgivings about it deepened. As a result, much of the narrative in *From Flushing to Calvary* is a clear foreshadowing of Dahlberg's later "baroque" style which clashes much more violently with the rough vernacular of the dialogue than it does in *Bottom Dogs*. The decade began when Dahlberg's writing style would undergo its total metamorphosis.

NOTES

1. Interview: E. D., April 18, 1973.
2. Interviews: E. D., April 18, 1973; Michael Sands, Sept. 19, 1972.
3. Interview: E. D., April 17, 1973.
4. See *transition workshop*, ed. Jolas (New York: Vanguard Press, 1949), and Kay Boyle and Robert McAlmon, *Being Geniuses Together* (Garden City, N.Y.: Doubleday, 1968).
5. Kiki was actually the famous nude model who married Man Ray.
6. Interview: E. D.: April 17, 1973.
7. Interview: April 19, 1973. Miss Barnes would not respond to inquiries about Dahlberg.
8. Interview: E. D., Sept. 16, 1972.
9. Robert McAlmon: A Memoir," *Alms for Oblivion* (Minneapolis: University of Minnesota Press, 1964), p. 45.
10. Ibid., pp. 46-47.
11. "Beautiful Failures," *New York Times Book Review,* 72 (Jan. 15, 1972), 4.
12. *Confessions,* p. 191. Carnevali's disease was actually encephalitis lethargica.
13. "Beautiful Failures," p. 36.
14. Drawings by Miss Moorhead and others by Francis Picabia show Walsh sunken-cheeked, with carrot hair and enormous eyes staring out from over his large nose and toothbrush mustache.
15. *Being Geniuses Together,* p. 195.
16. "Beautiful Failures," p. 4.
17. Ibid.
18. *Confessions,* p. 191. Interview: E. D., April 17, 1973. There is no evidence that Miss Moorhead really disliked any of these authors; in fact, she published all of them.
19. While Dahlberg's work had been accepted by early 1927, the magazine did not appear until the spring of 1929. By that time, Walsh had died.
20. *This Quarter,* 4 (Spring 1929), 216-23.
21. "Beginning and Continuation of Lorry Gilchrist," pp. 61-101.
22. The fragments are entitled "November Blues" (pp. 193-95) and "New York" (pp. 196-97).
23. Dahlberg claimed he was once given a letter of introduction to Joyce, but he never cared to meet the man.
24. *Pagany,* 2 (Summer 1931), 80.

25. Interview: E. D., April 19, 1973.
26. *Confessions,* pp. 192-93.
27. Dahlberg sometimes insisted that Miss Barnes stole the material from him, despite the fact that she published *Ladies Almanack* in 1925—long before Dahlberg had published a book.
28. Interview: Feb. 17, 1973.
29. Confessions, p. 192.
30. Interview: E. D., April 19, 1973.
31. *Confessions,* p. 209. Mrs. Webb is not identified by name, but only as "the near kin of a Cleveland industrialist, a professor of greed" (p. 208).
32. Interview: E. D., April 19, 1973.
33. Interview: Nov. 2, 1972.
34. Interview: E. D., April 19, 1932.
35. Edward Dahlberg, "The Expatriates: A Memoir," *Alms for Oblivion,* pp. 55.
36. Ibid., p. 55.
37. Although Dahlberg claims that Carnevali was mortally ill at the time (1927-28), he did not die until after 1940.
38. Interview: E. D., April 19, 1973.
39. Dahlberg was responsible, nearly forty years later, for the publication of the autobiography.
40. *The Autobiography of Emanuel Carnevali* (New York: Horizon Press, n.d.), p. 194.
41. Letter: Walter Lowenfels, Oct. 17, 1972.
42. Interview: E. D., May 3, 1973.
43. Interview: E. D., April 19, 1973.
44. *Confessions,* p. 211.
45. Interview: E. D., April 19, 1973. Read's book was published in London by Routledge & Company in 1943.
46. Interview: E. D., April 19, 1973.
47. Interview: E. D., April 19, 1973.
48. Letter: Harry T. Moore, July 7, 1973. Professor Moore edited *The Collected Letters of D. H. Lawrence* (London: William Heinemann, 1962).
49. *Letters,* II, 1108-9.
50. Ibid., January 11, 1929, II, 1115-16.
51. Ibid., p. 1131.
52. *Bottom Dogs,* introduction by D. H. Lawrence (London: G. P. Putnam's Sons, 1929), pp. xviii-xix.
53. Letter: Walter Lowenfels, Oct. 17, 1973.
54. *Letters,* II, 1147.
55. Interview: E. D., April 19, 1973.
56. *Confessions,* pp. 216, 207.
57. Fred Moramarco, *Edward Dahlberg* (New York: Twayne Publishers, 1972), pp. 33-34.
58. Interview: E. D., Nov. 11, 1972.
59. Interview: E. D., March 20, 1973.
60. Letter: Walter Lowenfels, Oct. 17, 1973.
61. He claimed, in fact, to have no recollection of it.

62. Interview: E. D., Feb. 17, 1973.
63. "Hart Crane," (review of *The Letters of Hart Crane, 1916-1932,* ed. Brom Weber) *New York Review of Books,* 5 (Jan. 20, 1966), 19.
64. Interview: E. D., May 3, 1973.
65. "Hart Crane," p. 19.
66. Interview: E. D., May 3, 1973.
67. Voyager: A Life of Hart Crane (New York: Farrar, Strauss & Giroux, 1969), p. 13.
68. Clarence Crane was indeed a candy manufacturer who had a passionate nature. (Unterecker, pp. 9-14.) Grace Crane apparently turned more and more to her religion as her troubles with her son and husband worsened. (Ibid., pp. 553-563 *passim.*)
69 Interviews: E. D., Feb. 27, 1973; May 3, 1973.
70. "Hart Crane," 19-20.
71. Interview: E. D., Sept. 16, 1972.
72. Unterecker, p. 599.
73. *Confessions,* p. 222.
74. Interview: E. D., May 3, 1973.
75. *Bottom Dogs,* pp. xiv-xv.
76. Interview: E. D., Dec. 8, 1973.
77. *Bottom Dogs,* pp. 2-4.
78. Ibid., pp. 9-11.
79. Interview: E. D., Dec. 8, 1973; pp. 9-11.
80. Interview: E. D., Dec. 8, 1973; p. 50.

4.

A Stranger at Home: 1929-1937

In the spring of 1929, embittered that not even the limited British edition of *Bottom Dogs* had reached publication, Dahlberg spent what remained of his eight-hundred-dollar advance for the novel to return to the United States in nearly total anonymity.[1] Fortunately, he did not know at the time that the stock market collapse on October 29 would postpone publication until the end of the year and eventually doom the sales of his first book, both in America and in England. Though poor once again, his most serious preoccupation was with what he began to perceive as the deficiencies in his colloquial "street-Arab" style. He was eager to cover his tracks with a newer and, he thought, revolutionary style pioneered by James Joyce.

The prospect of starvation was narrowly averted when an invitation came for Dahlberg to spend some time at the Mac-Dowell Colony at Peterborough, New Hampshire.[2] He was thoroughly pleased with his little wooden cottage, where a sandwich was left every day at 1:00 P.M. at his door.[3] His project was to assemble the beginnings of a new novel, to be entitled *From Flushing to Calvary*: "I had to write and rewrite, but even rewriting didn't help me very much.[4] I had not learned to let the feelings take care of the words, but hoped that with luck the book would be all right. But I was maimed by innovations, a farrago of misbegotten brand-new words." [5]

As it happened, Dahlberg accomplished little writing, good or bad, since he was almost immediately hospitalized in Peterborough for appendicitis. The doctors could not fathom the reason for his slow recovery: "Now, what really occurred, and I never divulged it (and why should I disclose this to a doctor who wouldn't understand it anyway?)—I was so ill over *Bottom Dogs* that I must have had a great desire to die." [6] He did indeed languish at the hospital. Isadora Bennett Reed, another writer then in residence at the colony, recalled that "he managed to capture my husband Dan and make him walk miles to the hospital to bring him delicacies that he thought he needed. And *my* writing went by the boards because I ended up being Dan's secretary." [7]

Though he claimed not to remember the Reeds, Dahlberg never failed to acknowledge his debt to Marian MacDowell, the founder of the colony and the widow of Edward MacDowell, for paying for his hospital care.[8] But he seems to have misapprehended thoroughly the characters of both the colony and Mrs. MacDowell, whom he saw as "an erect, spare woman, her hair the color of granite, and with a face as sharp as her measure of people. I thought her eyeglasses were waspish. Past her middle sixties she was given to a few stony words. . . . [She] was as austere a lawgiver as Lycurgus." [9] He added years later that "She was a darling woman, but you would never know it. She had a puritanical, rocky exterior." [10]

Dahlberg felt extremely out of place at the colony and his perceptions were distorted accordingly. Dr. Arnold T. Schwab, Marian MacDowell's biographer, was quick to correct Dahlberg's insistence that she was a spartan who ruled her "bleak" colony with a heavy hand.[11] Dr. Schwab depicts her as having been "lively, personable, and attractive . . . [with] a lively sense of humor about people, especially artists." [12] Isadora Bennett protested more stridently than Dr. Schwab, saying that Mrs. MacDowell was "a totally free and open person, . . . one of the greatest women I have ever known—and I have known great women, including Harriet Monroe, Helen Morrison, and Susan Wilcox." [13]

Dahlberg also projected his anxiety onto other members of the colony, including its most prominent resident, Edwin Arlington Robinson. Dahlberg identified with the poet, to him the only artist at the colony who was "positively not average," and saw him as having "much hidden feeling," although he was, according to Dahlberg, isolated, gloomy, and an ex-alcoholic.[14] Isadora Bennett, however, insisted that Robinson, a lifelong friend, was most chipper at the colony: "He and I used to hold hands and walk to our separate cabins together. . . . He was certainly not a 'dour' man at all!" [15]

As his three allotted months at the colony were coming to an end, Dahlberg felt increasingly persecuted by the grande dame of the colony. Perhaps he had in some way offended her: "Was I a trial to her, and did I in some way oppose her conservative code? . . . Doubtless she had some real inkling of my nature but was resolved to rule the colony as she saw fit." [16] But Mrs. MacDowell apparently had the skill to handle both Dahlberg's fears and his vanity. Miss Bennett commented that she was "a tolerant person who understood every eccentric who misbehaved on the plantation including Edward Dahlberg!" [17]

On the eve of the Great Depression, Dahlberg returned to New York, eager to establish himself among the literati. He enlisted the aid of his American editor, Clifton Fadiman of Simon & Schuster, to supply him with useful connections. One of the people who came to know Dahlberg through Fadiman was Lionel Trilling, who had recently married and was living at One Bank Street. Professor Trilling recalled an early encounter:

[My wife and I] both admired *Bottom Dogs* and, as I recall it, were rather engaged by Dahlberg himself, doubtless the more because of his having known D. H. Lawrence. By the autumn of 1929, at the latest, the winter, the sense of catastrophe following the stock market crash was dramatically borne in on us when one day Dahlberg presented himself at our door in what seemed a state of extreme distress: he was unshaven and unwashed and very shabbily dressed and apparently was suffering from exhaustion and hunger. He asked if he might come in to rest and explained that he had been living on the Bowery. My wife of course at once set about making a meal for him, which he ate in silence, and we both undertook to make him comfortable and to cheer him as best we could, appalled by the thought that a man of such notable gifts should be so reduced. It was not until the end of the visit, when our concern and sympathy had been fully given, that it emerged that the sojourn on the Bowery had been wholly voluntary and of brief duration and had been undertaken for journalistic purposes—he had been commissioned to do an article on the consequences of the Depression.[18]

Dahlberg was actually far from homeless at the outbreak of the Depression. While still at the MacDowell Colony, he had decided to settle in New York with his mother, who had been complaining bitterly in her letters to him of her fear of death, and with Michael Sands, who had a fair income as a draftsman. Dahlberg had become aware that a number of writers, including Horace Gregory, Babette Deutsch, Adam Yarmolinski, and many people on the staff of the *New Republic,* had settled in an "artist's community" in Sunnyside, which was at the time a suburban section of Queens. Dahlberg imagined he could make an easy transition from the charming MacDowell Colony to this "bucolic" settlement.[19] In reality, Sunnyside Gardens, as the development was known, was the brainchild of city planner Lewis Mumford, who had arranged for his favorite architect, Sir Patrick Geddes, to build houses similar to those the latter had designed in England for London workmen.[20] Mumford states that it was not at all a "colony," as Dahlberg had supposed, but a "mixed community" in which a number of writers happened to live.[21]

Dahlberg was aghast at the "up-to-date slums" which bordered on the huge Calvary Cemetery, crowded with "cut rate Virgin Marys and Christs." [22] The "job-lot stucco houses" appalled him: "They were two-story boxes with a scrap of dirt in the back and maybe a few deranged flowers." [23] Actually, Horace Gregory explained, the quarters, whose design was inspired by Ruskin, were "too Spartan" to attract "model workmen":

Workmen were lured to another Long Island development, called "Little Venice," that had swimming pools lightly designed as miniature lagoons, and houses that looked like blocks of Neapolitan ice cream. Sunnyside's inhabitants were taxi-drivers, artists, writers, actors waiting to be booked. . . . Viewed superficially, Sunnyside, with its youthful trees and bright green gardens and lawns, seemed an extraordinary hothouse and breeding grounds for cranks. This was not bohemia but several stations away from it, for the red-brick rows of villas gave the place an air of quiet industry and virtuous calm.[24]

Dahlberg's quest for the tranquility and companionship he craved was frustrated in Sunnyside. Occasionally he went to the nearby community of Astoria, where Daniel Reed was employed producing movies on a lot owned by Paramount Pictures, but the company had no use for Dahlberg's services.[25] Sands and he quarreled bitterly over finances, responsibilities, and women.[26] To make matters worse, Lizzie, like her son Edward, became dejected in the hectic surroundings, so she provided little comfort for either son. She resigned herself to scanning obituary columns in the newspapers and examining—less avidly—the "Help Wanted" sections.[27]

Dahlberg attempted to become friendly with Lewis Mumford, who was also a Jewish intellectual and Anglophile.[28] Mumford, however, quickly recognized in Dahlberg "a man of real talent, who, through some perversion of his own genius, managed to stand in his own way again and again."[29] Dahlberg replied to this coolness by denouncing Mumford's interest in "urbanology" as "impure" and mechanical. Mumford recalled: "We saw very little of each other, corresponded briefly, but not with any great intimacy. . . . [Later] he broke off his relation with me as he did with other people, denouncing me as a worthless person unable to appreciate real talent, one who consorted only with mediocrities and thus couldn't possibly consort with him." [30] Before the split, Mumford introduced Dahlberg to the writer Horace Gregory and his wife, Marya Zaturenska, both of whom suffered from more than their share of obscurity. Dahlberg and Gregory, a classical scholar, were attempting to promote American speech as a respectable and dynamic literary idiom. Dahlberg was awaiting the publication of *Bottom Dogs* in America, while Gregory had rendered the odes of Catullus in the American vernacular. Like

Bottom Dogs, the *Odes* had seen its sales nearly obliterated by the depression. Almost simultaneously, the income of the Dahlberg household was wiped out when Michael was thrown out of work. Sands admitted that his brother, with his racy wit and love of popular music—he had grown fond of singing popular ballads—cheered up many a gloomy evening, although his neighbors in Sunnyside tended to be unsettled by his fear of death and his constant preoccupation with his health. They found it even stranger when he took to carrying a medicine case, since he developed stomach ulcers and he seemed constantly to be gargling with Lavoris.[31]

Horace Gregory, who was writing reviews for the *New York Herald Tribune* book supplement, and Dahlberg, who had access to the pages of the *New Republic*, wrote reviews of each other's books. Though Dahlberg later boasted that *Bottom Dogs* received "fantastic notice"[32] on its American appearance in February 1930, Gregory wrote one of the few accolades; he attempted to distract prospective readers from Lawrence's discouraging introduction (ironically, this review appeared on March 2, 1930, the day of Lawrence's death):

> As Mr. D. H. Lawrence fails to point out in an exciting introduction, Mr. Dahlberg has laid hands upon a remarkable and accurate prose style. It is American speech, precisely formalized, intent upon disclosing the actual character of our vernacular and the voices that we hear below us in the street.[33]

The book enjoyed almost no sales. "Remaindering" of leftover copies was unknown in the 1930s. They were quickly removed from the shelves and reduced to pulp.[34] Dahlberg's indelicacy with the public and his stubborn pride did not help:

> Simon & Schuster arranged for me to talk at the Barbizon. . . . There was a galaxy of beautiful girls for whom I was asked to inscribe books. . . . All this was arranged by Clifton Fadiman (of all people!). All I said, being inordinately naive, "Why should I inscribe my books to a lot of girls I've

never even seen before?" So they were infuriated with me, but still I declined—I didn't autograph a single book. . . . I had been so terrified of making public speeches, and it took me some while to learn how to speak before an audience.[35]

Dahlberg was rescued by Eduard Lindemann, an editor of the *New Republic*, who obtained for him a $1,000 grant[36] from the organization which supported the magazine, the Willard Straight Foundation.[37] With this money, Dahlberg, and a new acquaintance, an enchanting young dancer named Sara Mazo, rented a house at 571 Commercial Street in Provincetown, Massachusetts, near the home of Edmund Wilson.[38] Miss Mazo, who adopted the name "Sara Dahlberg," later married the painter, Yasuo Kuniyoshi, whom she met at the home of Michael Sands.[39]

Sands, who by this time had succumbed to his brother's insistence that he adopt the name "Michael Dahlberg," hitchhiked to the Cape to visit Edward, and returned to Sunnyside to tell of the vibrant literary friendship that had grown between his brother and Wilson. A neighbor in Sunnyside recalled a brief conversation with Lizzie at this time: "I met her on the street and asked, 'How is Edward?' She said, 'Edward is giving a lecture. Edmund Wilson is giving the introduction and talk, but Edward is going to be the whole cheese.' " [40] At the beginning, Wilson had considerable respect for Dahlberg and even included an essay, "Dahlberg, Dos Passos and Wilder," dated March 26, 1939, in *The Shores of Light*. Speaking of *Bottom Dogs,* Wilson proclaimed: "We read the book . . . with wonder to see how the rawest, the cheapest, the most commonplace American material may be transmuted by a man of talent, so submerged in it that he can only speak its language, yet acting upon it so strongly, so imbuing it with his own tone and texture, that he can make it yield a work of distinction." [41] It would be unreasonable to expect the egotistical Dahlberg to remain content in the shadow of the great Cham of American letters; but at first he was amply impressed by an "admirer" who he thought would soon be regarded as "a la Bruyère of our literature—a great figure": "Wilson was very friendly to me, and I definitely liked him. He would give me cases of books which he didn't care to review, and I would go down to Fourth Avenue and get money for them." [42]

After a few weeks, however, the relationship began to sour, and, years later, Dahlberg observed:

> When I first mentioned Lawrence's *Studies in Classic American Literature,* he [Wilson] scoffed at me (and so did Van Wyck Brooks). But as soon as Melville looked like merchandise to him, he included the thing [in *The Shock of Recognition,* which Wilson edited]. Wilson absolutely *fleered* at it when I mentioned it, and Brooks said, "It's just Freudian nonsense." Now it's not a sustained book, but Lawrence never wrote a sustained book. He was simply incapable. . . .
>
> And then Wilson sent me the galleys of *The Dead Sea Scrolls;* one of the lines was, "Oh, isn't Genesis wonderful!" or something like that. I wrote, "My God, Edmund, how can you write such a bathetic line?" And I never got a reply. That was the last I ever heard from him.[43]

Dahlberg later ascribed his contempt to Wilson's physiognomy:

> Wilson had thin, leafy hair of a rust-colored hue, a lisp, a caustic chin, and a mouth too niggardly clothed for his vocation, literature. I had the utmost faith in his faculties . . . but had uneasy feelings about his physiognomy. . . . The thought comes to me that American literature might be different had Edmund Wilson had carnal lips.[44]

Dahlberg's grant and his small royalties from Simon & Schuster and Putnam's sustained him for less than six months in Provincetown. Sara earned a few dollars giving dance lessons. Meanwhile, Michael wrote that Lizzie had been forced to return to Kansas City because they could no longer afford to maintain the house in Sunnyside. He took the only job he could find, with the Department of Public Works in Albany, but he was forced to return to Sunnyside and seek shelter with the Gregorys after state funds ran dry. Dahlberg was able to convince Max Lewis to hire Michael as an assistant at his already fashionable spa in the Mojave Desert.[45]

Late in 1930, Dahlberg and Sara moved back to New York City. Since the depression had produced an abundance of vacant apartments, they easily found a spacious and comfortable flat at 76

Bank Street in Greenwich Village. Dahlberg was eager to cultivate the friendship of Richard Johns, who had founded a fine magazine of experimental writing called *Pagany*, named after William Carlos Williams's poem, "Voyage to Pagany." [46] Johns's wealthy father (Dahlberg claimed he ran two burlesque houses in Boston [47]) had funded the magazine. Williams, Hart Crane, Gorham Munson, William Saroyan, and many others had a hand in the original concept, but for the three years of its existence Johns performed most of the editorial duties and handled the correspondence with his contributors.[48] Dahlberg was hopeful that exposure in this "gamy sheet," as he termed it, would arouse publishers' interest in his second novel, which was virtually pieced together at this time. Johns had expressed enthusiasm for his manuscripts,[49] and Dahlberg prodded him to speed publication while complaining of the countless misfortunes which had befallen *Bottom Dogs*:

> My own book, "Bottom Dogs" has never appeared in its original form, not even the first limited English edition. . . . And in its American form it was highly bowdlerized; so that I hardly know what I'll do with my next book Flushing to Calvary [sic], when I am done with it. I don't like underground or sub rosa circulation.[50]

By 1931, Dahlberg was quite willing to accept the potentially valuable notoriety he had gained as a "bottom-dogs" writer and as "a disciple of John Dos Passos and realistic follower of D. H. Lawrence." [51] While he has always denied the influence of Lawrence's novels, Dahlberg never denied "liking" Dos Passos: "He did not lack probity; he spoke out of the shallows because he was mediocre, and he could do nothing else unless he were a hypocrite." [52] Despite this repudiation, Dahlberg's writing during the 1930s bears the unmistakable imprint of Dos Passos's montage techniques. Harcourt, Brace, which was considering the manuscripts of *From Flushing to Calvary*, applauded this frenetic method of narration:

> For most people, this book would be simply what it appears to be, an uncommonly gross and detailed story of revolting, filthy, unmentionable people. The central characters are an

old woman named Lizzie Lewis, formerly a lady-barber, and her son Lorry, clerk in a commission house and worker in a subway newsstand. Incidental figures are an Argentinian bicycle-dealer, a boy who writes ads, Irish neighbors, Jewish shopkeepers, all the rundown godforsaken shabby and abysmally ignorant people who—we are dismally aware—live somewhere in or about the suburbs of New York.

There is an endless procession of these people ... but Dahlberg is able to marshall it, to pour a steady cleansing stream upon this human material. It takes shape, the details are clear and unforgettable, and against our will, against one's taste and choice even, sympathies are aroused for these most miserable, these godforgotten.[53]

Johns agreed to publish extensive excerpts from *From Flushing to Calvary* in forthcoming issues of *Pagany,* and Dahlberg invited him to a summer home he had rented in Provincetown:

The Dahlbergs [Edward and Sara] were eager to show the Johns the entire range of summer living, and Johns went back to Cape Anne with a kaleidoscopic picture of the beaches, art exhibits, night clubs, where the entertainers were generally transvestites, and finally the quiet simplicity the Dahlbergs had set up for themselves in the midst of the seasonal jamboree.[54]

While he was attracted to the debauchery of his neighbors in Provincetown, Dahlberg also enjoyed feeling superior to them: "I realized nobody was supposed to do anything except vomit, fall on the floor, or insult somebody." [55]

After the Provincetown summer of 1931, Dahlberg was frequently separated from Sara, who occupied herself almost entirely with her dancing career. The galleys for *From Flushing to Calvary* had already been corrected and returned to Harcourt, Brace. Uncertain about his future plans, Dahlberg journeyed to Victorville to visit Max Lewis and Michael, who was employed at Lewis's Lucerne Supply Company. The sting of poverty and his loneliness still pricked at Dahlberg. He outlined his sufferings in the "bottom-dog" idiom in a letter to Johns:

> By the way, Dick, would it be a hardship for you to send now what check you think is due me to Sara. It's her birthday, and as the publishers are giving me a very small monthly stipend and I'm absolutely busted all the time. If you can manage it, would you please sent [sic] it to Sara Mazo Dahlberg, Care of Refrigier, Woodstock, New York.[56]

On the way to California, Dahlberg probably stopped in Kansas City,[57] where Lizzie may have given him funds to continue his journey and to tour his home state, which he had not seen since he was in college. He proceeded on to Hollywood, where the film industry seemed to have reawakened his ambition to corner the lucrative filmwriting market. He sought out a young writer named Michael Blankfort, who had written a favorable review of *Bottom Dogs* in V. F. Calverton's radical magazine, the *Modern Quarterly*, of which Blankfort was the coeditor.[58] Blankfort recalled the meeting warmly: "I remember, gratefully, Edward going over a manuscript of mine, the first pages of a still unfinished novel, and editing them with red ink. In those few pages he taught me a good deal about the economy of writing." [59] Blankfort, who corresponded with Dahlberg until the latter's death, commented in 1973 on some of his friend's quirks:

> He now . . . despises with unaccountable venom, even for him, anybody who lives or works out here. It doesn't matter to him that I haven't written a film in seven years; he thinks that I can't be much of a novelist because I have been corrupted by the industry. But he has his private sancta and he lives by them.[60]

A month later, Dahlberg headed back to New York, presumably to rejoin Sara and to collect an advance from Harcourt, Brace for his novel. He also felt that Johns, who had published a portion of that novel, "Coney Island Angelus Bells," [61] owed him a fee. Another excerpt, "Graphophone Nickelodeon Days," had been published in the winter issue.[62] This piece strongly supports the contention of Ruthven Todd, a onetime friend of Dahlberg, that "Dahlberg's prose relies upon good usage of words rather than imagery," mainly because his weak eyesight led him to rely on aural perceptions rather than visual ones.

"Graphophone Nickelodeon Days" laces Dahlberg's memories of the Eighth Street barbershop with strains of the dancehall and popular music which he loved all his life.[63] He could hold forth with practically any Al Jolson melody, and one of his favorite songs was "Hello Central, Give Me No-Man's Land." [64] The episode takes the narrator (presumably Lorry Lewis) through the Kansas City "West Bottoms," "a wiry and rusty rat trap," and George Washington Public School on Independence Avenue, into the Cleveland orphanage. The raucous nickelodeon melodies which permeate the earlier part of this montage ("A Hot Time in the Old Town Tonight," "O Gee, Be Sweet to Me Kid," etc.) give way to the grim, almost martial anthem sung in Germanic Yiddish at the Jewish Orphan Asylum: "*ist das nicht das weisenhaus, ya wohl, das ist das weisenhaus. . . .*" [65] This orphanage, unlike the one in *Bottom Dogs,* is emphatically Jewish. Dahlberg reaffirmed his roots as he installed "Doc" Wolfenstein, the Old Testament Jehovah, at the head of the home.

The narrator drives at a galloping pace through the topography of the orphanage and memories associated with it: "Diphtheria pond, becker's stalecakes, herman mush tate's dictionary of sure-fire words earthier than the bible, . . . goulashy every-other-wednesday sausages." [66] Transitions are supplied by a discordant medley of songs, chanted at the JOA by its hapless inmates: "i pledge alliance, *o tennenbaum, o tennenbaum, die kuchen schmekt so gut,*" followed by a song signaling Lorry's confirmation and graduation: "good bye J.O.A., i say good bye to you, without the least regret" This merges into George M. Cohan's martial refrain, "The yanks are coming . . . the yanks are coming," [67] and a number of disjointed sexual allusions: "puberty skyscraper erections, the vaginal walls of jericho are falling." [68] By the end of the episode it is apparent that the prose poem has been a surrealistic stream of associations in the mind of Lorry Lewis. The irritating, noisy memories have been triggered by the narrator's visit to Coney

Island, located very close to Bensonhurst, where Lorry (and, of course, Dahlberg) lived.

According to Stephen Halpert, there was no middle ground in the critical reception of the Dahlberg contribution to *Pagany*: "it was either liked or hated . . . It wasn't meant to be easily accepted as average run-of-the-mill work. For Johns, Dahlberg's piece was a prose poem of horror, dredged by a sensitive, loud-speaking man out of the scraps of recollection during one searching and indelibly etched day." [69] Convinced that he had indeed discovered an American Joyce, Johns never forsook his conviction that he had isolated a singular and promising genius despite Dahlberg's usual nagging and bullying manner. Dahlberg wrote to him on February 8, 1931:

> I wish myself that you could change the name [of Pagany]. Dos Passos feels as I do as a number of others do that there are so many goddam mushroom halfassed periodicals around town that one is leery of all of them. I told Dos Pasos [sic] that the only way to make a magazine good is to have first rate writers contribute to it.[70]

By February 1932, Sara Mazo had left Dahlberg and moved into an apartment on Waverly Place, near the Little Red Schoolhouse, where her sister, Dorothy Diamond, was a teacher. Dahlberg, furious at having been abandoned, was able to find himself a spacious apartment at 2 Grove Street, in one of the oldest and most charming areas of Greenwich Village. This location was ideal, since most of his new left-wing friends either lived or spent much time in the Village. These people included José Calderón, an importer of Spanish olives, who eventually went to fight with the Lincoln Brigade in the Spanish Civil War; Luis Muñoz Marín, who became governor of Puerto Rico during the 1960s; a beautiful young woman named Ladine (Dina) Young; her lover, Walter Durante, who wrote for pulp magazines; and Sara and Max Cohn, by then Dahlberg's oldest friends in New York City.[71] But despite his friends' ardor for the various brands of left-wing ideologies, Dahlberg could admit to being no more than a "fellow traveler" in 1932.[72] His difficulty in facing audiences and his general lack of social grace no doubt increased his reluctance to commit himself to a movement which submerged the individual beneath the anonymity of the masses.

The celebrity attached to being a card-carrying communist was becoming more attractive, however. Dahlberg began eating his meals at Stewart's Cafeteria on Sheridan Square, "where you would pay five cents for coffee, then get free coleslaw, beets, and relish," and at the Proletco Cafeteria (short for Proletarian Cooperative), located in the basement of the Communist party headquarters on Union Square: "They served very hearty and inexpensive dishes: rice, kasha, potatoes. Everyone went there to eat." [73]

At about this time, Dahlberg met two sisters named Dora and Rosa Shuser, who agreed to share his Grove Street apartment. Rosa was a quiet woman, but a meticulous housekeeper and excellent cook, while Dora (who committed suicide in 1972) was a dynamic and independent woman who supported the trio with the earnings from her excellent job as a buyer for a large department store.[74] Max and Sara Cohn, who lived in the same building as the Dahlberg ménage, recalled that Dahlberg soon convinced Dora to abandon her involvement with the capitalistic retail store and become a social worker. Almost immediately she became an ardent communist, and soon large dinner parties were being given at the Grove Street apartment. At first the food was free, then twenty-five-cent and later fifty-cent "contributions" were requested—"to raise money for the cause." [75] As the dinners grew larger, and the need for additional space became apparent, the three found larger quarters at 49 Bank Street, directly across the street from the Bank Street School. One of the apartments on a floor above was occupied by Kenneth Burke and his family.[76] He was such an avid Ping-Pong player that he had installed a table in his apartment in which he beat Dahlberg, who was only a fair player, in nearly all of their frequent matches.[77] Burke recalled how the relationship developed:

> Though Ed and I used to haggle a lot, and I was aware that to be on good terms with him was but the first stage of being hated, I had the impression that we got along quite well. . . .
>
> And I remember how, day after day while we strove at

pingpong, Ed kept singing "Any little girl that's a nice little girl is the right little girl for me," etc. That's a good sentiment, yes?

Ed was twisted in his way, and I was trying to pull myself out of the tangle I had got myself into (as per my novel, *Towards a Better Life*). And all told, we somewhat ended by changing places, as he pushed me towards the political Left, then himself moved towards his own variants of the aphoristic style (such as, in my way, my novel had been in line with).[78]

Like many other people, Burke recalled "Ed's sudden terror of rodents, apparently due to his early experiences in an orphanage." But Burke accepted these eccentricities as an essential aspect of the phenomenon that was Dahlberg: "I came to have great respect for his kinds of agitation, which he has dealt with eloquently." [79]

One of the most memorable of the Dahlberg fund-raising dinners involved Burke's family on Thanksgiving Day, 1932. James T. Farrell and his wife, John Chamberlain of the *New Masses*, and Sara and Max Cohn were among those invited. Mrs. Cohn was in the kitchen helping Dora and Rosa prepare dinner when Burke, who had recently caused a sensation by divorcing his wife and marrying her sister, arrived at the party with his new wife, his ex-wife, and his mother-in-law, all of whom amazed the entire gathering with their utter delight with the arrangement.[80]

The Ping-Pong matches with Burke were transformed into the finest episode in Dahlberg's third novel, *Those Who Perish*.[81] In this book, the hero, an exceedingly pompous but self-hating Jew named Eli Melamed ("Eli the teacher") has been invited to an elegant party by a grotesque Anglo-Saxon aristocrat named Edgar Briarcliff. An unrelenting anti-Semite, Briarcliff taunts Melamed (whose mannerisms and appearance closely resemble Dahlberg's) by persistently mispronouncing his name "Mel-ah-mede." Unwittingly Briarcliff gives Melamed a chance for retaliation by challenging him to a Ping-Pong match. Melamed startles the socialite guests with his prowess:

> He had a short, inching, sniping serve, which Edgar was unable to pick up. Melamed won the first five points. The people standing around the table stopped talking and began

to watch. Edgar cork-screwed his serve which twisted and landed in an askew cut. But Melamed coolly waited for it to hit the table and then slammed it back across the net with the speed of a football player. Melamed, whenever Edgar returned the ball, ran from one part of the rim of the table to the other, picking up the ball, and lunging after it with quarterback alacrity and the confidence of good fleshly poundage across his shoulders.[82]

But Melamed suddenly makes a fatal error by recalling that he is an intruder in alien territory. His desire to please the very gentiles whom he hates and envies eclipses his lust for victory:

> Melamed sent the next three balls wildly off the table, and did not see the following one which Briarcliff lightly popped over the net. . . . Troubled and unhinged by the silent, tense faces around the table, Melamed felt like an oppressed minority people engulfed by a hostile imperialistic power.[83]

In an incredible turnabout, Melamed actually joins his "persecutors" in making anti-Semitic comments while Briarcliff vanquishes him: "he was enormously thankful that it was Edgar Briarcliff and not he who was winning. Melamed gazed at Briarcliff's aristocratic Nordic eyes, mouth, teeth, and cravat, which were of one piece and felt this was as it should be." [84] *Those Who Perish* is Dahlberg's only major work in which he attempted to deal both with anti-Semitism and with his own strangely ambiguous feelings about his Jewish ancestry. As we shall see, Dahlberg was at no time in his life as conscious of the problems of being a Jew as in 1933, when he wrote this novel.

Dahlberg was also attracted to other members of Burke's family, especially his twelve-year-old daughter, about whom he nurtured some fairly exotic fantasies:

> She came to my apartment and pretended to faint. You see, she was in the rutting season, so I just put cold compresses on her head. I was really very taken with her—it was tempting all right!

[Years later] I met her in the park. I was so woeful that day!
I never told her that I really was in love with her.[85]

It is perhaps no coincidence that a minor character in *From
Flushing to Calvary* acts upon such lustful fantasies. An inarticulate
Italian from Buenos Aires, Jerry Calefonia, desperate for a woman,
attempts to seduce Lizzie Lewis, even though she is old enough to
be his mother. Later, in the most pathetic scene in this rather
gloomy book, he clumsily molests a fourteen-year-old girl and
smothers her "with tender phallic kisses." [86] Dahlberg seemed to
insist upon the innocence of Calefonia's motives, since the latter is
suffering from sensual deprivation; he is justified in feeling
persecuted when he is convicted of attempted rape and sent to jail
for five years. He echoes the author's sentiments as he sullenly
blames his Bensonhurst neighbors for their callousness and intolerance: "Cheap peoples live here." [87]

Dahlberg was determined not to have his second novel pilloried
by the critics as the first had been. Meanwhile, the tiny White
Horse Press in Cleveland agreed to publish ninety-five copies of his
beautiful and highly animated prose poem, *Kentucky Blue Grass
Henry Smith*. Illustrations, which were pasted into most of the
copies, were supplied by an artist named Augustus Peck.[88] The
opportunity of bringing his finest new stylistic techniques to bear
against his oldest foe, the man who replaced him in his mother's
affections, delighted Dahlberg. A simultaneous celebration and
indictment of Smith, this tour de force sings of his seductive skills
("he would always have a woman never fear that" [89]), while his
callousness in casting off lovers is treated flippantly: "Oh dear, how
they boohooed again and again. Oh dear." [90] The poem moves
against a background of verses from "Meet Me in St. Louis," as the
reader gains increasing awareness that this elegant but useless
gentile, this "Kentucky gentleman," after shamelessly philandering
and flirting with Lizzie's lady barbers, loses his job on the
steamboat and quickly degenerates into a parasite totally dependent upon Lizzie. After impoverishing her, he hastens her death by
abandoning her just as she is about to undergo surgery: "Then she
was strangely and medically divided, one part of her trailing away
from the other. She was being unribboned, unravelled. She floated

away from herself." [91] Dahlberg's mother had suffered her third
fictional death in this novella, the third of his major publications.

Although a vehicle for Dahlberg's continuing literary experiments, *From Flushing to Calvary* is directed at a left-wing audience, as
is apparent from its stridently political tone, its abundant communist jargon, and the "pessimistic determinism" of proletarian
naturalism throughout. In order not to be overlooked by the then
powerful Communist party, Dahlberg arranged for the controver-
sial literary magazine, *Contempo*, to devote most of its January 1933
issue to *From Flushing to Calvary* and to allow him ample space in the
October 1932 number to defend himself against past and antici-
pated left-wing criticism. Dahlberg began by attacking one of "the
small insurgent magazines" that listed *Bottom Dogs* among "defeatist novels." Although he admits that his characters are "doomed,"
he denies that they can be condemned as "defeatists," "because
that implies a choice, which they never had, simply because they
never knew they had one." These wretched individuals could never
become communists because they never heard of communism. The
protagonists in *Bottom Dogs* (and, by implication, in *From Flushing to
Calvary*) are so devastated that they are scarcely human, merely
"kick-about-figures . . . [who] never act but [only] react upon their
environment." Dahlberg declares triumphantly that he is depicting
something more than "American Bolsheviks" have ever had to deal
with—people who have surpassed all the history of suffering in the
rigor of their lives: "What the author has tried to indicate here is
not Lawrence's *Look! We Have Come Through*, but 'Look! What has
come through us.' " [92]

Aside from defending his book from critics and from partisan
detractors, Dahlberg was shrewdly announcing that although he
was gradually embracing party doctrine the communists could not
expect his flamboyant individualism to be submerged in their
orthodoxy. He apparently believed then, as he always did, that
"Man changes his creed but never his character." [93]

From Flushing to Calvary was released by Harcourt, Brace on
October 6, 1932, and in England by Putnam's in January 1933,
but the depression doomed this novel as it had *Bottom Dogs*. To
make matters worse, President Franklin D. Roosevelt's Bank
Holiday was declared on March 6, 1933. [94]

Dahlberg's initial dissatisfaction with his "early" style of writing eventually grew to the point where he melodramatically bewailed his apprenticeship fiction as his lifelong disgrace: *"From Flushing to Calvary* was a heap of pleonasms, misconceived metaphors, outrageous similes, and 'new' conceits. Most volumes of our 'costermonger age' are joyless and industrial products." [95] Dahlberg may have deceived himself as to the improvement he managed (although privately he was far less stringent in his criticism of the early books). Much of the prose in *From Flushing to Calvary* could easily be taken for an early draft of his masterpiece, *Because I was Flesh*, written more than thirty years later. For example, in the earlier novel, Dahlberg describes Bensonhurst:

> In the winter the ashen stucco houses shaped like Camel cigarette-boxes before the bensonhurst [sic] mist. Bensonhurst, low, flat, rheumatic marshland, is a realtor's reclamation project.... At one corner is Gravesend. In the cold neutral months it has the dumbmuted stare of an empty tincup.[96]

Although *Because I was Flesh* shows obvious refinements in style and attitude, the overall improvements are not so great as Dahlberg later imagined. The vocabulary and metaphor employed in the two novels are often identical:

> In 1926, my mother had decided to join me in Astoria, a cheap German borough with grum and gritty delicatessen and hardware stores and the dead bricks of tenements. But after a year in Astoria we moved to Bensonhurst, then a rheumy marshland. A low, squab mist hovers over the bay which damps the job-lot stucco houses.[97]

The critics did not rush to welcome another *Bildungsroman* about the sensitive young artist, Lorry Lewis, and his stifling attachment to his long-suffering mother. Horace Gregory politely declined to review "Blushing for Calverton," as he wryly called it,[98] although he consented to write a blurb insisting that *"Flushing to Calvary* establishes Dahlberg's right to be considered as an important young novelist." [99] The *New York Herald Tribune,* however, denied the book even guarded praise: an anonymous reviewer complained that *From Flushing to Calvary* "is hardly a novel; it is rather a series of character sketches."[100] The *Philadelphia Public Ledger* declared flatly that "the lower than middle class about whom [Dahlberg] chooses to write has no absorbing qualities."[101] A perplexed reviewer in the *New York Times* was aware that "Mr. Dahlberg has power of a kind, [but he] too often gives the effect of a runaway horse, frightened at its own freedom":

> One mistake Mr. Dahlberg makes . . . is trying to write a proletarian literature in terms of proletarian speech. It ties his hands in two ways: first, it makes his protagonists too self-consciously literate and, second, it confines his own expression as an author. The field is too wide for him.[102]

But it was precisely Dahlberg's handling of what was considered to be "proletarian" material that won him the slight critical praise he was to receive. Even this, coming mostly from the Left, was not undiluted. F. Wright Moxley, in *Contempo,* declared that all of Dahlberg's characters are lunatics and "lunatics alone are the one class of people who are not proletarians."[103] Others in the communist literary community were also disappointed that they had another Dreiser, not a Zola, in their midst.

With *Bottom Dogs* (and Lawrence's introduction) still fresh in their minds, reviewers were impatient with Dahlberg's highly experimental novel, which is actually a series of interconnected short stories similar to *Winesburg, Ohio.* Jerry Calefonia is only one of a number of minor characters who succumb to the sterility of Dahlberg's Bensonhurst; like James Joyce in *Ulysses,* the author interposes a large number of bestial individuals in order to paint a panoramic view of the marshy communities of Sunnyside and Bensonhurst. But the point of view set forth is distinctly that of Lorry Lewis, the young, damaged, and unacknowledged genius of *Bottom Dogs,* who is now working as a shipping clerk for the downtown New York Wharf Commission. The narrative quickly focuses on the cross Lorry must bear—his ill-starred mother ("only God knew what misery she had"), who has plunged deeper into desperation since her appearance in *Bottom Dogs.* Although she still halfheartedly pursues her quack medicine business (while simultaneously billing herself as a "beauty specialist"), she is devoting ever more time to absurd gestures aimed at entrapping her chronically evasive "suitors." Lorry, who spends an inordinate amount of time commiserating with his mother and unburdening himself of his own grief, seems little better equipped for the ugly struggle for survival in Bensonhurst. Unsuited for either manual or white-collar labor, he decides that he will supply all their wants by writing scenarios for silent films.

Lorry's adolescent daydreams contrast with the depression and disappointment he encounters in Bensonhurst, and in Astoria, Queens, where he, the ailing Lizzie, and a foolish German singer named Willy Huppert are sharing a two-room apartment in a tenement under the elevated train tracks. Though only in his early twenties, Lorry is becoming increasingly obsessed with the idea of death, a feeling which is hardly relieved by the fact that the apartment directly overlooks Calvary Cemetery, where "from the windows the neighbors can see every day the slick mahogany limousine hearses motor by. Hilly mounds of flowers foam over the top of 7-passenger Packards. . . . The tenants pass the time away watching" (p. 95).

His dreadful boredom with life in Queens is largely the product of Lorry's feeling of total incompetence. With no training for any job, no education, and his terror of strangers, his few job interviews are disasters: " 'Is there any opening here please?' The 'please' was tacked on and came out as a defense; for mentally his arm went upward to ward off the answer" (p. 123). He no sooner lands a menial job than he succumbs to depressive fits and neurasthenic attacks: "The horns blared against his ears. The autos, the swing of chevrolets, fords, buicks, buses, were an ethersong through his brain. It swam through him and benumbed him" (p.238).

Lorry's ultimate response is to retreat from the outside world and fasten himself more securely to his mother, whose cynicism has hardened to the point where she is equally willing to sue a suitor for "heart balm," or breach of promise, as to snare him in matrimony. Inevitably, all but "Hervey," the most pathetic of her suitors, are frightened away by her aggressiveness, her vulgarity, and the almost passionate alliance between her and Lorry. Hervey is duped into taking out a marriage license, but once Lizzie feels she has him securely in hand she drops her guard and becomes shrewish. When Hervey senses that he may be in some danger, he searches her belongings, where he finds some old letters in which

Lorry seems nearly hysterical about the state of his mother's health. Thus Hervey finds a convenient escape from his dilemma: he cannot marry a "sick" woman.

At this point, approximately two-thirds through the book, malignant forces overcome both major and minor characters in the book. Huppert, after failing miserably in his singing career, develops first venereal disease and then hemorrhaging ulcers; a neighboring gravedigger's wife, Mrs. Roonan, dies of a combination of malnutrition and despair. Lizzie degenerates beyond the point of no return while her son looks on in muted horror:

> She complained more than ever of pains and weakness. When he passed her to go into his own room, he couldn't raise his eyes on a level with hers. His eyes x-rayed her, passed through her, and somewhere inside of him was an accurate photographic plate of her broken-winged mouth, her dead hair, the dye on it, the burnt-out soot on her pots, her slick embalmed chin. Vaguely, he knew; somehow, he saw her, the photographic negative of her, as if in running water. He didn't want to look too close; for he didn't want his eyes to tell him anything more.

The abundant death imagery in this passage, projected against the backdrop of the immense Calvary Cemetery with its "iodine weeds," signals Lizzie's surrender to death. Her masochism reaches incredible heights as she actually comes to look forward to surgery. As if to increase her son's panic, she rehearses a forthcoming operation: "Each night she drew finger-diagrams across her abdomen to show Lorry how the cut would have to be made" (p. 195).

With Lizzie's death already a foregone conclusion, Dahlberg attempted experimental narrative techniques which he never again employed. The first and weakest of these is an obvious borrowing from Dos Passos, a montage of newspaper extracts entitled "Daily Graphic Slabs." They form a rather heavy-handed attempt to underscore the central theme of death by interspersing obituary notices, tragic news items, and mortuary advertisements with vignettes of the dissolution and death of several of the characters in the book. In each case, as with Willy Huppert, these deaths are as unnecessary as they are unnoticed—they transpire before the lifeless eyes of a factory-made society, symbolized by the hulking marble orchard of Calvary Cemetery. Despite its august name, no saints or messiahs are interred beneath its cheap monuments.

The book reaches its climax while his mother is under the knife. Lorry suffers an apparent nervous breakdown after a horrifying nightmare. This "dream stuffed with ratty secondhand furs, holey shoes, [and] red-blooded suitcases lying in the show-window of a 14th-Street pawnshop" apparently abstracts all the fears and psychic injuries which have oppressed Lorry since his early childhood. Symbols of abandonment, poverty, and death run rampant:

> There were trapdrum moons, basedrum streetlamps, gilded grapefruit pawnshop balls, all lit up by diamond electric lights.
>
> Out of that he had suddenly come into a room full of mahogany furniture; it had the slick mahogany finish of Calvary hearses. Then he was stopped short by a woman who pointed to a skinny toothpick heap underneath a white sheet on a brassy saxophone bed. He knew it was his mother. The tears ran down his cheeks. He ran to her and knelt down and petted and fondled her; than he tickled her underneath the chin, as if with a dandelion, and asked her whether she liked butter. He tried to get nearer and nearer to her. And when he couldn't reach her, and he couldn't mix his warm breath with hers, for she didn't have any, not even a cigarette wisp of breath, for she was a dead oilswamp sea, he wept more and more, as if his heart, stone-still, had been touched by a mosaic rod. The tears, sweet-sour and bitter in his mouth, were a passover bitterness. (p. 201)

Within the dream, Lorry seems to be singing an incestuous epithalamion, both tender and infantile, though sullied by images of commercialized death. These latter blend easily into Part IV of the novel, "Coney Island Angelus Bells" (see Chapter III), in which the mechanized fun-making at the amusement park symbolized the falseness, pretense, and inhumanity of the whole of Lorry's environment. Is it possible that even Lizzie's chronic illnesses are psychic constructs designed to blackmail her son emotionally?

Dahlberg never answers this question; instead, he thrusts us into a Joycean *Walpurgisnacht*, celebrated in the neon glare of Times Square as well as the deafening noise and delirious movement of Coney Island. He may have been recalling that, when Maxim Gorki visited his amusement park, he was horrified that Americans turned to machinery for their entertainment.[104] Lorry, who has suddenly awakened from his nightmare, turns briefly to the New York Bible Society for help, but his abhorrence of institutionalized religion only drags his thoughts back to Calvary Cemetery's "daily graphic chewinggum slabs which were as pale as the Holy Ghost." By now he is certain his mother has left him. He is driven far back into his hated past: "Up the subway station stairs, gardenseed-cereal went pouring out of his mouth, the dead Wolkes in the sick orphan boy's mind. The vomit on the stone. His mother's oatmealy, scribbled, and shriveled-up throat. He didn't want to go back" (p. 238). But his panic forces his memories along in rapid succession. Infuriated that his mother has betrayed him by dying, Lorry takes a surrealistic walk along "Death Avenue," where he is haunted by childhood memories of sleeping in the same bed as his mother, of the depravity and violence of Kansas City, and of "the snoring silas-marner ivanhoe schoolhouse" at the JOA. Inevitably, Simon Wolkes, Lorry's other oppressive parent figure, steps forth, and with him, all the wrath Lorry has hoarded against the superintendent. Unfortunately, Lorry is forced to acknowledge that Wolkes is now dead and can never be brought to account for his cruelty. Lorry must endure both his and Lizzie's "betrayals":

> and now wolkes was dead and now a thousand times and much more he wished it was otherwise. And yet now what was the difference—now that he knew what death was; how it was; now that it had sunk into his bones like a cold sluggish serum seeping through them at a hesitant brassband funeralmarch time. (p.249)

The book ends with a shortened version of "Kentucky Blue Grass Henry Smith," in which we learn the grim details of Lizzie's *actual* death, and her son's obsession with her decaying body: "He had heard, he thought, hinge-creaking of bones, his mother's gravebones roomily skidding like a key in a rusty lock" (p. 289). After selling her furniture for eight dollars, he considers traveling, though he cannot summon the initiative to go anywhere. By chance, he wanders into the midst of a pitched battle between the police and communists on Union Square, where he is knocked to the ground: "About to straighten up he saw something out of the corners of his eyes which looked to him like an auctioneer's red flag. Then it went scooping down, bloodstreaming floppily. Something hit hard against his head" (pp. 290-91). Lorry seems only slightly more dazed than he was before the crack on the head. This brief encounter with revolutionaries bent on saving the world makes no impression on him, since he hasn't the capacity to emerge from the devastation of his personal life. He is no potential working-class hero, no sturdy but downtrodden peasant, but a being so damaged that there is no energy left in him. Half unconscious, with blood streaming from his head, Lorry picks himself up and sings an orphan-asylum hymn, while the communists break into a revolutionary anthem.

Despite its few unsuccessful experiments, *From Flushing to Calvary* was a decided improvement over *Bottom Dogs*. In the later book Lorry Lewis is certainly not the "kick-about" figure Dahlberg claimed he was, but a complex (if compulsive) personality. The sinister, even malignant nature of Lorry's attachment to his mother is far more interesting and convincing than in *Bottom Dogs*. Only in *Because I was Flesh*, which was begun more than a decade after Lizzie Dahlberg's death in 1946, would Dahlberg again attempt to unravel this relationship, which dominated his entire life.

Unlike his character Lorry, Dahlberg was not floating in a political and social vacuum. By 1933 he was as close to being a communist as one could be without carrying a card. He made speeches before the John Reed Club, which had been founded in 1932 as the literary organ of the Communist party,[105] and his friend Joshua Kunitz had persuaded Dahlberg, Rosa (who by now was using the name Dahlberg), and Dora Shuser to rent a cottage for the summer of 1932 in Croton-on-Hudson, a left-wing artists' colony at the time. Besides Kunitz, Max and Cristal Eastman, Walker Evans (who photographed nearly everyone at Croton),

Aaron Copland, and the illustrator William Gropper of the *New Masses* were in residence.[106] Dahlberg claimed he was asked to give lodging to one of the white women "alleged to have been violated by the black Alabama peasants" at Scottsboro: "When I laid eyes on her I was dumbfounded. She was the most rancid and used-up whore I had ever seen. Her face was laced with pimples and boils and she looked so diseased that after she used the toilet I would not go there until I had thoroughly disinfected it." [107] He needed no further proof of the innocence of the "Scottsboro boys."

His desire to avoid becoming an active minion of the Communist party may have been one reason which prompted Dahlberg to visit Germany as Hitler was assuming power in February 1933. Although the express purpose of his trip was to investigate Nazi violence and the alleged beatings of American citizens, his exact reasons for going and his method of financing the trip have never become clear. The *Times* of London, the *Deutsche Allgemeine Zeitung* (which was still courageously printing uncensored news), and Michael Sands stated that Dahlberg had been sent to write articles for *Scribner's Magazine*.[108] Dahlberg later claimed, however, that the newspapers were guilty of "specious reporting," [109] and in *The Confessions* he offered the explanation that "In 1933 I wrote a piece on travel for a steamship line, urging Americans to go to Europe while it was still extant. For this writing I received a round-trip ticket to Germany and forthwith embarked for Hamburg and from thence by rail to Berlin." [110] Still later, he insisted that he financed the trip himself.[111]

He arrived in Berlin at the most dangerous time possible, a few days after the burning of the Reichstag on February 27, 1933. During his sixteen days in that city, he set about frenetically interviewing newspapermen, the kaiser's former pastor, spartacists, socialists, and communists:

> Someone suggested that I see the foreign correspondent of the Baltimore *Sun*, a man named Boulton. He disclosed that he had been on friendly terms with Hitler, said the Fuhrer had read a good deal of ancient history, and that eighty-three percent of the German students supported him. He advised me to see Edgar Ansel Mowrer.[112]

When I set foot in Mowrer's office, he declined to present

himself. Baffled, I found the reason was most plausible. He detested Boulton and so did I, and when I was able to explain that I had known nothing of Boulton until I met him, we became friendly. . . . Mowrer said one could hear the groans of tortured Nazi victims in Berlin every day.[113]

Evidence of Mowrer's allegations was all too available. Dahlberg observed boycotts of Jewish-owned shops in Berlin, "the Nazis preventing, by physical violence if necessary, the entrance of any customers." [104] After hearing Nazis shout, "Awake Germany, exterminate the Jew," Dahlberg beseeched his Jewish friends, including the novelist Egon Irwin Kisch to flee the country. Communists, Dahlberg concluded, were in comparable danger: The Alexanderplatz, which had been Communist party headquarters, was now a no-man's-land where a swastika flew in place of the red flag.[115]

Dahlberg had already become certain that Jews were being secretly murdered in Germany when, on the evening of Saturday, March 11, 1933, as he was emerging from a cafe on the Kurfurstendamm, a young man in Nazi uniform, yelling *"Juden Schweinerei,"* set upon him viciously with a wooden sword.[116] At first Dahlberg thought he was caught in the midst of a general riot, but soon he was able to perceive that the crowd was mostly sympathetic to him and that only one drunken Nazi was assaulting him. His screaming brought a policeman, who examined Dahlberg's passport, and then dragged both the victim and his assailant to the police station. Dahlberg later complained to reporters from the *Deutsche Allgemeine Zeitung* that the policeman had allowed the Nazi to continue the beating until other officers lost patience and took the stick from the Brownshirt.[117] Although he was allowed to return to his hotel room, Dahlberg was astonished when another police officer visited him and requested that he keep the whole affair secret. The following day, the distraught wife and daughter of the Nazi begged him to drop charges, since the young man was in danger of losing his job as a butcher's assistant. Dahlberg, however, refused to believe that his assailant had been drunk, as his relatives contended, and proceeded to press charges.[118]

Pictures taken of Dahlberg at the time suggest that he had

somewhat of a rabbinical appearance—receding curly hair, dark-rimmed spectacles, with the Gottdank nose extending over a small Chaplinesque mustache. A truculent and intoxicated Nazi could conceivably have been provoked by his Semitic appearance. Covered with bruises, and justifiably frightened by the possibility of future beatings, Dahlberg fled Berlin. In Bremen, sixteen days after his arrival in Germany, Dahlberg stated to the press that he "assumed the case was dropped because he did not remain in Berlin 'to see it through.' " [119]

Although it did not quite become "an international *cause célèbre,*" [120] the beating was reported in all the major newspapers and eventually it became a State Department matter. Michael Sands, who had gone to stay with Lizzie in Kansas City when the Bank Holiday (March 6, 1933) cost him his job, recalled seeing a copy of a letter written in Hitler's name to Dahlberg's publisher, requesting copies of his books and information about the author. [121]

Immediately upon his return to New York, the *Times* requested that Dahlberg write an article recounting in detail the terror he had witnessed in Germany. The thorough yet succinct analysis which he produced of German national hysteria did not conceal his conviction that the Communist party was the strongest line of defense against the Nazis. He noted that since 80 percent of the students are Nazis, "The Communist Party has been driven far underground." Therefore, "a general strike of the working classes in Germany may occur, but at present it seems remote." Dahlberg then explained to a public just becoming aware of Nazism the function of the Brownshirts ("Herr Hitler's private army"), the *Stahlhelm,* led by the old Junker, Alford Hugenberg, "who is at present a member of the Hitler Cabinet," the death of trade unionism, the oppression of Jewish businessmen, and the censorship of the press, which "is so close that the average American reader of the newspapers knows more about conditions in Germany than the majority of German people do." Dahlberg concluded with what was probably one of the strongest anti-Nazi statements to appear in a major American newspaper up to that time: "The Nazis have left no stone unturned to suppress opposition." [122]

Dahlberg was far from displeased that the international attention he received meant that for once he would not have to quibble with publishers to have another of his novels published. The John Day Company commissioned him to write a novel with an anti-Nazi theme, and, with unprecedented speed, he produced the first book of its kind, which preceded Sinclair Lewis's more popular *It Can't Happen Here* (1935) by almost a year. Unfortunately, *Those Who Perish* is a clumsy, mismanaged work—in many ways Dahlberg's worst, because even in a novel of protest he could create only characters that are composites of himself and his mother. The heroine of the story, Regina ("Queen") Gordon, embodies all the maternal qualities which Dahlberg tried to perceive in Lizzie Dahlberg. An attractive, urbane, London-born Jewish woman, aged thirty-nine, her permanent home is on Rivington Street, the very place where Lizzie originally met Saul. She is married, although by supporting her husband, she bribes him to remain hidden from herself and her retarded child.[123] Dahlberg reserved his most luxuriant style, usually reserved only for Lizzie, in rendering this "sorrowing Hagar": although Regina "was of an inferior race, and neither assimilation, politics, nor convictions could annihilate the dark, smutty Mediterranean bloodstream that ran through her veins . . . her teeth [were] the inside flesh of a snow apple and [she had] young pillowy breasts" (pp. 12-14).

Regina's gifted but self-tormenting lover is her boss, Dr. Joshua Boaz, of the Jewish Community House in New Republic, New Jersey—obviously Hackensack.[124] Although the Community House is mainly concerned with aiding mentally retarded Jewish children (Regina and Boaz each have one),[127] Boaz has diverted most of his energies to counteracting the prevailing opinion in backward New Republic that "The Nazis are the last dyke against Communism" (p. 46). Regina vigorously supports his stand, not only because they are lovers, but because her first cousin, Julius Halevy, a student at the University of Berlin, has recently been murdered by storm troopers, and she has an uncle in a Nazi "torture camp" (p. 141).

Like Regina, the Jews of New Republic are a neurasthenic, self-defeating lot; most of them are rendered satirically, like Mr. Irwin Mouser, "who had vague blond hair, [and] had taken up colonic irrigations and Schopenhauer and was now a devotee of Mary Baker Eddy" (p. 38). Even Boaz is emotionally mangled, so that he quickly comes to depend totally on Regina: "Could one have psychologically X-rayed Joshua Boaz, then he would have witnessed a mental cinematography of a child writhing and squirming on the floor and bitterly crying: 'I don't want to be dependent on people! I don't want to touch them. Just leave me in my corner and don't torture me!' " (p. 88).

The only truly interesting character in *Those Who Perish* is Boaz's distant cousin, Eli Melamed ("Eli the Teacher"), Dahlberg's unmistakable self-portrait. Tall and angular like his creator, he is an easily provoked yet sensitive and intelligent graduate of Columbia University. Socially inept, he offends people either with his excessive politeness or with his rudeness; he will go to incredible lengths to avoid dealing with strangers. When he tries to borrow $500 from Boaz, he hopes his cousin will mail him a check so that he will not have to pass the telephone operator in the office. This revulsion extends to most of the physical world. Like Dahlberg, Melamed has a hard time with excrement, odors, insects, and especially sex: "his first boyhood introduction to amorous desires had been connected with a house of prostitution which seemed to emit an alcoholic odor which he endeavored to allocate and grasp whenever he passed below its windows" (pp. 85-86).

Such a morbid and decadent trio fail pitifully in trying to lead the "Jewish Resistance," a movement which disintegrates the moment the first swastika is seen. Boaz proves immediately willing to submit to the Nazis. He then collapses and goes to the hospital after Regina attacks him for his cowardice.

Melamed is, incredibly, even more feeble. Unable to find a job or involve himself with anything, he takes refuge on Rivington Street, where he feels "united with his race" (p. 185). By this time, he lacks even the will to live and throws himself from the Brooklyn Bridge. Meanwhile, Jewish boycotts are easily broken by storm troopers with truncheons, and headlines appear predicting war with Germany and Japan. Regina and Boaz are totally sapped by this string of crises and quickly follow Melamed to the grave: Boaz dies of a heart attack, then Regina poisons herself.

Those Who Perish suffered badly from divided aims. Though Dahlberg wanted to write an important protest novel (or at least a highly successful potboiler), his lingering infatuation with decadence dulled the impact of his book and confounded the reviewers. Ford Madox Ford reported that the novel sold only two hundred copies and ruined Dahlberg's chances of being published again.[125] Perhaps, as James T. Farrell has suggested, Dahlberg's "underlying worship of self-pity" [126] may also have doomed the novel, at least as a vehicle for protest. Certainly, a stuffy preoccupation with the sentimental tribe of neurotic individuals precluded any coherent exploration of social issues. Daniel Aaron added, "in the strictest sense, Dahlberg could never produce 'proletarian' fiction, if we accept Martin Russak's contention that such literature must deal with the working class alone, not 'with the emotions and reactions of the upper or middle classes or the *lumpen proletariat.*' " [127]

Critical appraisals were guarded. Many felt Dahlberg's craft had degenerated and refused to make any comments.[128] John Chamberlain was generous in praising Dahlberg as the "Proust of the lower and middle depths of society," but he was fearful that readers might be put off before they reached the "climactic" scenes.[129] Edmund Wilson, who especially admired the Ping-Pong episode in the book, seized upon Dahlberg's startling images of death and hailed him, rather illogically, as a proletarian Huysmans. Although Wilson's comment was printed on the dustjacket of *Those Who Perish,* Dahlberg later rejected this "corrupt encomium": "I admire Huysmans. He's a remarkable French writer, but Edmund Wilson was a liar. I couldn't come near Huysmans at that time—Huysmans was a master of style. Who wants false praise? Furthermore, Wilson always praised people he knew. He was very weak-witted and he couldn't write." [130]

Wilson, whose talent Dahlberg came to devalue only in later years, was obviously trying to encourage a young novelist in whom he saw much promise. But Dahlberg was seriously disheartened by the commercial failure of his three novels. His decisions to abandon fiction and to join the Communist party came simultaneously. By December 1934 he was officially a member, and he threw himself frenziedly into party activities, spending much of his time consorting with party "regulars," many of whom had been introduced to him by Dora Shuser. His bravado, cynical humor, and flash temper appealed to the more anarchistic individuals in Greenwich Village. They would meet at Stewart's Cafeteria on Sheridan Square, pay five cents for coffee, and then get free Coleslaw, beets and relish or at Proletco [131] for even more earthy repast.[132]

People who knew Dahlberg during his one year as a Communist agree that he was wasting his time picketing and delivering lengthy speeches in Harlem and on Union Square.[133] Apparently the party itself regarded him as something of a buffoon, since he avoided the "worker's movement" and often used rhetoric too lofty for the simple folk in his audiences. He preferred to act alone, as he always had, in the role of a literary messiah given to pronouncements such as, "I am an artist. I do not make mistakes." [134] On one occasion, he stormed out of the office of Earl Browder, executive chairman of the Communist party, after the latter (no doubt feeling somewhat messianic himself) informed Dahlberg, "I have only two minutes for you!" [135]

A severe test of Dahlberg's willingness to support the workers' cause came when he was asked, along with Nathanael West, James T. Farrell, Sol Funaroff, Edward Newhouse, and Herbert Kline, to picket Ohrbach's Department Store at the height of the Christmas season in 1934. The protest was intended to break a labor injunction against striking employees of the store, which was located directly across Union Square from party headquarters. Dahlberg, who was rapidly acquiring a bad reputation for pinching attractive females on picket lines—several fistfights nearly resulted[136]—recalled: "We were in a queue. Many writers were there, perhaps twenty-five. Then, what we called 'the Cossacks,' the police, came on horseback. Farrell was in this group and grew waxen and blanched. Why I didn't run, I don't know. But I didn't. *He* ran."

Locked up in a cell with West, Dahlberg had a "thin but friendly acquaintance with him." [137] Farrell, however, insisted that he did *not* run and was arrested—not for breaking a labor injunction, as the party had wished—but on charges of disorderly conduct. Farrell made a speech at the trial, at which he was convicted and given a suspended sentence. Charges against Dahlberg were dropped.[138]

Despite his most flamboyant efforts in public, Dahlberg enjoyed only limited exposure in the radical press. He wrote brief reviews of Horace Gregory's translation of *The Complete Poems of Catullus*, Robert Cantwell's *Laugh and Lie Down*, James Farrell's *Young Lonigan*, and Erskine Caldwell's *Tobacco Road*.[139] He had also contributed a slightly longer article to *The Nation* on the Bonus

Army which marched on Washington,[140] but he came to feel that his talents were being neglected in the existing left-wing magazines, so he began to explore new outlets for his writing.[141]

His attention was drawn to a new "magazine of party opposition," *The Partisan Review*, which was being formed to consider " 'theoretical and practical problems of proletarian culture' too specialized for *The New Masses* readership." [142] In actual fact, the magazine was intended to counteract the strident and often lowbrow tone of *The New Masses*, which, according to Daniel Aaron, had formed the practice "of excusing bad writing on the grounds of political expediency." [143] *The Partisan Review* was also founded as the literary organ of the John Reed Club, which itself had been organized in 1929 as a program for developing promising artists of the proletariat. Since he had already given numerous talks to John Reed audiences, Dahlberg felt he had earned a statutory right to be a part of the new journal.[144] Later he claimed that since his name was listed on the editorial board in both the first and second issues of *The Partisan Review*,[145] he had founded the magazine: "I came in before [Phillip] Rahv and [Wallace] Phelps. They were asked to join me, and I walked out. There was no other reason. I thought they were such ambitious and cormorant ignoramuses that I wanted no part of them." Dahlberg went on to explain that the Central Committee had personally selected him and Saul Funaroff, another communist writer, to organize the journal.[146] However, William Phillips (the former Wallace Phelps) utterly contradicted Dahlberg: a dozen or more people were originally listed on the editorial board, but since most of them did little or no work their names were soon dropped. Dahlberg's name was stricken in the third issue (June-July 1934), and he neither published in the journal nor had a book reviewed.[147]

Dahlberg began writing for the less literary *New Masses*, which was never ashamed to exploit standard Marxist rhetoric to drive home its messages. For awhile, he hesitated at incorporating the magazine's gothic excesses into his own writing. His first, very brief article noted obvious parallels between the followers of Hitler and "the comic opera insurrectionists" of the South, the Ku Klux Klan.[148] By the June 12, 1934 issue, some of the worst features of the ponderous left-wing jargon which Dahlberg later de-

nounced [149] had crept into his style. In the following passage, he
styles himself as the "Chairman of the Committee Investigating
Fascist Activities, 163 West 23rd Street, New York City":

> The work the committee is doing is of paramount importance.
> By means of leaflets and pamphlets as well as the issuing of a
> biweekly bulletin, it fights the menace of the Fascist plague. It
> also has as one of its tasks the building and maintenance of a
> complete set of archives pertaining to Nazi and Fascist
> activities.[150]

Evidence of the further compromise of Dahlberg's style is not hard
to discover, as this review of Kenneth Fearing's *Poems* appallingly
illustrates:

> The tinfoil hopes and thwarted aspirations and Hol-
> lywoodesque ikons of the hopeless middle class are disclosed.
> It is an involved procession of recumbent rooming house souls
> soaked in mazed sanitarium dreams but forever being
> awakend by evictions and hunger.[151]

Dahlberg's willingness to indulge himself in such empty metaphors may be excused because of his desperate need for acceptance
by the left-wing press, especially since he could no longer be
reviewed by "the bourgeois papers." [152] He later admitted that it
took him years to extricate himself from bad habits acquired on
the *New Masses*. But despite his compromises, Dahlberg was
berating, in the very same issue as the Fearing review, Marxist
language and rhetoric, especially as they affected literature:

> What has happened, among other things, is that reporting, a
> doggerel, slangy prose, has taken the place of a literary
> vocabulary. As a method of chronicling and as a stenographic
> record of surface relations and tabloid events, the use of
> Americanese is often highly effective. But it imposes definite
> limitations upon the writer, so much that a conscientious
> critic must constantly remind the reader that the prose, and
> the cerebral processes are not the author's mind. Conse-

quently, insights, nuances, and graduated perceptions cannot be gotten even out of a very highly formalized journalese.[153]

This attack was by no means gratuitous, since Dahlberg followed his own precepts in his prose writing if not in his journalism. Several critics, including Farrell, saw Dahlberg as the only original prose stylist on the Left. Farrell commented: "[Dahlberg's] imagery in many cases is derived from words and associations taken from urban sights and sounds, and from comparisons between objects that are regularly seen by those whose experience is also urban." [154]

Dahlberg soon fell afoul of another critic, Granville Hicks, whose book, *The Great Tradition* (1933), had become a touchstone for Marxist literary criticism, and who was probably the most powerful member of the *New Masses* staff. While Hicks was living in upstate New York and visiting the magazine offices infrequently,[155] Dahlberg helped design a questionnaire entitled "Author's Field Day, a Symposium on Marxist Criticism," [156] which was distributed to twenty-five writers who had been reviewed in the *New Masses*. Dahlberg maintained that he had inaugurated the project as a device for attacking Hicks, who "was making the most outrageous remarks, calling this man a defeatist and that man a Trotskyite and that man a furtive Fascist." [157] In his own response to the symposium Dahlberg screamed:

> Sometimes one actually gets the impression that Hicks dislikes good writing, and that the nuances and pigments of prose are, if not offensive to him, altogether baroque. Often the reader feels that Hicks would like to annihilate several centuries of sensibilities and start anew.[158]

Hicks thrust back angrily:

> Edward Dahlberg's statements that I make "no graduated distinctions between writers except political ones," and that "one actually gets the opinion that Hicks dislikes good writing," are as ridiculous as they are bad tempered and deserve no comment.[159]

The bitterness generated between the two fiery critics endured for at least forty years. Hicks wrote in 1972:

> I have been told that Dahlberg said of my review of "Truth Is More Sacred" [160] that "Hicks had been waiting 20 years to get me." As a matter of fact, I read the book because the publisher argued strongly that I had been unfair to Dahlberg and ought to examine his new book. It has always been easy to convince me that I was biased about this man or that in the thirties because I know how sectarian I tended to be in those days. [161]

Not mellowing, but confirmed exasperation was the result of Hick's renewed encounter with Dahlberg's critical attitudes:

> Dahlberg's failure to respond [to the writers under considera-tion in the book] is so complete that we look for an explanation. It seems to me that he is writing out of hatred and jealousy as if Lawrence, James, Eliot, and Pound have done him some harm. And perhaps they have, just by being what they are, which is so much more than he could ever be. [162]

Dahlberg's vituperation in the *New Masses,* coupled with his arrogant manner on the lecture podium,[163] eventually alienated all but a few of his friends and associates on the literary Left. He annoyed V. J. Jerome by courting Archibald MacLeish,[164] and his comments in general came to be regarded as injurious to the cause:

> I spoke in many universities on Proletarian Literature, [but] of course not to the satisfaction of the Communists. I attacked every Proletarian writer and that did not endear me to them.
> Actually, I never meddled in their politics because I didn't know what their politics was. We were just used, as Max Eastman (whatever esteem or disesteem he merits) realized,

that the so-called intellectuals were being used by the Communists. We were just little boys.[165]

Ironically, Dahlberg also clashed with Farrell, a potential ally, since the latter was in 1935 accusing "would-be Marxist writers, Russian and American, of committing every sin in the book." [166] The two men had at times competed for women, but in 1935, at approximately the time Farrell separated from his wife Dorothy, there was an explosive encounter which ended the friendship forever.[167] The incident may be retraced in Farrell's morbidly humorous story, "Literary Love." The main character is the oafish "Carl Waller," obviously Edward Dahlberg, "who was almost a forgotten legend in New York literary circles":

> He had written with a strange and neurotic power, and he had impressed some critics and the more discerning of the literary minded. But he had gradually written in a more and more obscure manner, until his work had disintegrated into a chaos of strange and fantastic words, into a kind of frenzied and solipsistic verbal fantasy that barred others from gaining understanding or sustenance from it.

His precise selection of details in this tightly woven story reflect how well Farrell knew Dahlberg: "He was a bitterly disappointed writer, and a bitter man inclined to violent anger. He seemed obsessed by the necessity to destroy all his relationships."[168] Carl becomes more lonely as he wanders through life, "fighting, insulting, threatening a violence he never carried out. . . . His sexual obsessions intensified and tended to become almost the entire content of his life. He continually needed new girls and women in order to gain a sense of personality and fulfillment." Ultimately, he befriends a woman named Millicent, who detests him on sight, but gradually reverses her opinion after a friend convinces her that he is "a new American Melville" (p. 167). Carl soon begins to court her, succeeding in charming her despite his unctuous manner and overcultivated voice. His pomposity and belabored gravity ("Of course, we live now in a time of chain-store culture . . . ") amuse Millicent until he heavy-handedly attempts to seduce her, all the while pontificating: "Why should we not act as man and woman? It is beautiful, it is natural. It is the crowning moment of unity between two sensitive natures. It is not to be crudely described as sleeping together" (pp.170-71).

Hardly able to suppress laughing at Carl's banality, Millicent removes his hand from her thigh and tries to direct his thoughts to Melville, whereupon he changes his tack and pronounces that she is not "worthy" of savoring the great American writers: "You are crude and insensitive. Don't you dare ever use the name of Melville. You commit a sacrilege if you dare even mutter his name." With bewildering speed, Carl again reverses his course, trying to soothe Millicent with an offer to "make" her worthy of understanding Melville; she breaks free of his viselike grip by biting his tongue. Shocked and humiliated, he flees her apartment, looking like a "ghoulish old man," and taking with him the signed copy of a book he had given her (pp. 172-74).

Dahlberg's personal, ideological and aesthetic difficulties with the Communist party were compounded by the decision, made in 1935 at Earl Browder's headquarters, to liquidate the John Reed clubs.[169] Founded in 1929, these clubs established, besides *The Partisan Review,* a number of militant magazines which featured the work of "undiscovered writers and artists, mimeographed leaflets, improvised 'skits for mass rallies,' " and so on.[170] The clubs were to organize a National Congress of Writers "within the next six or eight months ... to strike a blow at the growing Fascist enemy." The task would be rendered more effective, hard-line communists thought, by dissolving the John Reed clubs and enrolling "writers of some standing." [171] "Crude Trotskyite agit-prop" was to be strongly discouraged, and a respectable anthology, *Proletarian Literature in the United States,*[172] was contrived to implement these ideas.

Dahlberg was crushed when he discovered his exclusion from this anthology of "protest" literature, which included writers of such renown as Erskine Caldwell, John Dos Passos, Muriel Rukeyser, and Clifford Odets, as well as more obscure figures such as Herman Spector, Harry Alan Potemkin, and Robert Gessner. Dahlberg came to blame Phillips and Rahv for this "insult": "They worked together with Alexander Trachtenburg and they saw to it that I was totally excluded." [173] It seems more likely, however, that by late 1935 Dahlberg had alienated the majority of the American Writers on the Left; his erratic behavior and temper tantrums are remembered by virtually everyone who knew him at this time.

One of his closer acquaintances was a left-wing painter named Ephraim Doner, whom Dahlberg had met shortly after the publication of *Those Who Perish*. Dahlberg, his wife Rosa, and his sister-in-law were then living on West Sixteenth Street, and they invited the poverty-stricken Doner to join their household.[174] Doner, Dora, and, to a lesser degree, Rosa were still enthusiastic communists, and the combined pressure from all three may have deferred Dahlberg's decision to quit the party. But Dahlberg, as he made clear even in his writing for the *New Masses*, was yearning for tradition and a sense of the past. As early as 1934, he had begun taking notes for a book which would improve on the attempts of Lawrence's *Studies in Classic American Literature* and Williams's *In the American Grain* in searching for what is noble and enduring in American culture.[175] He was rapidly convincing himself that, contrary to radical dogma, "everyone wants to be original, but originality is just another word for obscenity." [176] Our ideas should be moving backward, not forward: "Nations without stable forms and deities are brutish. . . . People that are not Janus-faced remember little, because they are always changing their customs and calling it Progress which is a sly word for Mammon." [177]

Dahlberg ultimately felt that his creative energies had been blocked by his involvement with the proletarian movement. In an essay written in 1936 or 1937, he concluded that communism was "necrophilic" and could only cheat and destroy humanity, since "the People" become "the ritual bull that must be eaten so that society, the cadaver-flesh of the masses, can be reborn!" Sociologic, proletarian literature, lacking myths of rebirth and cosmological mystery, cannot ennoble the reader; it can only defraud him:

> The dogma of the naturalistic novel will not permit imaginative flights beyond the so-called bounds of the characters presented; so that we can invariably foreknow what will be done, said [and] how it will be uttered. The touchstone of the "realistic" novel is imitation, mediumistic imitation, and not utterance; the American writer does not express or dynam-

ically sculpt the world; he copies it and lets it sieve through
him—there is no more dismal misconception of creation, or de-
energizing act, than this mediumship, this sieving of the
times.[178]

In short, the writer must not let his ideas be formed or suggested by
society or nature. He must stand fast and transform his surroundings, by violence if necessary, in order to relate them to the past
and have them conform to his personal standards.

In 1936, Dahlberg began the first of his two long periods of
literary silence. Having ruined his chances of being published in
either the left-wing or establishment presses, he succeeded only
twice between 1936 and 1950 in having work accepted by
magazines. *Do These Bones Live* (1941) was his only major publication until *The Flea of Sodom* (1950), a bitter satire in which he
discharged fifteen years of accumulated rancor against former
friends in the Communist party and the Machine Age in general.
By the latter date, his politics had shifted as far to the right as they
formerly had been on the left.

In the spring of 1936, Dahlberg published a short piece of fiction
in a remarkable little magazine called *Signatures: Work in Progress,*
which included "experimental" pieces by Kay Boyle, Katherine
Anne Porter, Sean O'Faolain, Farrell, and Dorothy Richardson.
Dahlberg's contribution consisted of two chapters from "Bitch
Goddess: a novel of literary New York," a book with which he later
"just became discouraged and left off." [179] Although this fragment
does not accurately forecast the "baroque" style of his later career,
it clearly indicates that at this time the author's major concerns
were stylistic, since he could dredge up no new autobiographical
themes. Thus, he became almost obsessively preoccupied with
style: "Style is another name for perception and wisdom." [180]
"Your ideas are composed of the words you employ. You can't
separate a man's thought from his style." [181]

Like the earlier novels, this piece concerns a young Dahlberg-like
writer named Eugene ("well-born"), who is infatuated with the
"Bitch Goddess," success. As the story opens, Eugene's mother has
just died as he tries to assuage his grief with a prostitute. The
encounter degenerates into a morbid burlesque as Eugene's

clumsiness and thoughts of his mother thwart his sexual pleasure. Images of death and lust become hopelessly tangled in his mind:

> He painfully measured the slur of water at the rim of the crockery pitcher in the basin on the paint-puling washstand. He rubbed his fingers against the quilt and then against his pants. [The prostitute] had left the room to douche downstairs. He could not rise. As he thought of the whole sexual act it came over him like the dead churning and deterioration of gravebones. He wanted to flee; he had already paid her. He owed no one anything. As he thought of himself on the bed in a dirty sexual gasp, his own blood, feverless and stung with bottomless remorse, wretchedly brooding over his poor beautiful mother, who was already turning and churning. O the word, wipe it out, the flesh of her sexually creaking into bones.[182]

The comedy falters and the characters are too predictable to be funny as Dahlberg attempts to convert his narrative into a satire on the literary and artistic life of Greenwich Village. "Ellen McIntyre" is obviously Alice Neel, who is depicted as "a ham painter ... with her little punk, Kennedy McKenna," who was, according to Ms. Neel, Kenneth Doolittle, her lover at the time.[183] In the following passage, Ellen is trading insults with Eugene's Marxist friend, Alex Salter:

> Alex got on his feet, looked at his army shoes, size five, and put out, testily said: "Ellen, you would sell your whole life for a cheap pun; you've done that already with your art. That's why you paint Joe Gould with nothing on but his glasses and his scrotum. The next thing you'll do is Maxwell Bodenheim with pipe piper and penis [sic]." [184]

Alice Neel actually painted a portrait of Joe Gould with three sets of genitals. Ellen, a huge and frightening earth mother with "pumpernickel breasts," ". . . let out a clear high-pitched laugh and smashed her full-fleshed thighs: 'Alex, that's the trouble with you Communists: you have no sense of humor. You hate too much to love life: you're for the proletariat but you're dead against people.' " [185]

In 1937, Dahlberg's domestic situation had become at least as chaotic as his literary experiments and his politics. Dora Shuser's ardent communism had become subdued to the point that she was having an affair with Lawrence Dennis, author of *The Coming of American Fascism* (1936), while Rosa Dahlberg and Ephraim Doner were already enjoying the warm friendship which would eventually culminate in their marriage.

His publishing prospects appearing bleaker than ever before, Dahlberg began to seek new literary alliances. His one meeting with Van Wyck Brooks, "author of 'The Deflowering of New England,'" was brief and disappointing: "If one of the Peabody sisters stepped into a manhole, this, for Brooks, was an extremely fine piece of literature," Dahlberg opined.[186] But he was exuberant after meeting Theodore Dreiser, whom he came to regard as both mentor and benefactor.[187] Eager for approbation more than advice, he trundled his manuscripts and notes to the older man even though he had contempt for his writing:

> I thought it was very miserable of me to bring a manuscript to Dreiser. . . . If I had reread his books, I would have had to assail him, so I did a more miserable thing—I offered him the manuscript. Of course, it was a very woeful and crass thing on my part to do this; I wanted to do a portrait of Dreiser, but I couldn't. Although his human understanding was great, his critical faculties were impoverished. . . .
>
> I was terrified! To show a man a manuscript [of *Do These Bones Live*] in which he does not appear? What kind of admiration is that? [188]

Dahlberg was to describe Dreiser's naturalism as "cloacal," [189] but actually the philosophies of the two men were not dissimilar. Dahlberg might have been speaking of himself when he said:

> Because a man has a pessimistic viewpoint, he's not necessarily morose. The two don't go together. I used to go up to Mount Kisco to see him or to the Rhinelander Apartments

where he had a sparse two rooms. . . . I found him to be a lovely man, a wonderful companion, who laughed constantly. . . . He was *not* gloomy as Swanberg [190] said. He was a marvellous man! I wish I could have told him that.[191]

Dahlberg insisted that there was "too much of the early ragtime sentimentality in Dreiser"—ironically, a quality which Dahlberg only faintly perceived in himself. The older man would outrage his protégé by insisting that "Beethoven was as good as 'Little Annie Roonie.'" But Dahlberg never relinquished his conviction that "Dreiser was actually a sovereign in his day. It was still a time when people believed in an American Rennaissance." [192]

Dahlberg also became the frequent companion of Sherwood Anderson at this time. He had met Anderson through Frank Morley, the son of Herbert Morley and an editor at Harcourt, Brace, who went with him to spend the Christmas weekend of 1937 at Anderson's house in Marion, Virginia. Anderson contrasted charmingly with the intense radicals and urban sophisticates who had been Dahlberg's friends for the last decade: "He wasn't rustic in his manner, just completely unassuming." [193] The two men seem to have complemented each other in comical ways. Paul Metcalf, who knew Anderson in the late thirties, related an anecdote about them:

> Anderson, who was very suspicious of anyone from big cities or from the east, was walking through New York City with that other boy from the Midwest, Edward Dahlberg. Dahlberg was carrying on in his usual way; "With what malevolence this city was conceived!" Anderson just drawled in reply, "Aw, no—it just happened." [194]

Dahlberg fancied he saw in Anderson a "money-fear" similar to his own:

> Anderson cowered before money, fearing it might destroy what was fecund in him. When he was in New Orleans, the publisher Horace Liveright asked him to write a novel,

offering him a hundred and twenty-five dollars a week while he was working at it. . . .

When Liveright came to see him, he asked, "What's the matter Sherwood? You look so gloomy. Has somebody asked you $150 for the book?" "No," replied Anderson, "that's not it. But Horace, you've got to stop sending me all that money; those checks are killing me! I can't write!" [195]

Like many of Dahlberg's accounts of the literary titans, this account shows signs of his imaginative embroidery. But, as with Dreiser, the chimera of money became (at least from Dahlberg's point of view) an obstacle to their friendship: "The worst book Anderson ever made, the one about Negroes [*Dark Laughter* (1925)] brought him lucre, $10,000, with which he built the house on the outskirts of Marion, Virginia. This began the literary demise of Sherwood Anderson." [196]

Despite Dahlberg's curious notion that "wealth is an obstacle to a man's understanding" and his dubious assertion that he never wrote "a line for lucre," [197] the problem of supporting himself while studying and writing his essays had become his major concern by 1937. Since he was sure it was infested with communists, he avoided the Federal Writers' Project as a source of income, but finally he contacted Jerre Mangione, the national coordinating editor.[198] Mangione and Dahlberg remembered their dealings very differently. Dahlberg claimed, "I was amiable with Jerre. I liked him, but I did not really know him," [299] while Mangione wrote:

In the thirties I knew him well, but I have not seen him since. A few years ago, in answer to a letter I wrote him about the Writers' Project, he explained his experience on the Project had represented "a stigmata of shame" and for that reason he had pushed it out of his memory. It was rather a beautiful letter, and I should have answered it sooner than I did. I think he may have become offended by my delay, for I have not heard from him since.[200]

Mangione put Dahlberg in touch with James McGraw, the director of the New York Project, who arranged for him to become part of the program. Special arrangements were made for Dahlberg, since writers were mostly involved in assembling "state guidebooks" and were required to remain within their native locales.[201] He was an exception:

> In the Federal Writers' Project I was writing a part of *Can These Bones Live.* I went to Mexico when I wasn't supposed to do that, but I was one of six or seven writers who were permitted to do their own work. After I left the Project, I think that they curtailed or amputated funds and became very patriarchal.[202]

Mangione thought that Dahlberg's story may well have been accurate:

> It is true that he was on the secret creative writing unit that was established in the NYC Project for the sake of those writers, like Dahlberg, who had already published. And it's quite possible that he arranged, with the connivance of some sympathetic Project supervisor, to go to Mexico and have his salary check sent to him.[203]

With the intention of devoting his energies exclusively to his new book, Dahlberg departed for Taxco early in the summer of 1937. During the six-day voyage to Vera Cruz, he met the novelist Eleanor Clark. Apparently, according to Miss Clark, he had not abjured communist doctrine, even if it might have been a drawback in impressing attractive young women: The party line "would certainly *not* help in amorous conquests," especially of the secretary types on that boat, "who hoped to hook a respectable dentist. . . . Dahlberg couldn't conceal his views no matter what he would lose by it":

> He was a Stalinist and I a Trotskyite, so of course we avoided each other until the very last morning, approaching Vera Cruz. By that time, as I interpret it, we were both fed up with the petty bourgeoisie and it drew us into brief communica-

tion. A certain common Marxist view was for the moment stronger than our violent differences.[205]

Characteristically, the encounter transpired quite differently in Dahlberg's memory. He was attracted to Miss Clark, especially since "she was not without culture: she had read Sir Thomas Brown's *Urne Buriall.*" However, fearful of being "outwitted" by her, he "fled from her when we got to Mexico." [206] Dahlberg's trepidations about "cultured" women were operating in earnest.

At Vera Cruz, Dahlberg decided to take a bus to Mexico City. It was "one of those tin buses that roll from one precipice to another and you look down the sheer declension and close your eyes." The irritations of traveling and the sultry atmosphere of Taxco combined to convince him that he had erred seriously in leaving New York:

> Taxco was a kind of travelogue town which you enjoy looking at but not living in. It was terribly lonely. It dropped from 7500 feet in Mexico City, where you would have a divine climate were it not for the altitude. The altitude really affects you enormously.... Your head is on the table if you're writing daily.[207]

He soon found himself unable to write a line in the noisy little town: "I'd wake up every morning at ten and hear 'Take Me Out to the Ball Game' while I was writing the essay on Thoreau." [208] In a letter dated August 9, 1937, he complained bitterly to Dreiser:

> Taxco is colonized by Americans. They do nothing, read nothing, and only defecate, I am certain, when afflicted with dysentery. Also in Taxco is the Polish minister; he is a little dry flaky man, who clicks his heels and make his bows, not so much to the people he greets as to himself. The pinochle minister of eleven vest-pocket Latin American countries, he is a fair representative of the kind of diplomatic intelligence which rules the world. I ask him: "What do you think of the Spanish Situation?" He replies: "I think it is quite a situation...."
>
> I need a change, as you may doubtless surmise.[209]

Dahlberg returned from Mexico, sun-blistered and frustrated that he had accomplished almost nothing. Convinced, as was the Dies Committee which finally abolished it,[210] that it was "a nest of Reds," Dahlberg quit the Writers' Project. James McGraw was certain Dahlberg left of his own volition:

He was always very strange. All I remember is that he was on the Project and he was very difficult. I don't think he was removed—he removed himself, because I was in charge of hiring and firing and I know if I had ever fired Ed Dahlberg I would have heard about it.[211]

NOTES

1. Interview: E. D., March 20, 1973.
2. Mr. Conrad S. Spohnholz, General Director of the Colony, confirmed the fact that Dahlberg was in residence there in 1929. Letter: May 17, 1973.
3. *Confessions*, p. 238.
4. Interview: E. D., March 20, 1973.
5. *Confessions*, p. 238.
6. Interview: E. D., April 26, 1973.
7. Interview: E. D., June 18, 1973.
8. *Confessions*, p. 241.
9. Ibid, pp. 237-39.
10. Interview: E. D., May 19, 1973.
11. *Confessions*, pp. 238-39.
12. Letter: May 26, 1973.
13. Interview: Isadora Bennett, June 18, 1973.
14. *Confessions*, p. 239. Professor Wallace L. Anderson is editing the letters of Robinson, but he has found no Dahlberg-Robinson correspondence. Letter: July 6, 1973.
15. Interview: Isadora Bennett, June 18, 1973.
16. *Confessions*, p. 242.
17. Interview: Isadora Bennett, June 18, 1973.
18. Letter: June 18, 1973. In another letter (October 23, 1972, Trilling denied that he had met Dahlberg while they were students at Columbia, as Dahlberg repeatedly claimed.
19. Interview: E. D., Jan. 12, 1973.
20. Interview: Lewis Mumford, Feb. 6, 1973.
21. Interview: Lewis Mumford, Feb.6, 1973.

22. Interview: E. D., Jan. 12, 1973; *Because I Was Flesh*, p. 208.
23. Interview: E. D., Feb. 17, 1973.
24. *The House on Jefferson Street* (New York: Holt, Rinehart & Winston, 1971), pp. 178-79. See also Clarence S. Stein, *Toward New Towns for America*, introduction by Lewis Mumford (New York: Reinhold Publishing Corp., 1957). The designers of Sunnyside had intended to plan communities in the same way as Frederick Law Olmsted had planned Central Park (p. 16).
25. Interview: Isadora Bennett, June 18, 1973.
26. Interview: Michael Sands, Feb. 20, 1973.
27. *Because I was Flesh*, p. 209. Dahlberg and his editors telescoped the last twenty years of Lizzie's life (1926-46) into one chapter (Ch. XII) of this book. Dahlberg fictionized many of the events of this period and distorted the chronology.
28. Interview: Walter Arnold, June 12, 1973. Mr. Arnold was Dahlberg's editor at Dutton.
29. Interview: Lewis Mumford, Feb. 6, 1973.
30. Interview: Lewis Mumford, Feb. 6, 1973.
31. Interview: Michael and Minnie Sands, March 10, 1974.
32. Interview: E. D., May 19, 1973.
33. *Books* (March 2, 1930), pp. 5-6.
34. Interview: Theodore Wilentz, Mar. 8, 1974.
35. Interview: E. D., May 4, 1973.
36. Interview: Michael Sands, Feb. 20, 1973.
37. *Confessions*, p. 248.
38. Letter: Lionel Trilling, June 18, 1973.
39. Ms. Mazo indicated her preference not to talk about her relationship with Dahlberg.
40. Interview: Feb. 12, 1973. This individual prefers not to be identified.
41. (New York: Farrar, Straus & Giroux, 1972), p. 446.
42. Interview: E. D., Dec. 28, 1973.
43. Interview: E. D., Dec. 28, 1973. Wilson and Dahlberg did not see much of each other, so this incident may well have been a fabrication.
44. *Confessions*, p. 245.
45. Interview: Michael Sands, Feb. 20, 1973.
46. *A Return to Pagany*: 1929-1932, ed. Stephen Halpert with Richard Johns, introduction by Kenneth Rexroth (Boston: Beacon Press, 1969), p. 3.
47. *Confessions*, p. 251.
48. *A Return to Pagany*, p. xvii.
49. Ibid., p. 207.
50. Ibid., p. 207. This is the only claim Dahlberg ever made that his books were censored.
51. P. 332. Dahlberg is quoting, in a letter to Johns, reactions of various publishers to the manuscripts of *From Flushing to Calvary*.
52. *Confessions*, p. 249.
53. *A Return to Pagany*, p. 333.
54. Ibid., p. 335.

55. *Confessions*, p. 248.
56. *A Return to Pagany*, p. 452.
57. Another letter to Johns bears a Kansas City address (p. 333).
58. See Daniel Aaron, *Writers on the Left* (New York: Avon Books, 1965). Dahlberg approved of Calverton's politics, which are described by Aaron as "oppositionist" (p. 310).
59. Letter: Feb. 13, 1973.
60. Letter: Feb. 13, 1973.
61. *Pagany*, II (Summer 1931), 77-89. This item was discussed in Ch. III.
62. *Pagany*, II (Winter 1932), 38-47.
63. Interview: Oct. 30, 1972.
64. Interview: Gilbert Sorrentino, Sept. 27, 1972.
65. *A Return to Pagany*, p. 247.
66. Ibid., p. 249.
67. Dahlberg left the orphanage in 1917 and enlisted briefly in the army (see Ch. I).
68. *A Return to Pagany*, p. 248.
69. Ibid., p. 303.
70. Ibid., p. 256.
71. Interview: E. D., Nov. 16, 1972. Many of these people were satirized in Dahlberg's *The Flea of Sodom* (see Ch. VI).
72. Interview: E. D., May 25, 1973.
73. Interview: Sara and Max Arthur Cohn, Feb. 13, 1973.
74. Interview: Sara and Max Arthur Cohn, Feb. 13, 1973.
75. Interview: Sara and Max Arthur Cohn, Feb. 13, 1973.
76. Letter: Kenneth Burke, Jan. 6, 1973.
77. Interview: E. D., Sept. 16, 1972.
78. Letter: Jan. 6, 1973.
79. Letter: Jan. 6, 1973.
80. Interviews: Sara and Max Cohn, Feb. 13, 1973; E. D., Jan. 14, 1973.
81. *Those Who Perish* (New York: The John Day Co., 1934).
82. Ibid., p.114.
83. Ibid., pp. 115-16.
84. Ibid.
85. Interviews: E.D., Nov. 21, 1972, and Jan. 14, 1973.
86. *From Flushing to Calvary* (New York: Harcourt, Brace, 1932), p. 38.
87. Ibid., p. 41.
88. The text is a few paragraphs longer than the virtually identical final chapter of *From Flushing to Calvary*.
89. *Kentucky Blue Grass Henry Smith*, p. 8.
90. Ibid., p. 6.
91. Ibid., p. 20.
92. "From Flushing to Calvary," *Contempo*, 3 (Oct. 25, 1932), 1-4.
93. *Confessions*, p. 164.
94. Interview: Michael Sands, Feb. 20, 1973.
95. *Confessions*, p. 216.

96. *Because I was Flesh,* p. 3.
97. Ibid., p. 208. Here the author expands the occurrences of several months to several years.
98. Calverton was the famous "oppositionist" in American radical politics. He founded the *Modern Quarterly,* which was severely criticized by hard-line communists for its "eclecticism" (Aaron, p. 345).
99. *Contempo,* 3. (Jan. 10, 1933), 5.
100. "Books" (Oct. 9, 1932), 17. "Books" was the review supplement in the Sunday edition of the *Herald Tribune.*
101. Quoted in *Contempo,* 3 (Jan. 10, 1933), 5.
102. *Contempo,* 3 (Oct. 23, 1932), 15-17.
103. *Contempo,* 3 (Jan. 10, 1933), 1-5.
104. Lecture: CCNY, Dec. 12, 1973.
105. Aaron, p. 297.
106. Interview: Walter Arnold, June 12, 1973. Mr. Arnold, of E. P. Dutton & Co., lives near Croton in Ossining, New York.
107. *Confessions,* p. 279.
108. *Times* (London), (Mar. 14, 1933), 13; *Deutsche Allgemeine Zeitung* (Mar. 13, 1933), 4; Interview: Michael Sands, Dec. 9, 1972.
109. Interview: E. D., May 9, 1973.
110. *Confessions,* p. 175.
111. Interview: E. D., May 9, 1973.
112. Mowrer, who won the Pulitzer Prize for journalism in 1961, was at the *Chicago Daily News* bureau in Berlin when Dahlberg met him.
113. E. D., quoted in the *New York World Telegram,* Mar. 29, 1933, p. 1.
114. Ibid., pp. 1 and 7
115. Ibid., pp. 1 and 7.
116. Reported in the *New York World Telegram,* Mar. 29, 1933, p. 1.
117. Paraphrased in the London *Times,* Mar. 14, 1933, p. 13.
118. Ibid.
119. *New York Times,* Mar. 30, 1933, p. 13.
120. Interview: E. D., May 9, 1973.
121. Interview: Michael Sands, Dec. 9, 1972.
122. *New York Times,* April 19, 1932, p. 20.
123. P. 57.
124. The main street in Dahlberg's fictional town is "Hackensack Boulevard."
125. Quoted in Harold Billings, "Introduction: Cabalist in the Wrong Season," *Edward Dahlberg: American Ishmael of Letters,* ed. Harold Billings (Austin: Roger Beacham, 1968), p. 17.
126. Interview: James T. Farrell, July 6, 1973.
127. Quoted in Aaron, p. 310.
128. Interview: Anonymous, Feb. 12, 1973.
129. *New York Times,* Sept. 7, 1934, p. 19.
130. Interview: E. D., Sept. 16, 1972.
131. One of the characters in *The Flea of Sodom* is named Ajax Proletcult, an obvious pun on the name.

132. Interview: Max Arthur Cohn, Feb. 13, 1973.

133. Interview: Max Arthur Cohn, Feb. 13, 1973.

134. James T. Farrell, "Literary Love," *An American Dream Girl* (New York: Vanguard Press, 1950), p. 169. A discussion of this story follows.

135. Interview: Michael Sands, April 19, 1973.

136. Interview: Edwin Seaver, Dec. 26, 1973.

137. Interview: E. D., Jan. 14, 1973.

138. Interview: James T. Farrell, July 6, 1973.

139. All appeared in *The New Republic*, vols. 68-71.

140. "Hunger on the March," *The Nation*, 135, (December 1932), 642-44.

141. Interview: E. D., May 9, 1973.

142. Aaron, p. 313.

143. Ibid.

144. Interviews: Lou Gilbert, Feb. 13, 1973; Kenneth Rexroth, Feb. 17, 1973; and William Phillips, May 20, 1973.

145. (February-March 1934, and April-May 1934).

146. Interview: E. D., May 9, 1973.

147. Interview: William Phillips, May 20, 1973.

148. "Nightgown Riders of America," *New Masses*, 10 (Jan. 30, 1934), 17.

149. *Confessions*, p. 251.

150. *New Masses*, 11 (June 12, 1934), 22.

151. *New Masses*, 15 (April 23, 1935), 22.

152. Interview: E. D., June 16, 1973.

153. "Waldo Frank and the Left," *New Masses*, 15 (April 23, 1935), 22.

154. "In Search of the Image," *New Masses*, 13 (December 1934), 21.

155. Letter: Granville Hicks, Oct. 9, 1972.

156. *New Masses*, 12 (July 3, 1934).

157. Interview: E. D., June 17, 1973.

158. *New Masses*, 12 (July 3, 1934), 28.

159. Ibid., p. 32.

160. Dahlberg's exchange of letters with Sir Herbert Read (New York: Horizon Press, 1961).

161. Letter: Oct. 9, 1972. Dahlberg's actual remark, in a letter to Josephine Herbst (April 23, 1961), was "Did you see Granville Hicks' review of the book by Herbert Read and me; he has been lying in ambush for me for twenty-eight years" (*Epitaphs*, p. 165).

162. *Saturday Review* (April 18, 1961), 20.

163. Interview: Lou Gilbert, Feb. 13, 1973.

164. *Confessions*, p. 294. MacLeish wrote: "I remember Dahlberg not, as I apparently should, with shudders, but with warmth." (Letter: Oct. 14, 1973.)

165. Interview: E. D., June 17, 1973.

166. Aaron, p. 317.

167. Max Cohn guessed that this woman was Hortense Alden, who married Farrell after he divorced Dorothy, whom he remarried in 1955.

168. *An American Dream Girl*, p. 166.

169. Aaron, p. 299.
170. Aaron, p. 358.
171. Aaron, p. 300.
172. Ed. Granville Hicks, Michael Gold, Joseph Freeman et al. (New York: International Publishers, 1935).
173. Interview: E. D., June 17, 1973.
174. Interview: Ephraim Doner, May 27, 1973.
175. Interview: E. D., Dec. 31, 1972.
176. Interview: E. D., Oct. 17, 1972.
177. *The Flea of Sodom* (London: Peter Nevill, 1950), p. 97.
178. "The Helmet of Mambrino," *Do These Bones Live* (New York: Harcourt, Brace, 1941), pp. 55-57.
179. Interview: E. D., Sept. 16, 1972.
180. *Alms for Oblivion*, p. 101.
181. Interview: E. D., Dec. 29, 1972.
182. *Signatures*, 1 (Spring 1936), n.p.
183. Ibid. Doolittle, a sailor, once in a violent fit slashed all of Ms. Neel's paintings. (Interview: Alice Neel, June 28, 1973.)
184. *Signatures*, 1 (Spring 1936), n.p.
185. Ibid.
186. Interview: E. D., Jan. 29, 1973.
187. W. A. Swanberg, in his biography, *Dreiser*, states that Dreiser, "who needed someone to replace his late admirer, George Douglas, exchanged visits with the novelist Edward Dahlberg, who lived nearby on West Sixteenth Street." (New York: Charles Scribner's Sons, 1965), p. 446.
188. Interview: E. D., Jan. 29, 1973.
189. *Epitaphs*, p. 12.
190. See note 187 above.
191. Interview: E. D., Jan. 29, 1973.
192. Interview: E. D., July 15, 1973.
193. Interview: E. D., Jan. 29, 1973.
194. Interview: Dec. 1, 1972.
195. "My Friends, Stieglitz, Anderson, and Dreiser," *Alms for Oblivion*, pp. 10-11.
196. Interview: E. D., July 15, 1973.
197. Quoted in Phil Casey, "Writing What He Must, Getting By—But Barely," the *Washington Post*, June 18, 1973, p. 23.
198. Jerre Mangione, *The Dream and the Deal: The Federal Writers' Project, 1935-43* (Boston: Little Brown, 1972), p. 3.
199. Interview: E. D., April 2, 1973.
200. Letter: Mar. 3, 1973.
201. Mangione, pp. 149-150.
202. Interview: E. D., Feb. 11, 1973.
203. Letter: Mar. 3, 1973.
204. Letter: Eleanor Clark, May 25, 1973.
205. Letter: Eleanor Clark, May 25, 1973.

206. Interview: E. D., May 25, 1973.
207. Interviews; E. D., Feb. 17 and 19, 1973; May 25, 1973.
208. Interview: E. D., Feb. 11, 1973.
209. *Epitaphs*, p. 11.
210. Letter: Jerre Mangione, Mar. 3, 1973.
211. Interview: James McGraw, Mar. 16, 1973.

5.

Searching for a Center: 1937-1950

The apartment at 2 Grove Street was a bleak place when Dahlberg returned to New York in the autumn of 1937. The rooms no longer echoed with the brave talk of his former comrades, and Ephraim Doner was virtually courting Rosa Dahlberg, who now recognized that her husband had lost interest in her. Dahlberg, perhaps to relieve his boredom, frequented An American Place, the famous gallery of Alfred Stieglitz at 509 Madison Avenue. Dorothy Norman, a young photographer and writer in Stieglitz's circle, recalled that she was amazed when Dahlberg began visiting Stieglitz, since she had remembered that in the early 1930s, when she had first met him, Dahlberg had vilified the famous photographer.[1] Now Dahlberg seemed to be espousing pacificism and civil liberties as passionately as he had formerly embraced communism. He may have adopted this stance simply to win friends, although he never became close to those associated with An American Place.[2]

Mrs. Norman, an ardent civil libertarian, was in the process of founding a periodical which would emphasize "art and action," support freedom of expression, and denounce such undemocratic processes as racial discrimination and the persecution of conscientious objectors. The thoughts of Thoreau and Gandhi set the tone of this magazine, which came to be known as *Twice a Year*. The publication was supported by Mrs. Norman from her own funds and produced at a loss since her intention was to sell the issues at a price which college students could afford. All editing was done at her home in New York, at Wood's Hole on Cape Cod, and at An American Place. But the early days were not easy, since she had made Dahlberg one of the editors after Stieglitz had pleaded with her to do so.[3] Preliminary stationery was printed, indicating Dorothy Norman as editor, Edward Dahlberg as associate editor, and Mary Lescaze as assistant editor of *Twice a Year*, "a semiannual journal of literature, the arts, and civil liberties."

Initially, there was little discord. Dahlberg wrote letters to a number of people, including Dreiser and Emma Goldman, soliciting manuscripts for the new publication. By now, he had evolved into a steadfast anticommunist, and Dahlberg and Emma Goldman mourned the murder of the translator, José Robles, by the communists. Although Robles is best remembered as a good friend and translator of Dos Passos, Dahlberg claimed that he had also been engaged in a translation of *Bottom Dogs*. The Primo de Rivera dictatorship suppressed the book in 1930, and Robles was executed shortly thereafter.[4]

Dahlberg became genuinely infected with Stieglitz's love of the writings of the World War I anarchist, Randolph Bourne.[5] He no doubt identified strongly with Bourne, a grotesquely disfigured outcast and an unrecognized genius who died in 1918. Accordingly, Dahlberg dedicated "To Alfred Stieglitz: A Living Intransigent" the first of four essays he was to write on this tragic "subversive" whose "problem was how to remain uninvaded by the war." [6] The last article by Dahlberg to be accepted by any periodical until 1950, this essay rambles and is far less intense and coherent than later versions, but it clearly reveals the reasons for his perverse attraction to Bourne, who was "five feet high, with malformed back and chest, with a stump of ear on the left side of his face." Dahlberg's fascination with the grotesque becomes manifest here: his favorite paintings were Velasquez's series, *The Dwarfs,* and he always had a morbid preoccupation with his own disfigured eye. Moreover, Bourne shared Dahlberg's poverty, his loneliness, his disappointing experiences with women, and his insatiable hunger for knowledge: "At Columbia University, [Bourne] had sat at the feet of Professor John Dewey, knelt there, and in 1913-14, as a holder of the Gilder fellowship from that same institution had received his baptism in those eclectic pre-war days in Europe." [7]

Dahlberg came to feel that he had rediscovered Bourne and became eager to move him to the front ranks of American literature. At the same time, Mrs. Norman, who also admired Bourne, was planning to print some of his work. She had learned of certain unpublished letters of the deceased writer and had gone to Princeton to get permission from his sister to publish them.[8] Dahlberg later insisted that he was destined to head the magazine, [9] but the fact remains that Mrs. Norman was founder, publisher, and editor of *Twice a Year.*

Arguments over editorial matters mounted. Dahlberg insisted on accepting only what he called "beautiful prose," and he reacted furiously when Mrs. Norman wanted to publish Roger Baldwin, who was not a great writer, but an outstanding civil libertarian.[10] Dahlberg also claimed that his friendship with Ford Madox Ford was damaged by Mrs. Norman's refusal to publish an essay by Ford on Stephen Crane.[11] Dahlberg's loyalty to and identification with Ford, whom he considered "the last of the Pre-Raphaelites" and "a hero of literature," is not difficult to comprehend. He felt that Ford was at war with academia; he admired the older man's taste in literature: Walton's *Compleat Angler,* White's *Natural History of Selborne,* and William's *In the American Grain,* which Dahlberg was attempting to supersede by writing *Do These Bones Live.* But Ford was close to death when Dahlberg met him. His mistress, Violet Hunt, had abandoned him, and now, old, impoverished, and monstrously overweight, he was, Dahlberg thought, already a "posthumous celebrity." [12]

Mrs. Norman denounced as "complete fantasy" Dahlberg's claim that she rejected an article by Ford; [13] she insisted that Ford was never even asked by her to write an article, and that a piece on Stephen Crane would have been outside the scope of the magazine.[14] Nothing in Dahlberg's correspondence with Mrs. Norman bears any reference to Ford, nor did she have any correspondence with the latter.[15]

Quite predictably, Mrs. Norman explained to Dahlberg that it was not possible for him to continue as coeditor.[16] He responded with a confusing series of letters which alternately denounced her and sought reconciliation. On one occasion, he insulted her viciously, condemning her for turning Stieglitz against him, but two months later he minimized their quarrels.[17] Two facts are clear from the correspondence: Dahlberg did not, as he claimed, resign from the magazine, and he wanted desperately to publish in it.

Stieglitz had no choice but to side with Dorothy Norman. Moreover, the photographer was growing weary of Dahlberg's importunate behavior. Having received a number of beautiful photogravures, Dahlberg persistently demanded more. At his death, Stieglitz left behind several of Dahlberg's letters with the envelopes still sealed.[18]

It took Dahlberg ten years to brew his "revenge" upon Stieglitz, which was couched in an ostensible tribute to "My Friends Stieglitz, Anderson, and Dreiser." In this essay, he grudgingly admitted that "Alfred Stieglitz had genius, but he was not a good man. I think he suffered from what has been called man's most malignant affliction, coldness." [19] Dahlberg's unpublished comments were more acrimonious: "Stieglitz was a remarkable, refrigerated man. ... He was a wonderful charlatan who did wonderful things for his artists who were also quacks." [20]

Dahlberg and Mrs. Norman managed to agree on one editorial issue: the publication of an essay by Dahlberg's first and best-known disciple, Charles Olson. Dahlberg had met Olson on August 9, 1936, when he was vacationing on Cape Ann, a half-day's drive around Massachusetts Bay from his favorite vacation spot, Wellfleet. Olson, on leave from his job as a mail carrier in Gloucester, Massachusetts, made a pilgrimage to meet Dahlberg, who, upon answering the loud knock on the door of his rented room, was astonished by the spectacle of this "giant near seven foot high." [21] After the two settled into conversation, Dahlberg was astonished not only by the young man's erudition but by his taste in literature, remarkably similar to his own:

Olson knew pages of Shakespeare's *Measure for Measure, Lear, Troilus and Cressida, Timon of Athens* by rote. A perfervid disciple of Herman Melville, he had devoured *Moby Dick, Mardi,* "The

Encantadas," "Bartleby the Scrivener," "Benito Cereno." He venerated the small spermal candle in American literature, Melville's "Hawthorne and His Mosses," and was the first to excavate many of Melville's epistles then in the possession of Mrs. Metcalf, Melville's granddaughter.[22]

Dahlberg submitted to Dorothy Norman an essay by Olson which had grown out of a long term paper written for F. O. Matthiessen at Harvard on the resemblances between Melville and Shakespeare. Eagerly and efficiently, Dahlberg helped Olson revise and cut the paper.[23] Mrs. Norman liked it at once, despite Dahlberg's contention that he had to oppose "a lioness with barking dogs for a belly." [24] This "lioness," actually the mild and soft-spoken Mrs. Norman, insisted "there was no argument or tampering with [Olson's piece,]" and she enjoyed a long and very warm friendship with Olson.

Almost immediately, Dahlberg's competitive nature asserted itself. In a letter, written after the Olson manuscript had been accepted, Dahlberg insisted he wanted to write about the same subject! [25] Indeed, an element of competition never was absent from the friendship: Olson was simultaneously impressed and oppressed by the man he initially idolized, and Dahlberg lived with the perpetual fear of being dethroned by his brilliant disciple. Paul Metcalf suggested that "one trouble with Olson and Dahlberg was that both wanted to be Ishmael." [26] In one of several unspecific indictments of Olson's "plagiarism," Dahlberg festers over what he calls Olson's "intellectual cuckoldry," and his "vowing the utmost fealty to a friend whilst breaking into his soul to get what he requires for his own ends." [27] Just what Olson "stole" from Dahlberg, or when these "crimes" were perpetuated, is never made clear. The friendship, which endured for almost nineteen years, grew increasingly turbulent as Dahlberg, by degrees, came to see Olson as the Ahab in his life. That he would come to feel betrayed by Olson, who was also solitary, moody, and often paranoiac, seemed inevitable. Dahlberg, while insisting that he "loved" Charles Olson and that "You can't have a patronizing relationship unless you're a maggot," demanded his complete submission: "I said to Olson, 'If you're not influenced by me, you'll be influenced by men other than me.' But he didn't listen. He went to Pound and then went to Williams—and that was the end of Olson. There was nothing left but for him to die." [28] In what seems almost a twenty-year campaign to destroy Olson, Dahlberg condemned the latter's literary opinions as well as his prophetic utterances, even though they often espoused an identical philosophy. For instance, Dahlberg repeatedly declared, "A man's character is his fate," a simple deterministic affirmation. Olson somehow arrived at a similar conclusion and cast it as "People don't change, they only stand more revealed." [29] This Dahlberg accepted as *prima facie* evidence of plagiarism. Eventually, even Olson's handshake came in for criticism:

> If a man hasn't a firm handclasp, there's something wrong with his character. . . . Olson had a poor handclasp and I said, "Well, look, Charles, learn how to shake hands with people warmly." So after that, he did so, and I said, "My God! I've taught him to be a dissembler!" [30]

At the height of their friendship, Dahlberg once commissioned Olson to visit Lizzie Dahlberg in Kansas City, [31] but his envy of Olson came to color the whole relationship. Although he finally admitted that " 'Lear and Moby-Dick' was entirely Olson's idea, not mine," he came to feel that many of the younger man's insights into Melville were cribbed from their conversations together. In fact, "Lear and Moby-Dick" contains material that Dahlberg may well have wished to have incorporated in the essay "Ishmael" which he was writing for *Do These Bones Live.* Dahlberg and Olson had spent many hours discussing the fact that, after having read *King Lear,* Melville, like Shakespeare, wrote a "wicked book." Ahab's problem, said Olson, is his identification with evil exemplified by the pact with Fedallah.[32] Ahab is a madman, but so close is his insanity to the occult arts ("theurgic magic") that the crew of the *Pequod* fail to recognize his mania. Pip's "more fathomable idiocy" is more accessible to the crew, although *his* madness is closer to "right reason" and more easily dismissed.[33]

Gilbert Sorrentino, a novelist who knew both men, felt that "Their interest in each other blossomed because of their mutual interest in Melville." [34] Both were searching for a new idiom in which to write American English, and, like Melville, they explored the past to find it. Also like Melville, both men had defective eyesight and yearned to write like Shakespeare: "What perils there are in originality!" exclaimed Dahlberg.[35] Both saw Ishmael as the commentator or "chorus" in Melville's dark drama,[36] while both were deeply concerned about the role of "sapient madmen" in literature:[37] Dahlberg dwelled repeatedly on Don Quixote, afflicted with idealistic "windmills in his head," while Olson wrote of "the necessary silence of truth," as expressed in Melville's Hawthorne essay, which Olson thought derived from the philosophy of the Fool in *King Lear*.

Over the years, Olson repeatedly acknowledged his debt to Dahlberg, especially in his dedication of *Call Me Ishmael* to "Edward Dahlberg, my other genius of the Cross and the Windmills,"[39] and in his essay on "Projective Verse":

> Now ... the *process* of the thing, how the principle can be made so to shape the energies that form is accomplished. And I think it can be boiled down to one statement (first pounded into my head by Edward Dahlberg): ONE PERCEPTION MUST IMMEDIATELY AND DIRECTLY LEAD TO A FURTHER PERCEPTION.[40]

Olson surely owed Dahlberg a substantial amount. Dahlberg helped him not only in forming and refining his ideas but with money. When Olson applied for a Guggenheim award in 1938, Dahlberg circulated reprints of "Lear and Moby-Dick" to gain publicity for the younger man.[41] But Olson, who had taken a teaching job at Harvard, felt stifled by Dahlberg's tyrannical manner and his genius for alienating people. (One of the lines cut from an early version of *Maximus* is "Loneliness is a goddam lie!"[42]) Olson especially deplored being dragged into the fight between Mrs. Norman and Dahlberg.[43] Emmanual Navaretta, who knew both men, attempted to analyze the tension between them: "Dahlberg's turning against Olson, and his denigration of Olson ... has more to do with the fact that Olson had attained an enormous notoriety and popularity, publicly and privately, as ... 'the king of the kids.' There wasn't one young poet on the east or west coast who didn't visit Olson at Gloucester, and Dahlberg was well aware of this."[44]

With Olson occupied in East Gloucester and Cambridge,

Dahlberg divided his time between writing and dallying with some of the younger writers he had come to know in Greenwich Village. One of the more intense of these friendships was with Harvey Breit, a charming young journalist and a friend of Hemingway and Faulkner. Dahlberg had met Breit in 1936 through Dorothy Norman, who had published several of his essays.[45] According to Clara Port, Breit's wife at the time, Dahlberg felt he had been her husband's "mentor," even though Breit had achieved fame long before he met Dahlberg. Miss Port thought the friendship had been harmful to her husband: "Edward would grab him and try to make mincemeat out of him—this brought about very stubborn resistance in him, although Harvey was imaginative and understanding." But Dahlberg's charm usually counterbalanced his arrogance:

> There was something about Edward that appealed to me—something very naive. Although he pretended to be sophisticated, he was a very provincial fellow. He wasn't sophisticated or worldly at all! All his feelings came from his provincialism and his emotions were tremendously involved in everything he did.

Having dealt with theatrical people for many years while writing *Playbill* for Shubert Alley, Miss Port was naturally fascinated by Dahlberg's divided and paradoxical personality. Despite the fact that he obsessively reiterated his hatred of homosexuals, she felt that he had a very "female" character, though the base of his creativity was "his tremendous anger against his mother." Dahlberg once threatened to kill Miss Port for saying this.[46]

When Dahlberg and Breit decided that a retreat might spark their literary inspiration, they rented a house on Fire Island, off the southern coast of Long Island, in the spring of 1938. The sojourn was not fruitful. Dahlberg, who was nearly impoverished at the time, seemed to resent Breit's having a wife to support him while he was writing. To make matters worse, Harvey fell ill on Fire Island and was bedridden for several weeks—Dahlberg found himself functioning as a nurse, a role which he did not relish.[47] Twelve years later, after Breit had either neglected or refused to review his *Flea of Sodom* in the *Times,* Dahlberg proposed writing a novel called *Harvey Corrupt*, [48] which was to be a lightly veiled allegory about "failed" writers. Guessing who would be the title character, neither Breit nor his wife offered any encouragement.[49]

By the fall of 1938, Dahlberg was desperately short of cash and willing to find an outlet other than writing for his energy. He approached a recent acquaintance named Oscar Cargill, a young professor at New York University, who was enthusiastic about Dahlberg's books and invited him to lunch. Dahlberg launched a display of erudition, which quite impressed Cargill, who thought he was a very good Latinist, "probably Jesuit trained," even though Dahlberg never learned any foreign languages: "He had a good knowledge of the 4th Century A.D. writers whom he ran into his rather astonishing talk." [50] Cargill presented Dahlberg's credentials to Dean Frank McCloskey, who appointed him to his first teaching position: part-time instructor of freshman English. It was the spring of 1939. Unfortunately, Dahlberg irritated many of his students and then had a "fearful quarrel" with the dean, "in which he publicly denounced McClosky. Under the circumstances I could not rehire Dahlberg at the end of the semester." [51] Cargill later discussed the incident with the dean and brought up Dahlberg's poverty, but McCloskey replied that Cargill was being sentimental, because Dahlberg wore Brooks Brothers clothes to his interview.[52] Dahlberg later claimed that he bought these garments to make a favorable impression.[53]

Dahlberg derived several fringe benefits from his first turbulent college appointment. On his way to the university, he would often meet Ford Madox Ford, "this immense, plodding Falstaff, strolling near his apartment at 10 Fifth Avenue." Dahlberg recalled that "Ford admired *Those Who Perish,* which I think was intolerably bad." He was often invited either to Ford's apartment or to have lunch with him at the Brevoort Hotel across the street. This friendship grew warm during the last months of Ford's life. So strong was Dahlberg's admiration for him that he came to regard the older man as "my one buckler. . . . Ford and I harangued one another over literary judgments, but never with one jot of malice. If kindness is one of the trees in the Garden of Eden, he was a branch of that tree." [54]

Ford easily reciprocated his young admirer's affection. In 1937, not long after they first met, he hailed Williams, Cummings, and Dahlberg as the three most neglected writers in America.[55] And, as Dahlberg related, Ford praised the manuscript of *Do These Bones Live,* and told him he would be delighted to write an introduction. He presumably took portions of the manuscript with him to France, but died before he could fulfill his promise.[56] His only published praise is preserved as a blurb on the dustjacket, which declares the book to be a "Work of genius. A most magnificent piece of criticism."

After Ford's death, Dahlberg relied more heavily upon the less bracing companionship of Dreiser, even though he was more aware than ever that he was simply replacing Dreiser's deceased friend, George Douglas.[57] He visited Dreiser's eccentric château, Iroki, at Mount Kisco several times, despite the fact that he found himself growing more resentful toward Dreiser's "whimsical attitude toward the language": "He was a cumbersome proser. He never learned to write, although I never harangued him about his writing. . . . Dreiser made a fortune and that was his disaster, since he had to appeal to the average mind to make that fortune." [58] Although he felt flattered by the old titan's attention, and he certainly never criticized Dreiser to his face (even letters were always signed "Your friend and admirer"), Dahlberg certainly implied condemnation of a ramshackle prose style by insisting: "Nothing I do ever quite satisfies me; but as I have no mania to rush into print I don't mind," and "I am the most insecure person imaginable. Each letter that I write is an ache or a doubt, misgiving and inchoate sleeplessness." [59] Dahlberg justly felt that Dreiser had no epistolary ability whatever and that "the reason for our rupture (which was not overt, just a separation), was, alas, my doing." [60]

Word of Ford's painful death on June 26, 1939, hurtled Dahlberg into a deep depression which spurred him to another furious jaunt around the country.[61] Work on *Do These Bones Live* had been erratic, and his marriage to Rosa—his third—had disintegrated. While still avoiding his mother, he was eager to remake old friendships, and 1939 seemed a propitious time, after a hiatus of seven years, to look up Max Lewis, who was now wealthy, but, unfortunately, sinking into seclusion. He traveled to Lewis's home in Altadena, where he was astonished to find an electrified fence surrounding the mansion. Unable to gain an audience with his old companion, Dahlberg's old resentments began to stir:

> He had been pursued by one bailiff after another. That had been the original reason [for his retirement]. When a man is furtive enough to you, the other extraneous reasons are of no consequence. He's furtive—I've never met anyone as envious. He had never met anyone who was his equal; but to meet someone whom he had tutored that had become his superior— he couldn't stand that! [62]

Dahlberg also visited Olson, who recounted to one of his students many years later what may have happened during the summer of 1939:

> Olson told me (us?) first me I think that he and Dahlberg were spending a great summer screwing girls in certain natural round depressions in the sand of Cape Cod. I picture a still sand whirlpool when he told this. . . . "but" says he "one of those girls was Italian and her father had a shotgun and [Dahlberg] had to marry her." I have the impression the girl was very young, about 16.[63]

Either Olson's or, more likely, the student's memory is faulty on at least one point. Dahlberg found himself in trouble not with an Italian girl but with a Scottish one whose name was Doris Huffam. Dahlberg was enchanted not only with the dimples of this young lady by the fact that she was probably related to Charles Dickens's godfather, Christopher Huffam, the well-to-do "Rigger in His Majesty's Navy." A native of Boston, Doris was regularly employed as a timekeeper in the programming department of a radio station in New York, City. Dahlberg moved into her apartment at 15 Christopher Street, where they were easily able to live on her salary of thirty-five dollars a week. But the couple were harassed by Miss Huffam's parents, who threatened to prosecute her lover under the Mann Act and for statutory rape unless Dahlberg could secure a divorce from Rosa and marry Doris. This he accomplished, and with his new bride Dahlberg seems to have

Edward and Doris, ca. 1939. (Courtesy of Clara Breit-Port.)

begun his custom of dressing his women in peasant blouses with full, gathered skirts.[64] In July 1940, when they were back in Boston, Dahlberg introduced Olson to Doris's half sister, Constance Wilcock, whom Olson soon married.[65] Olson, after leaving Harvard in 1939, moved to New York City in the spring of 1940 in search of a job. Dahlberg seemed exceptionally eager to aid and mold his young disciple by finding him an apartment on Christopher Street, giving him money, and reading additional chapters Olson had written on Melville, which Dahlberg called a "seed" for a book.[66]

It took Dahlberg well over a year, however, to see his own book in print. William Carlos Williams wrote to Louis Untermeyer on March 14, 1941: "Read Dahlberg's new book, Will [sic] these bones live? It seems incredible that he should have had difficulty finding a publisher. It's a book to swear by." [67] Williams had probably read either bound galleys or an advance copy of the book, which had been accepted by Frank Morley, an editor at Harcourt, Brace. Dahlberg received the page proofs by February

1941, but when he showed them to Olson he was accused of stealing his friend's ideas. Dahlberg immediately dedicated the chapter entitled "Woman" "to my very dear Friend, Charles Olson," [68] but Olson was not mollified. The two writers again became estranged and were not reconciled until 1947.[69]

Do These Bones Live finally appeared on April 10, 1941. The title, with the author's name, was boldly emblazoned in red on a dull black dustjacket. The biblical slogan, however, proved an immediate embarrassment to Dahlberg, who, on the advice of a purported "Hebrew scholar," had ignored the King James translation. One day, as Dahlberg was walking in Greenwich Village, Djuna Barnes stormed up to him and shouted, loudly enough to turn heads: "It's 'Can,' Mr. Dahlberg! Can! Can!' " [70]

Dahlberg felt that he had much more to defend than the title of his book, especially after his altercation with Olson. Reluctantly, he admitted that Williams "wrote one good book, *In the American Grain,*" [71] although he later firmly denied that he was ever influenced by Williams, who, he insisted, was uncultivated and "ill-languaged." [72] But early critics immediately compared the two books and awakened feelings of resentment in Dahlberg which blinded him to obvious parallels between *Do These Bones Live* and *In the American Grain*, especially in the section of the latter entitled "Jacataqua." Here Williams prefigures Dahlberg's most strident indictment of our culture—the American's perverted love affair with the Machine. Williams insisted that "Our life drives us apart and forces us upon science and invention—away from touch. Or if we do touch, our breed knows no better than the coarse fiber of football." [73] It seemed more than coincidence that Dahlberg also harped upon the American fear of physical contact throughout his book. Like Dahlberg also, Williams indicted prostitution, "hiding our indecent passion in meddling, playing," and violence: "America adores violence, yes. It thrills at big fires and explosions. This approaches magnificence!" [74] Dahlberg admired Williams's misogynistic appraisal of Emily Dickinson, "about the only woman one can respect for her clarity," who supposedly withered, isolated, and starved for affection "in her father's backyard." [75] Williams, like Dahlberg and Lawrence, also deplored the infantilism of American males and the "barrenness of American females": "Men who, when their friends disappoint them, grow nervous and cry all night. It is because there are no women." They augment each other's deficiencies: "A man without a woman finds one. She immediately starts to torture them [sic]. It's all they can do." [76]

Invidious comparisons may also have prompted Dahlberg to dismiss Lawrence's *Studies in Classic American Literature* as "mere buffoonery." Although he confessed that *Do These Bones Live* could not have been conceived "without a literary parent," he later insisted that Lawrence was a very minor influence.[77] However, even a cursory reading of Dahlberg's book reveals that he scrutinized Lawrence closely. The fact that the latter wrote in an offhand, almost slangy prose, seems to have been enough to have blinded Dahlberg to his many debts.[78] For instance, Lawrence insisted that the taste for violence in America breeds pederasty and that the American writer is unable to portray women.[79] Lawrence blamed this failure on Puritanism, as did Dahlberg. According to the latter, the American writer is doomed to be an *"isolato,"* since "Puritanism sundered men from one another." [80] Since our men never ripen, they cannot possibly create female characters: "In almost a hundred years of American literature, we do not have one feeding, breeding sexual male, not one suffering, bed-pining Manon Lescaut or a Shulamite." [81] Dahlberg later admitted that the logical conclusion of these ideas is that all American writers are "covert homosexuals," a notion which he steadfastly maintained was stolen by Leslie Fiedler.[82] Ironically, however, Dahlberg denied any resemblance between his ideas and those of Freud: "I can tell you *I* was never influenced by Freud. I would surely feel very disheartened if I were. Better say some of Freud's ideas bear superficial resemblance to mine. I study mythology, not Freud! " [83] But Dahlberg's objection to Freud, like his objections to Lawrence and Williams, seems mostly to be grounded on the issue of language—Freud employed "neologisms" and clinical jargon which became anathema to Dahlberg. By the time he was preparing *Do These Bones Live,* he had convinced himself that modern, and especially contemporary, American English, is an "off-scouring," [84] a corruption of the pure vehicle of the "Masters," whom contemporary man, bereft of customs and tradition, has foolishly forgotten. The writer Irving Rosenthal remembered his advice to "Rob graves, don't make babies," [85] and to turn to Shakespearean and seventeenth-century English for models. Such stylistic theory placed Dahlberg in the ranks of brave if eccentric authors such as Djuna Barnes, Ronald Firbank, and Holbrook Jackson, who attempted to reconstruct Elizabethan and Jacobean language and use it as their standard idiom. But Dahlberg, like Melville, was the only one of the four who was not seeking a basically comic effect. He believed that "newfangled" words are symptoms of a sick society, blighted by the fetish of progress: "When everything is changed every week or month, the whole nation is unstable, and the people become testy and hysterical." [86]

Why, then, did this idolater of antiquated English devote so much of his book to considering nineteenth-century American literature, which was rife with many of the mannerisms he most despised? The answer may be twofold. For twelve years he had wanted to revenge himself upon Lawrence. Dahlberg still nursed the "injury" he imagined he had suffered from the introduction to *Bottom Dogs*. He also felt the compelling need to challenge Williams, whom he secretly detested at the time, even while he professed to be a strong proponent of the poet's work: "Williams could not be anyone's friend unless that friend were useful to him. He was a cold and perfidious person." [87]

Of much more significance than these personal, and mostly illogical, vendettas was Dahlberg's throbbing ambition to become America's greatest author. He forced himself into competition not only with his contemporaries, but with authors of the nineteenth century, especially Melville. By criticizing them, often harshly, Dahlberg hoped to unseat them all and fill the great void with his own work. Sadly, his emphasis on style tended to obscure his own deficiency—an absence of content or something to say.

Dahlberg's diagnosis of the ills of modern society was simple. He borrowed the notion of Thorstein Veblen, whose prose and life-style he admired, that the decay of civilization is the direct result of the death of "the spirit of workmanship": "All work is to lard the cupidity of the employer." Language is the surest barometer of how far our society has fallen: "Words in the seventeenth century derived from trades that were salubrious. Now, no work is replenishing. New words, you see, are really whorish. They have to do with avarice and carnage." [88] Dahlberg, like Lawrence and Williams, often tended to employ metaphors of venereal disease to dramatize what he viewed as the worst symptom of "the great American sickness": loneliness. He had totally reversed his Marxist stance when he declared: "The rabble are going to give us a remedy, but it will be a palate of promiscuity and venereal disease." [89]

The facts of Dahlberg's own life were never far from his mind in *Do These Bones Live*. In the first essay, "The Man-Eating Fable," which is mainly Dahlberg's reading of *Hamlet*, he portrays Shakespeare's hero as the archetypal victim, especially of the opposite sex. Ophelia, like his mother and all women, is a "villainess"; Gertrude herself is the victim of her own depravity, with which she infects her son: "Hamlet runs into her room, the contagion of her lewdness feeding his wrath—the bone and flesh pity of the son overpowers all else—and pours forth: 'mother, mother, mother!'" (p.5). Thus Dahlberg introduced a theme most basic to his work: the cannibalization of man by woman and his sexual sufferings therefrom.

The theme of "author as victim" provides the transition into Chapter II, "Thoreau and Walden," where Dahlberg again superimposed his own character upon this "giant of negations," a born "opposer" who was driven to action by his own frustrated ideals. Dahlberg saw Thoreau as shunned for being a misanthrope and crank, but "we wholly misconceive Thoreau, for his virtues were heady enough; it was nature in him that was so diluted" (p.10). People of the twentieth century should turn to the Hermit of Walden, who could nourish their lives of quiet desperation, rather than to "those weedy and unkept affirmations in Walt Whitman's *Democratic Vistas.*" Though there was little tragedy or full-blown passion in his life, Thoreau is indispensable to twentieth-century man because he lacks faith: "Great lives are moral allegories and soon become deniable myths because we cannot believe that such good men could have existed in such an evil world" (p. 18).

Chapter III, "Randolph Bourne: In the Saddle of Rozinante," is the best of Dahlberg's essays on the "Christian anarchist" who fascinated him for over thirty-five years. Expanding Nietzsche's revolutionary maxim that "War is the health of the STATE," Bourne knew, "like the mighty seed of Abraham, [war] will beget war in ceaseless succession." A remedy for the violence of modern times does not lie in the American Constitution, which has made "democratic Ishmaels" out of common men, since they are forced to live without tradition; nor can they turn to the cruel hoax of communist teaching, which submerges "the individual identity into the herd will of the fatherland" (pp. 21-26). By the end of this brief essay we are well aware that Dahlberg was writing more about his own mission than about Bourne, although he invokes the latter "to guide us, as Virgil led Dante from one fiery circle to another, through the infernal limbo of American Culture where Thoreau, Melville, Whitman still clamour for the ripe warm light of this world" (p. 28).

The prophetic voice again predominates in the title essay, "Do These Bones Live," which intones solemnly: "There has been no more clinkered land for the artist to live in than America." Like Williams, Lawrence, and Van Wyck Brooks, Dahlberg blamed puritanism for the "polar privacies" of Hawthorne, as well as the "naked loneliness" of Melville, which finally numbed his creative energies. American artists are so stunted and misdirected that, instead of canonizing myths as they should, they are "image-breakers, iconoclasts who demolish Revelations, all mystery, doubt, confounding legends."

Dahlberg's antidote to mechanism, rationalism, and puritanism seemed to have been a vague blend of medieval mysticism and eighteenth-century humanism. But before declaring himself an exponent of the latter philosophy, he paused to denounce the foulest outgrowth of the former—naturalism: "To the naturalist man is an accursed and evil smell."

Central to Dahlberg's vision was his sense of the writer (or the "man of feeling") as the perennial victim and outcast. The sensitive man's imperfections paradoxically ennoble him, and no matter how much he may degrade or destroy himself, he is worthy of our pity and admiration. Within Dahlberg's scheme of things, Judas, not Christ, is the hero of the New Testament, since he was the man most cruelly rejected by our Lord, who "did not love all equally. Some men he despised; Judas Iscariot he hated." Judas was in fact *orphaned* by Christ, and his suffering, not unlike Dahlberg's, exonerates him!

> Was despised Judas "thief," "devil" and "unclean"? Were he foreordained "Satan," did he not require pity more than all? Was he not then God's malice, not his own? . . .
>   Did Judas betray Jesus for thirty pieces of silver? Nay. For a Kiss, Judas betrayed Jesus! (pp. 87-89)

Dahlberg perversely selected a madman, Don Quixote, as his own messiah, for Cervantes's hero is a perfect example of the "suffering somnabulist" and the "victim of Nature." Unlike Thoreau, Dahlberg distrusted animate nature, since he viewed it as his destroyer.[91] Thus, to be a true visionary, or "Quixotist," the poet must always be at odds with his time and environment, since he is obliged to affirm what is not. The Knight of the Doleful Countenance is obliged to live "with windmills in his head," fabricating his own environment, since he cannot live with barbers, curates, and prostitutes—the common masses who "will forever deny what *Is*" (p. 96). By implication, Dahlberg willingly donned the mantle of Don Quixote. How else could the bastard, outcast son of a lady barber hope to sally forth as the savior of American letters? Like Dahlberg, Quixote (who in reality was just plain "Peter Alonzo") hoped to resuscitate his countrymen with the "pure" language of a bygone era: "Don Quixote had hoped to recall all men to their original arcadian state, the meanest varlet, the curt roustabout, by the sweet cajolery of addressing them in a tender and polite tongue, in the medieval metre of a ballad or canto" (p. 100). At the end of this essay, which is the focal point of *Do These Bones Live,* Dahlberg noted with satisfaction that the rash knight proved to be too noble for this base world, and, after recanting his vision, died imploring Sancho to find Dulcinea. The artist-prophet must be martyred by his vision. But Dahlberg's rather appealing argument faltered thanks to his faulty reading of *Don Quixote.* At the end of Part II of the epic, Alonso Quixano, the former Don Quixote de la Mancha, dies avowing his "sanity"—it is Sancho Panza who tries to forestall the knight's death by reviving his romantic vision. Don Quixote dismisses this suggestion and insists on the reading of his will.

Dahlberg's hopes of becoming the savior-critic of American literature were soon frustrated. Despite an eloquent attempt by Alfred Kazin to defend the book's "experimental" English and fulminating tone, [91] and a publisher's announcement by Van Wyck Brooks which promised "a profoundly moving personal vision of American life and literature full of startling insights, with passages of superb prose," [92] *Do These Bones Live* went almost unnoticed and sold fewer than 375 copies.[93]

Nervous agitation as much as the thirst for publication launched Dahlberg, late in 1941, on a series of cross-country jaunts, the first of which took him up the California coast and then to Northmoor, a suburb of Kansas City, for a brief visit with Lizzie. He had not seen his mother in almost three years, and although she was self-sufficient financially [94] she clearly needed a nurse. Michael Sands seemed a likely candidate, but, nearing age forty-four, he was showing disturbing signs of wanting a family. Dahlberg made every attempt to sabotage his brother's wedding plans, and he extracted a promise from Sands that he would not marry. But Dahlberg's return to New York brought him the horrifying news that Sands had settled into a comfortable apartment at 15 Sheridan Square with his new bride, Minnie. The reason for Dahlberg's anger was patent—now there would be less money for Lizzie and himself.[95]

By 1942, Dahlberg had adopted a nomadic way of life, since he could no longer remain settled with Doris in what he termed a "barren union." He leaped at his publisher's offer to send him to Chicago, where he was to give a number of lectures and sign two hundred copies of *Do These Bones Live* for a bookseller who admired his writing.[96] He agreed to inscribe the books, but he refused to meet certain "celebrities" who had bought them.[97] His perverse refusal did not extend, however, to Harry T. Moore, a young instructor of English at Northwestern University, and his wife Winifed. As a Lawrence scholar, aware of Dahlberg's association with the novelist, Moore suggested that Dahlberg lodge with him. The vist was protracted after Dahlberg became excited by the attention he found the stunning strawberry-blonde Winifred was paying him: she was compelled by what she imagined was a startling resemblance between Dahlberg and Edgar Allan Poe.[98] Moore could not help but notice her very obvious infatuation, and, following a violent argument after which Winifred was hospitalized, she had no choice but to follow Dahlberg to New York.[99]

Doris was not immediately informed of her husband's new paramour. Instead, Dahlberg returned home unexpectedly on a cold winter's night and accompanied her to the apartment of the Cohns, where she had been invited for dinner. Max and Sara, who had been told that Dahlberg had gone "south" to recover from a cold, were startled to see him reappear: "But when we saw Edward and Doris together, we knew he had found someone new." [100]

Left with the disagreeable chore of easing Doris out of his life, Dahlberg deposited Winifred with George Kramer, a bookseller on Eighth Street. Understandably, Doris took the news of her displacement badly, but with the skillful mediation of the Cohns she agreed to a divorce. Winifred married Dahlberg quickly, and the couple assumed custody of ten-year-old Sharon Moore; a younger child was left with Moore.[101] Although Winifred was the first of his wives whom Dahlberg acknowledged, she is not mentioned by name in his "autobiography," *Because I Was Flesh*. She is simply "this woman." As the following passage reveals, his respect for the institution of marriage was hardly growing as he left the altar for the fifth time: "I needed sensuality as others require alcohol, tobacco, gossip, loose chatter, opium or faith. Were disreputable houses available and cheap, I should have relinquished all thoughts of wedlock." [102] Such sentiments were not wanting whenever he spoke of subsequent marriages.

Meanwhile, Sands and his wife had reluctantly agreed to assume custody of the rapidly deteriorating Lizzie: a letter from Sands to Dahlberg written at this time remarks how "frightening" their mother was in her tatters.[103] She moved to New York, but the three-room Sheridan Square apartment was overtaxed by the presence of the old woman, who obstinately refused to remove her huge steamer trunk from the middle of the living room. When it became apparent that Minnie Sands was pregnant in March 1942, Lizzie's removal became imperative. Lizzie's selfishness had become unbearable, as Mrs. Sands recalled: "She might have had a certain acuteness in taking care of herself, but other than that, I don't think she was too bright a person. She had a sort of animal cunning but certainly no emotional instincts of any great depth. Maternally, she was a complete washout." [104]

After two or three months, the couple found themselves exasperated by Lizzie's ceaseless complaining and erratic behavior. At times she would steal food (which was rationed at the time) to give to Edward.[105] To save their own relationship, the Sands moved Lizzie to a cold-water flat on East Ninety-sixth Street, which was all they could afford. After Lizzie's departure, Dahlberg and his new wife stayed briefly with the Sands, but the brothers argued violently when Dahlberg accused Michael of having thrown their mother out on the street. The Dahlbergs then moved in briefly with Lizzie, but their stay was not congenial. She, however, had somehow secretly acquired over the years five houses and other properties in Northmoor. Most of these she liquidated, and the money was combined with a moderate sum that Winifred had inherited to buy an automobile and a house on Cape Cod.[106] Dahlberg melodramatically altered this transaction in his autobiography:

> Then [Lizzie] drew from the depths of her breast a sheaf of hundred-dollar bills and she placed them in my hands. I stood there regarding this kneeling woman with stupefaction, but held fast to the money. What will she do if I keep it, I asked myself, choking the green papers between my fingers. I stuffed my pockets with these grassy maggots; then I got up and moved away from her as though I hoped distance might lessen my disgrace.[107]

The house in Wellfleet, which Dahlberg and his wife occupied for nearly six years, was not merely "old" (as in his description), but a beautiful clapboard cottage, built around 1700, on seven and one-half acres of land. Eventually, they restored it and filled it with antiques, pewter utensils, and Early American furniture, for which Dahlberg had developed a very refined taste.[108] Bad luck haunted the place, however, as two fires in rapid succession gutted the house and caused smoke damage to most of the furnishings. "Snowy seclusion" was all the demoralized Dahlberg had found in the wealthy resort town.[109] Furthermore, Edmund Wilson shunned him, and Dahlberg's hopes of reviving his friendship with Olson were frustrated, since the latter was busy working for the American Civil Liberties Union, the Office of War Information, and the Democratic National Committee.[110] Although his wife succeeded in flattering him by insisting that she wanted a child "by a man of genius," [111] Dahlberg, having no prospects of publishing, found he could write little. Sensing that he was all but a forgotten writer, he wept upon learning that Herbert Read concluded the final chapter of his book, *Politics of the Unpolitical,* with a quotation from *Do These Bones Live.*[112]

Dahlberg's isolation on Cape Cod was the most desperate he had ever known. He passed the long hours composing a satire on his neighbors, who, like Wilson and Conrad Aiken, steadfastly maintained their distance from him. "Methusaleh's Funeral" [113] focuses on the burlesque burial rites of a Cape Cod cat. Dahlberg always professed to despise felines of any sort; he felt that people who have affection for animals lack human sympathies, and so he depicted the chilly inhabitants of Cape Cod erecting "cat and dog temples of Ninevah brick" and of building "animal cemeteries . . . astonishing as the walls of Erech." [114] Departing from Christopher Smart's "A Song from Bedlam," and Diodorus Siculus's account of Roman worship of the cat, Dahlberg had his sterile New Englanders wracked with mock-biblical and mock-heroic grief "for Yankee Tabby Nimrod, the night hunter, who never impoverished the cupboard, for the toad, the fieldmouse, and the weasel were always with him," and for "Hagar, my Ishmaelite Maltese who slew single-footed five robbins from Brewster and Dennis." [115]

Little else of Dahlberg's writing survives from his years at Wellfleet. He claimed to have burned a novel, *Diary of a Nobody,* [116] after it was rejected by Harcourt, Brace. But his hours were spent mostly poring over books and assembling the first of his three separate libraries of several thousand volumes. Winifred never accompanied him on frequent trips to New York, where he visited Lizzie, but not his brother, from whom he was estranged.

Lizzie's letters from this period, identical in tone to Edward's, though composed in broken English, grieve constantly over her arthritis, her faltering hearing, and her poverty. Dahlberg allowed her to remain in the cold-water flat, and embarrassment over her condition apparently discouraged him from inviting her to Wellfleet. She probably never saw her grandson, Geoffrey Dahlberg, who was born in 1945, shortly before her wretched and lonely death.[117]

This grisly event, which Dahlberg had rehearsed a half-dozen times in his writing, finally transpired sometime early in February 1946—the month which he hated most. Although Dahlberg stated that her body lay for five days on a cot in her bare and dirty flat before a neighbor found her, [118] it is more likely, since the body was so badly decomposed that it clung to the bed, that she was not discovered for weeks. When Dahlberg received the news, he had his wife call Sara Cohn to ask her to identify the body. Having never met Lizzie, Mrs. Cohn was able to refuse this chore.[119] The Dahlbergs finally had no choice but to journey through heavy snow to perform the grim task. As the dreaded moment approached, Dahlberg grew nauseous at the thought of viewing his mother's body, and he forced Winifred to enter the morgue and make the indentification.[120] At the brief burial ceremony, during which Dahlberg nearly assaulted Michael Sands for having "killed" their mother, Lizzie Dahlberg was laid on February 26, 1946, in unmarked plot number 1711 in Beth Israel Cemetery, Woodmere, New Jersey.[121]

The law firm engaged by Sands to litigate Lizzie's estate consisted of a pair of Italian immigrants, Leo Calarco and Emanuel Popolizio. Popolizio, then a recent veteran of World War II, was willing to handle most of the details for a very nominal fee. He recalled Dahlberg as one of the most fascinating of his thousands of clients:

I remember . . . especially the kind of perpetual irritation that always seemed to move with him. . . . He was kind of tallish and lean. At first I thought he was dumb, but at the same time, I, being kind of square, sensed that this was a different kind of guy who had areas of sensitivity that I didn't dwell on but was aware of.

Then, at one point he irritated me because he felt that, since his brother was the "mover" in the estate . . . , Edward thought [Sands] should sign all the necessary papers. Suddenly Dahlberg asked for an informal accounting and he wanted to know everything that was going on. And at this time I knew he was not a dumbbell because he asked *all* the right questions.[122]

Popolizio, whose colorful speech bears the imprint of his Lower East Side background, became aware that the elegantly dressed and highly formal Dahlberg was most eager to let his brother do all the work:

> It seemed that Sands was more able in that direction and . . . that Edward resented this kind of busy efficiency and having to be grateful to the guy for actually doing all this stuff, then makes his feelings manifest in suspicion and hostility rather than a direct confrontation.

Eventually, Sands foolishly signed over to Dahlberg the administration of the estate, the size of which he never discovered.[123] But Dahlberg found he could neither manipulate nor bully the lawyer, who recalled:

> I think, because I don't give off intellectual sparks, and you can tell after a while with me that I've read books because there are people smarter than me and I want to know what they're talking about. And then, when you get a guy who's probably as bright as Dahlberg is, he becomes contemptuous of another wild nugget trying to smooth the edges. . . . [He] gave a feeling that he was slightly contemptuous of me and I, being an aggressive guy, always had lurking beneath the need to serve this client the feeling that "You go one step further and I'll bust you in the mouth!"

Open warfare never erupted, possibly because Popolizio worked mostly with poor clients and sympathized with broken, immigrant families like Dahlberg's:

> You know, a man who may say, "I haven't seen my brother in twenty years," I find this very shocking. So I understood Dahlberg's looking for his brother, whom he had never even

met! What's more, finding his brother affirmed what he knew about his mother.[124]

Dahlberg's problems in 1946 were compounded by the deterioration of his latest marriage. After he began blaming Winifred for his mother's death, she realized she would have to leave her husband. Furthermore, Sharon Moore was now an adolescent, and Dahlberg was making no secret of his attraction to her. By the summer, when Winifred realized she was pregnant again, she decided to protect her children by removing them from the household. An assault on Sharon strengthened her resolution.

One day, after a cruel beating, Winifred appeared at the door of the Cohns' apartment, begging for shelter for herself and her children. At first, Sara refused, observing that her home would be the first place Dahlberg would come looking. But she relented, allowing Winifred to remain a few days until she found a place to stay and a way of supporting herself.[125] Winifred rented a house in Croton-on-Hudson in Westchester County and found a teaching job in a private school (where one of her students happened to be the son of James T. Farrell). As predicted, Dahlberg came looking for his wife and left after denouncing the Cohns for refusing to comfort him in his troubles.

By 1947, Winifred had ruled out a reconciliation with Dahlberg. Their second son was born in February, but she decided never to allow her husband near any of her children again. Not until 1973, two years after his mother's death, did Joel Dahlberg meet his father.

During the two years it took Winifred to acquire a divorce, Dahlberg found himself, for the first time since his orphange days, utterly bereft of friends and family. His literary anonymity was relieved only slightly in July 1947 by the British publication of *Do These Bones Live* (as *Sing O Barren*), with a foreward by Herbert Read, who had convinced Routledge & Sons of London to take the book.

This small bit of good fortune was overshadowed by the appearance of Olson's *Call Me Ishmael* in the same year. Despite his bristling resentment, Dahlberg wrote to Olson, offering to renew their friendship and praising him effusively for his "triumph" in Melville criticism. The two men resumed their correspondence, but quarreled almost at once when Dahlberg complained that the book had not been dedicated to him.[126] Dahlberg's envy grew to the point where he openly accused Olson of plagiarism: "He took over, without quotation, my assertions in *Can These Bones Live* that there were no women [in Melville's books]." [127] Ironically, Dahlberg himself freely borrowed this assertion from Lawrence.

Dahlberg's only hope of supporting himself lay in finding another teaching position. He appealed once more to Oscar Cargill, and to Homer Watt of New York University, but they would not consider him. Cargill thought him "intemperate and unreasonable," [128] and Watt tactfully explained to him that "when I gave you an assignment in Freshman English for one semester, I was not moved to ask you to repeat the experiment because I was convinced that your artistry and creative intelligence were above the range of our somewhat immature youngsters." [129] But Watt prevailed upon Willis Wager, one of his former doctoral students teaching at Boston University, to find Dahlberg a teaching assignment there. Privately, Watt warned Wager that he would be "in for a headache or two" if he took Dahlberg on.[130] But Wager was willing to gamble, so Dahlberg found himself teaching in a "uniform" program in the two-year "general-education" college, in which all students had the same program and took the same courses. Dahlberg's course, "English and Humanities," had him spending three hours a week in a large lecture hall and two hours in section meetings with about twenty-five students. Wager recalled Dahlberg's debut:

> At the opening meeting of the year the new faculty members were introduced. I told some five hundred returning students (now sophomores) and some five hundred new freshmen that the distinguished novelist and critic, Edward Dahlberg, was on the staff. . . . He was present on stage. There was great applause, for many of the students felt that they wanted to write creatively. I told them that there would be a meeting of all those interested that afternoon at four.[131]

Herbert Miller, now professor of English at the City University of New York, was one of those students: "He taught like Jehovah! There were three hundred pupils at the first meeting. Edward bellowed: 'You are young, green and callow! No one here has read a book or can write a line!' Several girls burst into tears." [132] Wager recalled Dahlberg's reaction to this first encounter:

> at about 5:30 or 6 I happened across Edward on Huntington Avenue. He was obviously upset and seemed to be walking off his irritation at the way the meeting had gone. Apparently he had made quite a frontal attack on some of the pretensions of some of the people there, and the whole meeting had shortly assumed explosive proportions. There were subsequent meetings of this extra-curricular Creative Writing group, but the membership was now down to two or three. Herb Miller was one of the faithful; Paul Skaggs always came; and that was about it.[133]

Although Dahlberg had a few advocates who appreciated him as "the master of the gnomic line, the powerful metaphor, and the intuitive epithet," [134] he was by no means generally appreciated. Wager found himself in the midst of an incredible imbroglio:

> Shortly I was besieged by students who had got into explosive encounters with him and who wanted to get out of his section. . . . All sorts of rather existential happenings went on there. For instance, one of the students was a Boston policeman who had decided to come to college. When Edward heard this, he went to work on him. "What are you doing here?" "Well, I just wanted to see whether I couldn't be a better policeman." Actually, this student was a rather well-tempered, rather heavy-set fellow. I'm sure his motives were simply those of self-improvement; and there were other somewhat older students among the group. The fact that we admitted students on the basis of Intelligence Test scores and such evidences of ability rather than on high school records, and various other features of the program attracted a wide variety of students. But Edward couldn't accept the idea of this cop being there.

> The culminating incident occurred when one of the students reacted so violently to something Edward said that—at

least Edward maintained—this student had threatened to shoot him. Of course, many of the students were veterans—in fact, they almost all were. Many of them had been involved in a great deal of shooting. Whether or not this student actually threatened him in class, I am not entirely sure. But Edward felt that he had.

The policeman was interviewed, as were other students with grievances, but nothing was resolved and finally Dahlberg was fired. Wager had some hopes of keeping him on, since he had value as "a gadfly, like Socrates," and as a sort of "Minor Prophet, speaking out on many matters veiled by convention or egotism," but in the end he had to conclude that Dahlberg was just too much trouble.[135]

It was 1948 and Dahlberg decided to linger in Boston for awhile. Olson and he were on good terms again and their friendship actually seemed to broaden as their letters grew longer and warmer.[136] Dahlberg still had no hopes of publication, although he was assembling numerous fragments of an elaborate satire on modern civilization and communism, which by this time he had come to regard as the blight of the century. But the writing came hard—Dahlberg's private life was again barren. He was finally forced to accept the fact that Winifred wanted no part of him; though they were not yet divorced, she had already reassumed her maiden name, O'Carroll.[137]

By late summer, Dahlberg was willing to attempt anything, even a teaching stint at highly unorthodox Black Mountain College in Asheville, North Carolina. On the recommendation of the literary critic, Kenneth B. Murdock (who also gave the college ample warning of Dahlberg's eccentricities), he was given a year's appointment.[138] Black Mountain had, since its founding twenty-five years earlier, been a haven for maverick geniuses, but they were mostly on the opposite side of the political spectrum from Dahlberg: Black Mountain was probably the most liberal school in America at the time. Dahlberg, however, had been convinced from his stay at Boston University that "Democratic education is hemlock. If the teacher can't be the enlightened despot in the classroom, he won't teach." [139] Characteristically, he had no idea of what he was getting into, and his initial response to the college is described by Martin Duberman as "rhapsodic.":

> Soon after arriving he described Black Mountain's wonders in a letter to a friend with an ardor and cadence that can best be described as—well—biblical: "There are lakes, sweet creeks, and all the bucolic delights that I tried to communicate to you out of the *Iliad* and Genesis . . . a rare place for . . . tender human beings . . . to come to for the living waters." [140]

In another letter, perhaps intended as an indirect rebuke to Homer Watt, he wrote: "I cannot tell you how relieved I am to escape abhorrent bulk education." [141] But Dahlberg's boredom and bad temper dampened his enthusiasm in less than two weeks.[142] The setting as well as the students came to oppress him: " 'What homicidal foliage,' I remarked. And sure enough three students committed suicide there. It was very deathly foliage—trees can drive you to death!" [143] The freethinking Black Mountaineers "were lesbians and homosexuals, all of whom were totally rude," [144] he concluded. The students complained of Dahlberg's "abrasive, dogmatic manner," [145] to which he replied:

> I wasn't abrasive! These people didn't know anything! They would challenge me before I could consummate a sentence. I spent *hours* seeing them outside of the classroom, [and] my class went up in attendance. In spite of my so-called "abrasiveness," obviously they came! [146]

Rumors about Dahlberg ran rampant among the students, especially after they learned he was writing a book with the suggestive title, *The Flea of Sodom*.[147] That his escapades could be richly embroidered in the student's imaginations is evidenced in this memoir of Terence Burns, a student at the time:

> Nell Rice told me that Dahlberg had arrived at the college by night and tried to rape a student in the print shop. (I have always thought of this having happened in the little shed that once stood in front of the studies building). But it wasn't a student, it was a faculty wife and at the next meeting a

member of the faculty read "Edward Dahlberg has left." Nell made it sound as if all this happened within 36 hours, he arrived at night, the attempted rape, he left at night, and not many people at the college knew he had come and gone. Nell Rice didn't like Edward Dahlberg.[148]

Dahlberg probably assaulted no one during his brief tenure, though he defended his "occasional" rambunctiousness, with some justification: "What if an instructor did have a passion for a girl? Suppose I were interested in a young lady? What's so vicious about that?" [149]

Even though Nick Cernovich, a student interested in bookmaking, offered to publish *The Flea of Sodom* on his small hand-set press, [150] Dahlberg could not be convinced to stay. He left in a huff, announcing to the rector, Joseph Albers: "Let the students challenge each other, I'm getting out." [151] Despite his rancor, however, Dahlberg was responsible for providing the college with his successor:

> Now, Olson and I were very close at this time. I fathered him, I nurtured him, I had the very highest esteem for Olson. I said to Albers, "There's only one man I know of who can do the job. I'll go and ask him. . . ."
> Olson was living in a colored section of Washington, D.C., where he was paying twenty dollars a month for a little hovel. He had sworn he'd never teach again, but he had no money— he was living on pennies. So he agreed to move to Black Mountain and leave his ailing wife, Connie, in Washington. . . . But he never thanked me for pulling him out of desperate poverty.[152]

Olson, who eventually became the rector of Black Mountain, indeed did express his gratitude by requiring Dahlberg's books for reading in his classes and by trying to secure teaching positions for Dahlberg at Wesleyan University and elsewhere.[153]

Late in 1948, Dahlberg drifted back to New York, again an "urban nomad," [154] living at many addresses, fruitlessly seeking teaching jobs, and frequenting the famous abstract expressionists' "Club" on Eighth Street, run by the painter and art critic,

Emmanuel Navaretta. Unlike most of the patrons of the club, Navaretta was a serious student of literature who knew Dahlberg's work. Though the establishment usually restricted its membership to "plastic artists," Navaretta encouraged Dahlberg to mingle with the "regulars," who included such notable artists as Willem de Kooning, Robert Rauschenberg, and Leonard Baskin.[155] It was probably at the club that Dahlberg met a young Columbia University graduate student and writer for the *Saturday Review,* R'lene LaFleur Howell.[156] Some weeks later, at a party in the home of a fellow student, Chard Powers Smith, she was informed that "the Lion of the Day is coming." The "Lion" turned out to be Dahlberg.[157] He took an instant liking to this petite, outspoken young lady with huge brown eyes and a fanatical love of the works of Herman Melville. Before long, she would become convinced that Dahlberg was destined to become a second Melville. Not surprisingly, Dahlberg soon left with R'lene, who remembered: "Chard thought I had stolen his lion. He was furious and wouldn't talk to me for weeks!" [158]

A most intense courtship followed, during which Dahlberg called R'lene daily, bought her clothing, and courted her at Nat Simon's Penguin Restaurant on West Ninth Street. He also dedicated "Three Parables" in *The Flea of Sodom* to her, and, on October 14, 1950, the day the book was published and shortly after his divorce from Winifred became final, Dahlberg married R'lene (she later dropped the apostrophe) and began the most important marriage and literary collaboration of his life.

NOTES

1. Interview: Dorothy Norman, Sept. 17, 1973.
2. Interview: Dorothy Norman, Sept. 17, 1973.
3. Interview: Dorothy Norman, Sept. 17, 1973.
4. Interview: E. D., June 12, 1973. *Bottom Dogs* eventually appeared in Spanish, translated by E. Elizalde (Santiago: Ediciones Ercilla, 1940). Daniel Aaron writes that "Dos Passos gave his opinion that [Robles] had been murdered by the Communist controlled 'special section,' because 'Russian secret agents felt that Robles knew too much about the relations between the Spanish War Ministry and the Kremlin and was not, from their very special point of view, politically reliable.' " *(Writers on the Left,* p. 357.)

5. Dahlberg makes no mention before this period of Bourne.
6. "Randolph Bourne," *American Spectator,* 4 (February-March 1937), 11.
7. Ibid.
8. Interview: E. D., Jan. 29, 1973
9. Interview: E. D. Jan. 29, 1973.
10. Interview: Dorothy Norman, Sept. 17, 1973. Dahlberg wrote a condescending letter to Mrs. Norman on July 28, 1938, condemning her for her bad taste in liking Baldwin.
11. Interview: E. D., Nov. 5, 1972.
12. "Old Man Mad About Writing," review of *The Life and Work of Ford Madox Ford,* by Frank MacShane, *New York Review of Books,* 5 (Sept. 30, 1964), 3. Dahlberg also claimed to have founded, at Ford's apartment, "The Friends of William Carlos Williams," a group dedicated to promoting the publication of the books of Williams. (Interview: E. D., May 22, 1972.)
13. Fred Moramarco, in his book *Edward Dahlberg* (New York: Twayne Publishers, 1972), states that "When she refused to pay Ford for an article they had commissioned, Dahlberg withdrew from the magazine after working on only the first issue" (pp. 22-23).
14. Interview: Dorothy Norman, July 2, 1973.
15. Letter: Dorothy Norman, July 28, 1973; interview: March, 18, 1974.
16. Interview: Dorothy Norman, Sept. 17, 1973.
17. Letters: E. D. to Dorothy Norman, July 13, 1938, and Sept. 12, 1938.
18. Interview: Dorothy Norman, Sept. 17, 1973.
19. *Tomorrow,* 10 (May, 1951), 22-27.
20. Interview: E. D., Nov. 2, 1972.
21. *Confessions,* p. 257. Professor George Butterick, Olson's literary executor, stated that Olson had taken the summer off to meet Dahlberg. (interview: June 26, 1973.) Olson was actually only six feet eight inches tall.
22. *Confessions,* p. 257.
23. Letter: John Cech, July 13, 1973. Cech has written a detailed study of the friendship between Olson and Dahlberg (University of Connecticut, Storrs, diss., 1974).
24. *Confessions,* p. 258.
25. Paraphased in letter: Dorothy Norman, July 28, 1973.
26. Interview: Paul Metcalf, Jan. 29, 1973.
27. *Confessions,* p. 260.
28. Interview: E. D., Jan. 29, 1973.
29. *The Maximus Poems* (New York: Jargon/Corinth Books, 1960), p. 5.
30. Interview: E. D., Dec. 31, 1972.
31. Terence Burns recalls Olson's account of this visit: "When he knocked on the door (his best postman's knock) there was no answer, so he walked around to the side door and was going to knock there when he glanced through the window. At 6'8" he saw over the curtains, and there was Dahlberg's mother taking a bath in a tub in her kitchen. Olson went for a walk and returned at a more convenient time." (Letter: March 1, 1973.)
32. "Lear and Moby-Dick," *Twice a Year,* 1 (Fall-Winter 1938), 174.
33. Ibid., p. 175.

34. Interview: Sept. 27, 1972.
35. *Do These Bones Live,* p. 37.
36. Olson, "Lear and Moby-Dick," p. 178.
37. Interview: E. D., July 3, 1973.
38. "Lear and Moby-Dick," p. 167.
39. (San Francisco: City Lights Books, 194), p. 88.
40. *The New American Poetry,* ed. Donald M. Allen (New York: Grove Press, 1960), pp. 387-88.
41. Letter: John Cech, July 13, 1973.
42. Interview: Paul Metcalf, Jan. 19, 1973.
43. Letter: Charles Olson to Dorothy Norman, Sept. 6, 1938.
44. Interview: Oct. 30, 1973.
45. Interview: Dorothy Norman, Sept. 17, 1973. Breit was best known for his literary criticism in *Time* magazine and for his column, "In and Out of Books," which appeared in the *New York Times* from 1948 to 1957.
46. Interview: Clara Port, Jan. 18, 1973.
47. Interview: E. D., Jan. 22, 1973.
48. Interview: E. D., Jan. 24, 1973.
49. Interview: Clara Port, Jan. 18, 1973.
50. Dahlberg had, in fact, never learned Latin.
51. Letter: Oscar Cargill, April 12, 1972. Professor Cargill died two days after writing this letter, in which he seems to have confused Dahlberg's three appointments in three different branches of the university.
52. Letter: Oscar Cargill, April 12, 1972.
53. Interview: R'lene Dahlberg, April 13, 1972.
54. Interview: E. D., Sept. 23, 1973.
55. "The Fate of the Semiclassic," *Forum,* 97 (September 1937), 126-28.
56. Interview: E. D., Sept. 13, 1973.
57. Interview: E. D., Sept. 23, 1973 (Ch. IV).
58. Interviews: E. D., Sept. 16, 1973, and July 15, 1973.
59. Letters: April 22, April 28, 1938, *Epitaphs,* pp. 15-16.
60. Interview: E. D., Sept. 23, 1973.
61. Interview: E. D., Sept. 23, 1973.
62. Interview: E. D., Nov. 16, 1972. Letters which I sent to M. Lewis in Altadena were neither answered nor returned.
63. Letter: Terence Burns, Mar. 1, 1973.
64. Interview: Sara and Max Cohn, Feb. 13, 1973.
65. Interview: George Butterick, June 30, 1973.
66. Letter: John Cech, July 13, 1973. This book would, of course, become *Call Me Ishmael,* originally published in 1947.
67. Quoted in Mike Weaver, *William Carlos Williams: The American Background* (Cambridge: Cambridge University Press, 1971), p. 204.
68. *Do These Bones Live,* p. 104.
69. Letter: John Cech, July 13, 1973.
70. Interview: E. D., Nov. 10, 1972. Michael Sands related the same story on April 19, 1972.

71. Letter to Robert McAlmon: Nov. 16, 1963, *Epitaphs,* p. 135.
72. Interview: E. D., Jan. 17, 1974.
73. "Jacataqua," *In the American Grain* (1925); (rpt. New York: New Directions, 1956), p. 179.
74. Ibid., pp. 177-79.
75. Interview: E. D., Jan. 17, 1974; "Jacataqua," p. 180.
76. Williams, pp. 180-81.
77. *Confessions,* pp. 219-20.
78. Dahlberg, according to his wife R'lene, did read some Lawrence during the 1950s.
79. See especially Chapter V, "Fenimore Cooper's Leatherstocking Novels"; and Chapter XI, "Herman Melville's 'Moby Dick' ": "none of the Pequoders took their wives along" (1923; rpt. New York: The Viking Press, 1964), p. 93. Whitman, too, saw only "comrades," females, and "prostitutes"—never women (Chapter XII).
80. *Do These Bones Live,* p. 80.
81. Ibid., p. 81.
82. Interview: E. D., Sept. 30, 1972. Dahlberg is referring to Fiedler's study, *Love and Death in the American Novel* (New York: Criterion Books, 1960).
83. Interview: E. D., Dec. 18, 1972.
84. Interview: E. D., May 22, 1972.
85. Irving Rosenthal, *Sheeper* (New York: Grove Press, 1967), p. 123.
86. Letter to Robert M. Hutchins, Nov. 5, 1958, *Epitaphs,* p. 29.
87. Interview: E. D., Jan. 16, 1974.
88. Interview: E. D., Dec. 28, 1972.
89. Interview: E. D., Aug. 17, 1972.
90. Interview: E. D., May 22, 1972.
91. New York *Herald Tribune, Books* (April 13, 1941), 20.
92. Quoted in Mary Colum, "The Double Men of Criticism," rev. of *Do These Bones Live, American Mercury,* 175 (May-June, 1941), 765.
93. Harold Billings, "Introduction: Cabalist in the Wrong Season," *Edward Dahlberg: American Ishmael of Letters,* ed. Harold Billings (Austin: Roger Beacham, 1968), p. 18.
94. The only surviving letters from Lizzie to her sons date from 1942 and 1943. The ones to Michael Sands (who was then using the name Dahlberg) are brief and always request "the usual enclosure," i.e. money. The ones to Dahlberg tend to be longer and offer much affection and maternal advice. Sands believes that much of the money he sent to his mother was passed on to his brother. (Interview: Michael Sands, April 18, 1972).
95. Interview: Michael and Minnie Sands, April 18, 1972.
96. Interview: E. D.., Jan. 29, 1973.
97. Interview: E. D., Dec. 6, 1972.
98. Interview: Max and Sara Cohn, Oct. 30, 1973.
99. Interview: Michael Sands, Feb. 11, 1973.
100. Interview: Sara and Max Cohn, Feb. 13, 1973.
101. Interview: Sara and Max Cohn, Feb. 13, 1973.

102. *Because I Was Flesh,* pp. 228-29.
103. Paraphrased by Harold Billings, letter: Aug. 5, 1973.
104. Interview: Minnie Sands, Feb. 11, 1973.
105. Interview: Minnie Sands, April 3, 1973.
106. Interview: Sara and Max Cohn, Oct. 30, 1973.
107. *Because I Was Flesh,* p. 230.
108. Interview: E. D., Dec. 6, 1972.
109. Interview: E. D., Nov. 16, 1972.
110. Letter: John Cech, July 13, 1973.
111. Interview: E. D., Jan. 29, 1973.
112. (London: Routledge, 1943), p. 152.
113. Interview: E. D., Nov. 2, 1972. Dahlberg did not recall exactly when he wrote this piece.
114. *The Leafless American,* ed. Harold Billings (Sausalito: Roger Beacham, 1967), p. 76.
115. Ibid., p. 80.
116. Harold Billings notes that the University of Texas owns the first draft of a discarded novel, "Diary of a Social Man," which may date from the mid-1940s, but may have been written as late as 1952. (Letter: Sept. 9, 1973.)
117. Interview: R'lene Dahlberg, April 13, 1972. Winifred spent several days in 1970 with R'lene (who was then, like Winifred, divorced from Dahlberg) while the former was en route from Reno to Johannesburg, South Africa, where she died after open-heart surgery.
118. *Because I Was Flesh,* p. 233.
119. Interview: Sara and Max Arthur Cohn, Feb. 13, 1973.
120. Interview: R'lene Dahlberg, April 13, 1972.
121. Receipt for Opening of Grave, Feb. 26, 1946, Beth Israel Cemetery Association Second Street and Second Avenue, New York City.
122. Interview: Emanuel Popolizio, Nov. 29, 1972.
123. Interview: Michael Sands, April 19, 1973.
124. Interview: Emanuel Popolizio, Nov. 29, 1972.
125. Interview: Sara and Max Cohn, Feb. 13, 1973.
126. Letter: John Cech, July 13, 1973.
127. Interview: E. D., July 3, 1973.
128. Letter: Oscar Cargill, April 12, 1972.
129. Homer Watt: Letter to Edward Dahlberg, May 21, 1948.
130. Homer Watt: Letter to Willis Wager, June 6, 1947.
131. Letter: Willis Wager, June 5, 1972.
132. Interview: Herbert Miller, April 3, 1972.
133. Letter: Willis Wager, June 2, 1972.
134. Interview: Herbert Miller, April 3, 1972.
135. Letter: Willis Wager, June 2, 1972.
136. Letter: John Cech, July 13, 1973.
137. Interview: R'lene Dahlberg, Nov. 1, 1972.
138. Martin Duberman, *Black Mountain: An Exploration in Community* (New York: Dutton, 1972), p. 305.

139. Interview: E. D., Sept. 30, 1972.
140. Duberman, p. 305.
141. Sept. 3, 1948. Quoted in Duberman, p. 305.
142. Ibid.
143. Interview: E. D., May 22, 1972.
144. Interview: E. D., Nov. 5, 1972.
145. Duberman, p. 306.
146. Interview: E. D., Nov. 5, 1972.
147. Duberman, p. 307.
148. Letter: Terence Burns, Mar. 1, 1973.
149. Interview: E. D., Nov. 5, 1972.
150. Letter: John Cech, July 13, 1973. Interview: E. D., Nov. 5, 1972.
151. Interview: Martin Duberman with E. D., Nov. 3, 1968. Quoted in Duberman, p. 307.
152. Interview: E. D., Nov. 5, 1972.
153. Letter: John Cech, July 13, 1973.
154. Interview: E. D., Sept. 24, 1973.
155. Interview: Emmanuel Navaretta, Oct. 30, 1972.
156. She has since dropped the apostrophe from her name.
157. Interview: Rlene Dahlberg, Nov. 1, 1972.
158. Interview: Rlene Dahlberg, Nov. 1, 1972.

6.

The End of Silence: 1950-1957

Even people who had known Dahlberg for twenty years or more were startled when he ended his second period of literary silence with a stinging, though often obscure, satire on the Communist party. His ultraconservative stance was still more surprising since the former sentimental (though angry) bohemian had just acquired a dynamic and articulate young wife and an avant-garde publisher, James Laughlin, who had been known only once before—in the case of Ezra Pound—to sponsor an author with extreme right-wing views.

The year 1950, which saw publication of Dahlberg's tiny book of satires and parables, seemed most opportune since Sen. Joseph McCarthy had just charged that the State Department was infiltrated with communists. But for this very reason, Dahlberg had difficulty finding readers among his old or former cronies. Even Olson, who was friendly again and had promised to review the book, found various excuses to leave the job unfinished. When Olson failed to deliver a review by the fall, Dahlberg, reopening all the old wounds, accused his friend of "ingratitude, sloth, clandestine plotting, and lack of sincere friendship." [1] Olson was at the time thoroughly absorbed in his work at Black Mountain, and, in an attempt to avoid another blowup with Dahlberg, he sent a copy of *The Flea of Sodom* to the young poet Robert Creeley, hoping that he would be allured by Dahlberg's style. But Creeley was simply baffled: he knew that Olson had avoided the book because he was unsympathetic toward the prose, yet "didn't want to lay a bomb" on Dahlberg. Creeley sympathized with Olson's dilemma, and, since he preferred the work of Williams and Wallace Stevens at the time, his initial response to *The Flea of Sodom,* with its "wildly compounded, almost symbolic language," was, "I don't know what this man is talking about!" [2]

Unfortunately, Creeley's response was typical, [3] even though a reader familiar with Dahlberg's ideas should not be overwhelmed by the book. Herbert Read's touching introduction is mostly a tribute to the author himself rather than a key to *The Flea of Sodom,* which, like *Do These Bones Live,* wages quixotic warfare on modern civilization. In the book, however, "modern times" begin with the invention of the wheel! Dahlberg makes the hyperbolic claim that he is so far out of step with the twentieth century that he "was attacking the whole conception of the wheel, the greatest curse of the human race. The Aztecs knew the wheel, but never made profane use of it." [4] Thus a reader of *The Flea of Sodom* could do worse than to start with Part III, entitled, "The Wheel of Sheol." "Sheol," like "Gehenna" and "Hell," is the Hebrew counterpart of the Greek and Roman Hades.

The villain of this almost liturgical parable is Beliar, whose name Dahlberg said he discovered in the Jewish Apocrypha. Beliar is the embodiment of Disgust: his enlightenment comes, not from sweetness and light, but from degradation: "When Beliar's soul was miry with the waters of Styx he had an ecstasy" (p. 99). He is supreme commandant of all wheels, a sort of diabolic Prometheus, who stole "the burning, starry Wheels and turned them into the iron and rubber rings of horrid Sheol" (p. 104). Humanity, incurably corrupt, got what they asked for in dealing with this demon:

> The women wept for the Wheels and baked libidinous cakes for them. All lust was in the wheels, and there was no rest for the head or the bowels, and these Wheels were in men's eyes

which rolled in all directions. .... Nations hungered for strife,
pestilence, vermin, revolutions, and death because the Wheels
were in every land. (pp. 103-4)

Some of Dahlberg's best "biblical" cadences will be found in his
fulminating indictments of this mythical father of corruption.
Beliar is the very enemy of Wisdom:

> A ravine separates the Olive from the macadam meadows
> where wicked Beliar stares at Wisdom; her pure, delicate
> raimant makes him mad to possess her; and no man can look
> upon Wisdom and possess chaste learning. Though Beliar's
> intelligence is great, he has the rational faculty of Sodom and
> abhors Adam because he covered himself after he had eaten of
> the Tree of Good and Evil. (p. 102)

Beliar uses his wheels to disseminate his poison—he has quickened
the pace of life, depriving mankind of the time to think, "and
Beliar went everywhere his abominations took him."

Dahlberg, functioning in his favorite role as Old Testament
prophet, attempted to produce a mythology for the tradition-
starved masses of the twentieth century. He predicted an apoc-
alypse which will quash the desperate hurry of modern life, which
has alienated man from man and ruined our civilization:

> Dying Beliar is without his children, who detest age and the
> pillow of their mother and father because it smells, though
> man is the suffering earth that smells. The sons and daughters
> of Beliar are unsavoury, and their learning, which is without
> the water of life, has the evil odor of the world. (p. 105)

The most ludicrous of Beliar's offspring are pilloried in the
opening allegory of the book, the title piece, which begins with
what may be the most contemptuous line ever written about
America: "Let us admit, going over the Atlantic was a mistake" (p.
15). Dahlberg then undertakes to validate the motto of the book,
taken from Aristotle ("O my friends there is no friend") by
satirizing what he diagnoses as the diseases of American civilization: alienation, ignorance, perfidy, and immaturity. Cavorting

through these pages come greater and lesser known bohemians from New York in the 1930s. Ephraim Doner, for example, who married Dahlberg's third wife, Rosa, appears variously as the Marxist "Ephraim Bedlam," and as "Golem Patron," "the water-drinker and raw carrot and celery philosopher." Another prominent Marxist, who in real life was Ladine ("Deenie") Young, is portrayed as "Andromache." Bearing no apparent resemblance to the wife of Hector, this Andromache has a "fine neuter cohesion with Ajax Proletcult" (p. 51), [5] who, Dahlberg explained, represents a foreign correspondent named Walter Durante, who had lost his legs in a railroad accident: "He subsidized [Ladine] and she was grateful." [6] The narrator, presumably Dahlberg, resents being ignored by Andromache and her friend, Thais Collette, and makes a point of impugning their morality: " 'There go a pair of Dis-Graces,' I mused, as Ephraim Bedlam stood aside with bowed head" (p. 52). His disapproval extends to all the fatuous Marxists, who huddle together, frittering away their time devising impractical revolutionary schemes.

"Pilate Agenda" supposedly represents a man named Calderon, who carries on a long affair with a Texan beauty in the book. Dahlberg explained, "She's the one who used to wear mink coats during Communist demonstrations and always felt that she could not understand a writer unless she slept with him." [7] As his name would indicate, Agenda combines seduction and treachery with a deadly preoccupation with the mechanical, businesslike aspects of life. In the book, as in real life, he is a dealer in olives and olive oil; the narrator finds Agenda the most repulsive of all his creations, since this character tries to remain friendly with the communists while secretly carrying on trade with General Franco's fascist government: "When Pilate saw me . . . he put six chocolate bars in my pocket and stroked my coatlapel, and my soul was so lamed that I asked for another appointment" (p. 50).

"Thais Colette" is Dahlberg's satiric portrait of Dorothy Farrell (Mrs. James T. Farrell), who "took a room to entertain persons whose names had been compiled from the Agenda Brothers' list of merchants. But no one appeared except marxists and the people of Gomorrah." These fat and comfortable Marxists, however, are less upset about the treachery of the "merchants" (whom Dahlberg hated almost as much as the working class—the "garage proletariat") as with "Pilate's erotical eclipse" (p. 47). One of the guests at Thais's banquet is "a cartoonist celebrated for his drawings of bourgeois women with swinish buttocks" (p. 43). This is George Grosz, perhaps the only artist of this century whom Dahlberg admired.[8] Twenty years later, however, Dahlberg cast a far more puritanical eye upon his former friend:

> If one were a patron of the George Grosz proletcult museum he could gaze with a rising gorge at a pair of repulsive bourgeois women with fat blowsy posteriors. Should he afterwards step to a pornographer's bookmart he could browse through a George Grosz portfolio of female nudes with immense blossoming buttocks created to inflame the erotic appitite of the viewer.[9]

Interestingly, the characters in "The Flea of Sodom" section bear close resemblance to the caricatures of Grosz. Dahlberg's revolutionaries swarm through the pages of his satire, decimating each other and dispersing their energy on madcap schemes and fanatical, incoherent speechmaking for the Cause. Pilate Agenda, despite his poorly concealed dealings with the fascists, concocts an elaborate idea for collecting tinfoil from Hershey Bars to send to the Loyalist Lincoln Brigade in Madrid. With equal fervor he procures signatures "for a protest against a Bronx landlord and Japanese aggression" (pp. 47-48). Another character, the wealthy Thersites Golem (who may be Luis Muñoz Marín, who later became the governor of Puerto Rico [10]), combines idleness and profligacy with radical speechmaking: "What is so comfortable as the ordinary, adhesive filths of the brood. I love my profligate inertia; ye gods, give me Bacchus's sweet, and the squalid, goatish vices that are companionable" (p. 54).

The fall of the Spanish Republic and the rumblings of World War II cause little stir among the incestuous and absurd bohemian-revolutionaries:

> When Golem, wearing a walleted back, dropped upon Pilate's breast, crying out, "Barcelona has fallen!" Pilate handed him some consolatory Agenda Brothers' blotters. I then uttered

softly, "Gentle Sir Golem, Lute and dulcimer spirit of dying Europea," at which he joined two coffee merchants who wore fat hydrangeas that gave off a sleepy scent of money. (p. 44)

The narrator, who functions throughout the satire as a sort of Greek chorus, makes a standard Dahlbergian remark that, among the Sixth Avenue radicals, "Salutations were tepid because everybody feared an affront; none held out a hand lest he shake empty air" (p. 31). However, the satire is directed as much against Dahlberg's own writing of the 1930s and clumsy mechanics of the proletarian novel as anything else. As if to provide an object lesson, Dahlberg derides proletarian realism, which self-consciously attempted to imitate working-class jargon, by delivering highly bombastic mock-biblical homilies. While the naturalist "scientifically" develops a straightforward, clinically organized narrative, Dahlberg here writes virtually without transitions or connectives. The reader is hardly aware that the first satire has come to an abrupt halt when he finds himself beginning Part II, "The Rational Tree," which, Dahlberg explained, is "a Utopian novel grounded upon ancient Israel and an attack upon the American Mammon Commonwealth." [11] This series of short fables, which Jonathan Williams aptly likened to Hesiod's *Work and Days*,[12] is mainly preoccupied with the "tragedy" of the discovery of iron: "There was no iron in Eden. The Garden was an orchard of jubilant onyx, beryl, topaz, and the sardius" (p. 68). Although "Wood was savoury in bucolic Zion," Dahlberg notes with dismay that "Iron appears in Jeremiah, Job, and Daniel, the scriptures of weariness, and in Genesis, the lament for the Arcadia of Seth and Enoch": "Genesis, the poem on shepherds and husbandry, is it not of the time of agnostical Job and iron? Ratiocinative Babel and the Sodom and Gomorrah parable are didactic reflections on an Israel already rational and pederastic" (p. 69). In Dahlberg's mind, all forms of commerce and industry, including the profane uses of the wheel, metals, and fire, bred decadence, the worst form of which is homosexuality. Thus, by the time the Scriptures were composed, Israel was hopelessly polluted.

The book makes an easy transition from the decline of the Ancients (especially our "forbears," the Hebrews) to the "forgetfulness" of the Middle Ages and finally to the inevitable and total decline of Western civilization. Without the past mankind is nothing: "Fables and gods are a surety of man's sanity. Where Jehovah or the Cherubs is not contemplative Energy, it is health to the navel to have Jove give knowledge, Saturn keep sauces in his cruets, and Priapus guard virility" (p. 85).

"Bellerophon," Part IV, is an elaborate tribute to Charles Olson, whom Dahlberg likened to the Corinthian hero who, with the aid of Pegasus, was sent to slay the bellowing and incoherent chimera. Olson would presumably slay the literary chimera of *his* day, those writers of "caitiff" literature "who have fallen among the asps and fear to tremble." In trying to regain Olson's friendship, Dahlberg professed a faith in the younger man which he in fact no longer held, and his praise is coupled with a warning: "If a poem does not make the spirit shake as the reed in the wind, it is for infidel unfaith, for Pride, and if a man has not learned from heaven that verse is made in unclean tombs or at Cana, then let God write the BOOK, and men go down in the dust to read it" (p. 113). He concluded with a moving request that Olson return: "What is the mind that it should bray, or go proud and alone? . . . Go low, Bellerophon, come down, O learned Dust, Wisdom is our PRAYER" (p. 117).

Dahlberg's stinging and compact little satire was modestly priced at $1.50, but it was not destined to be a best-seller. The publisher lost money, [13] and the book brought fewer than fifty dollars into the author's pocket.[14] Although, largely thanks to Olson, the book became required reading at Black Mountain College,[15] Dahlberg had practically no readership, either in the general public or among his former literary friends. Ephraim Doner commented sourly on his own portrayal as "Ephraim Bedlam": "You're in Dahlberg's books, but you're not. Dahlberg doesn't know who anybody is. He doesn't know who *he* is, and thank God he'll never find out." [16]

Reviews of *The Flea of Sodom* were mostly polite but tentative, as if the critics were embarrassed to admit that they were unable to decipher the allegory. A brief anonymous notice in *The New Yorker*, for example, avoided discussing the book by linking it with Dahlberg's old nemesis: "With a fury and eloquence lost to us since the death of D. H. Lawrence, Edward Dahlberg attacks the blatancies of our culture in a series of oracular essays, although Dahlberg aphorisms are sometimes a bit too aphoristic." [17] One reviewer, a Sephardic Jew named Edouard Roditi, comprehended more than the others, but published, in *Poetry* magazine, the most virulent attack Dahlberg had ever endured. Roditi accused Dahlberg of being a fascist and coupled him with Pound and Lawrence in having "consciously advocated such fascist, anti-rational, or anti-humanist concepts as that of 'thinking with one's blood' or, as Dahlberg does now, of 'racial images,' 'racial memory,' and 'racial lore.' . . ." Soon Roditi, carried away with his argument, launched a diatribe worthy of Dahlberg himself, who is accused of being a "revivalist," a twentieth-century Cotton Mather or Joseph Smith, "who can but astound by the amateurishness and ignorance that are already revealed, even in a New Directions book that contains more than the usual New Directions average of printers' errors." The typographical mistakes are petulantly itemized, and Dahlberg is challenged "to draw on a blackboard, the cockatrice, for instance, that he so glibly mentions. If he cannot, he is no prophet but a pedant who borrows the style and the vocabulary of the ancient prophets." [18]

Readers of *Poetry* were no doubt delighted to find Dahlberg lustily defending himself in a subsequent issue. Although he does not condescend to mention his assailant by name, Dahlberg is clearly delighted for the opportunity to pummel Roditi in his most ornate language:

> This scribbler is a very august and subtle speller and has given me some hard fisticuffs for being a Bottom the weaver at my lettering. ... His spleen is up because Michiavelli appeared in my book instead of Machiavelli, and he is a choleric and flight wasp declaring that I should write Mephistophilus for Mephistophiles but should he look at the various Marlowe editions and Goethe translations he will find that Mephistophiles has three to four different ways of being lettered. Then I didn't spell eunuch the way he relishes it, for I put two n's in eunuch instead of one, to give this miserable word a kind of jocose priapic length. [19]

The charges of fascism are countered less effectively:

I am no working-class mystagogue who regards a riggish fruitdealer who sells carrots, peas and persimmons at four times their value as my benefactor, or the grubby grocer who changes his prices more often than Proteus his shape as my virtuous Cato. I do not care about the working classes, but what is essential to me is honest workmanship, learning and human poetry.[20]

Dahlberg's alliance with the right was solemnized when he joined forces with John Chamberlain, a former communist who had written a favorable review of *Those Who Perish* in 1934. In 1950 he began an ultraconservative periodical, the *Freeman,* in which Dahlberg contributed a regular column called "Second Harvest." There he found himself in the company of other lapsed communists such as Max Eastman and Robert Cantwell, who were attacking Stalin and defending Douglas MacArthur in the standard rhetoric of the McCarthy period. Rlene, who also contributed several articles, was not surprised that "Edward could find a home in a reactionary magazine." [21] Chamberlain himself lauded *The Flea of Sodom,* apparently for political reasons, since he said nothing about the book and merely paraphrased Herbert Read's extraneous comment that "[Dahlberg] . . . knows that Stalin's tanks stand ready to invade Tibet." [22]

Even if he now had a regular outlet for his writing, the struggling *Freeman* could by no means supply Dahlberg with sufficient funds to support himself and his new wife.[23] He again beseeched Oscar Cargill for a position at New York University,[24] but Cargill was able to obtain for him only a single course in the School of Education during the summer of 1950.[25] In the fall, Dahlberg decided to relocate to Santa Monica, California, where Rlene had found work as a part-time librarian at the University of California at Los Angeles. She recalled that her husband had to be "pried" away from New York City at this time, since he had just begun establishing roots there once again. Herbert Miller, his loyal disciple from Boston University, was now teaching part-time at New York University, and the two met nearly every day for lunch, which invariably consisted of liver and avocados. Since Miller was a most articulate speaker as well as a promising young writer, Dahlberg thought he had found a disciple to succeed Olson.

Miller, in turn, virtually idolized Dahlberg and was astounded by his titanic energy and linguistic resources; but he was at the same time aware of the dangers of becoming party to Dahlberg's relentless pessimism: "Edward preached failure, and if failure is your ideal, you must be content with failure," he remarked. But the younger man, until the late 1960s, stood very much in awe of his problematical mentor. Even Dahlberg's superstitious quirks were etched in his memory:

> If you have trouble unlocking a door, you don't want to leave. Once, we were riding in a cab and the driver was telling erotic tales. When we left the cab, Edward noticed that balloons were trailing from it. He remarked, "Those are testicles—that man is impotent!" [26]

In California Dahlberg was unable to find a university willing to offer him a position, so he busied himself as best he could with his writing. For *Tomorrow* magazine he wrote a reminiscence called "Hometown Revisited" about his childhood beneath the Eighth Street viaduct on Magee Avenue in Kansas City. In this article he was obviously refining his new "baroque" style, and simultaneously creating the germ of his masterpiece-to-come, *Because I Was Flesh:*

> Homer detested Ithaca, and let me admit, I hate Kansas City, which is still a wild, rough outpost town of wheat, railroads, packing houses, and rugged West Bottom factories. It is the burial ground of my poor mother, whose blood, like Abel's, cries out to me from every cobblestone, building, and street of Kansas City.[27]

Dahlberg was again taking mythic liberties, since Lizzie is buried, not in Kansas City, but in New Jersey. A corresponding passage in *Because I Was Flesh* shows the oracular voice (here soaked in phallic imagery) in even fuller bloom (and here, only Lizzie's hopes, not her body, are buried in Kansas City):

> Kansas City was my Tarsus; the Kaw and the Missouri Rivers were the washpots of joyous Dianas from St. Joseph

and Joplin. It was a young, seminal town and the seed of its men was strong. Homer sang of many sacred towns in Hellas which were no better than Kansas City, as hilly as Eteonus and as stony as Aulis. . . .

Kansas City was the city of my youth and the burial ground of my poor mother's hopes; her blood, like Abel's cries out to me from every cobblestone, building, flat and street.[28]

Dahlberg was also building his reputation as a wildly savage critic, as he launched attacks against Stieglitz,[29] and "Our Avant Garde Illiterates," which included Faulkner, Hemingway, and Caldwell as successors to Frank Norris's "cloacal" naturalism: "For all their avowed social purposes, [they] are vandals who pour bile upon nature, the human seed, and women." Dahlberg even whet his knife for his late "mentor," Dreiser, whom he assailed as "the erotica business writer whose books remind one of the Mount Kisco mansion he built to look like a Log Cabin Syrup can." Farrell, who, much to Dahlberg's chagrin, had delivered Dreiser's funeral eulogy in 1945, is derided as the creator of "Studs Lonigan [who] has the same sickness as [Faulkner's] Popeye, for how can Lonigan be a real stud in Farrell's unpigmented prose?" [30]

The most calumnious of the *Freeman* articles was, paradoxically, an attempt to win back the friendship of Charles Olson, who had again broken off correspondence with Dahlberg.[31] After admitting that he was "strangered" from Olson, Dahlberg stated that his object was to expose what Newton Arvin had "plagiarized," in his newly published study, *Herman Melville* (1950), from Olson's *Call Me Ishmael*.[32] Dahlberg later insisted:

I had no reason to come to Olson's rescue, for he had been an ingrate for years. But I picked up [Arvin's] book while I was teaching literature at New York University and wrote an article . . . which showed that Newton Arvin, who was a professor at Smith College, had lifted line after line from Olson's book. . . .

Then Hicks wrote to the editor that I had a sick and warped mind! [33]

Dahlberg accused Arvin not only of stealing Olson's insights— including numerous allusions to Melville's annotated and heavily marked Shakespeare and the stress on "womanless fiction"—but he itemized what he perceived as Arvin's thefts:

Olson	Arvin
"Structure, likewise. 'Moby-Dick' has a rise and fall like the movement of an Elizabethan tragedy." p. 66. "Melville makes little of the love of man and woman. . . . Melville had the Greek sense of men's love." p. 45.	"the book has a structural rise and fall like that of an Elizabethan tragedy." p. 155. "Melville implied inevitably a Greek-like cult of physical love . . . the beauty of the men especially." p. 56.
The "compact" between Ahab and Fedallah "is as binding as Faust's with Mephistopheles" Faust surrenders his moral freedom to Mephistopheles. p. 56.	"the diabolic Fedallah, to whom Ahab has surrendered his moral freedom, and whom Stubb quite properly identifies as the devil in disguise." pp. 191-2. p. 159

Olson responded to Dahlberg's apparent conciliatory move by thanking him for the article, but Dahlberg delayed answering and finally refused to bury the hatchet. Olson and he remained estranged until 1954.[34]

The Dahlbergs spent many of their leisure hours in the early 1950s touring California and visiting other migrants to the rapidly developing state. Once, they decided to meet Henry Miller at his home at Big Sur, but Miller, aware of Dahlberg's troublesome disposition, refused to let him through the gate. But the day was beautiful, and after Dahlberg flashed his most winning smile, he and Rlene were admitted to enjoy a pleasant afternoon and evening with Miller and his wife.[35] Miller remained solicitous and praised Dahlberg's work, but the latter threatened to live up to his reputation by retorting, "What you admire, I'm already ashamed of!" Dahlberg recalled being bored by Miller's company (but amused, it seems, by his own fantasies):

> He was then married to a young tigress, and, you know, she was *so* enchanted by my conversation! On one occasion, she was standing in the dark next to me. . . . There was no doubt

that there was something erotical that was passing between us, but I couldn't do anything about it.[36]

Another resident of California at the time was Robert McAlmon, whom Dahlberg had known in Paris: "At Santa Monica in 1952 I was told that McAlmon, entirely forgotten by his friends—and who else has the imperial privilege of ignoring us?—was an eremite on a sand dune, Desert Hot Springs." [37] In his youth, Dahlberg had identified with this man's aggressive and sardonic masculinity (see Chapter II), but now "McAlmon's obscurity hurt me":

> Full of bilge and wild disappointment, and ruttish to the end, McAlmon lamented his shrunken testicles. I suggested I might publish his book [a sequel to *Being Geniuses Together*] and asked if he would lend me the English edition of *Being Geniuses Together* and his unpublished manuscripts. He was uneasy. What could I pilfer from the fermented lees of his brain? [38]

Much of the pain which Dahlberg perceived in McAlmon must have been a reflection of his own, for, despite the beautiful climate and his growing circle of acquaintances, he could find nothing to interest him in California. Rlene was occupied in the library much of every day, and a much-hoped-for appointment to UCLA failed to materialize for him.[39] Dejected, Dahlberg returned to New York, pursuing the hope of part-time employment at Brooklyn Polytechnic Institute. But again he was not hired, and his growing disappointment was reflected in the magnified bitterness of his *Freeman* articles. One gratuitous attack was aimed at William Carlos Williams:

> Williams is an enormous deceiver, not because he tells almost everything, but because he reveals almost nothing of fundamental importance to the spirit. . . .
> Williams writes that he always has been a liar. But a man of sixty-eight is too old to lie. . . . He has lost his true memory and has become a weathervane admirer. . . . He has become mellow, which is another word for moldering.[40]

Dahlberg's grudges against D. H. Lawrence had mellowed only slightly by 1952: "Lawrence was a literary scold; he used to write me bullying, didactic letters when I was living in diggings in Chelsea, London. But when he suspected that I was not eating very often, he sent me a five-pound note." [41] Such reluctant charity to Lawrence contrasted glaringly with his sledgehammer attack in the same article on Richard Aldington and Witter Bynner, both of whom had written critical books on Lawrence: "I am almost totally at odds with Aldington's and Bynner's portraits. . . . These two bickering, gadfly books were written out of envy. Few can bear their own faults, and Aldington detests Lawrence's errors because his own have never been the leaven for a Quixotic trauma." [42]

Early in 1953, Dahlberg seized an opportunity to outdo himself completely in the writing of virulent criticism. Karl Shapiro, then the editor of *Poetry* magazine, commissioned him to write a review of Conrad Aiken's autobiographical narrative, *Ushant*.[43] The poet Isabella Gardner, who was associate editor under Shapiro, met Dahlberg at this time. Perhaps because he resented an interloper in the field of "autobiographical fiction," he embarrassed the editors of *Poetry* by delivering the most savage review they had ever been obliged to print: [44]

> *Ushant* is a long lotus sleep, and as the title suggests, it is not only anti-epical, but a florid, comic pun. . . . *Ushant* is an archive of piddling obscenities, and it is a loose-anecdotal recollection of puerile eroticisms.
>
> Conrad Aiken has selected Henry James as his master. As he himself is a residual, Jamesian hyphenate, what he requires are not the panicky, indecisive velleities of the old master, but a stable, and more roughly-hewn tripod. James is altogether anti-epical, and his irresolute style is canonical gabble. . . .
>
> All the panicky, Jamesian hiatuses are the result of impotency.[45]

This strangely phallic diatribe, which continued for nearly nine pages, left Aiken understandably hurt and bewildered. Sometime later, when she happened to be in the area, Miss Gardner drove to Aiken's house on Cape Cod, where she explained that the editors regretted having to publish Dahlberg's review, since neither of them agreed with his comments.[46]

In 1953, Dahlberg was still plagued with difficulties in marketing his work. He developed a very intense, though platonic friendship with Miss Gardner and sent her some of his poems, which she reviewed and commented upon. *Poetry* accepted two of these poems [47] plus a review of Lawrence's *Studies in Classic American Literature*. In the latter piece, Miss Gardner's mellowing influence seems apparent as Dahlberg reversed the position he took in the *Freeman* and actually eulogized his doppelgänger:

> Of his person I can say what Lord Bolingbroke asserted of Bacon, "He was so great a man that I do not recollect whether he had any faults or not. ... Though I have altered my thoughts regarding his gifts, let it be my portion when I retire to Erebus to have as companions the disembodied dust of Hesiod, Apollo, and D. H. Lawrence.[48]

Despite Miss Gardner's persistent encouragement, Dahlberg became increasingly irascible over growing piles of rejection slips. One of his particularly waspish (though Ciceronian) letters was never mailed to an unnamed female editor of a small magazine:

> Would it have not been more seemly to have returned the manuscript with some quiet words? It would be better for your own nature and more kind to any man so unlucky as to have fallen into your hands. This is a riff raff century, in which all people are supposed to be peers, and in which everyone claims to have talent. People write who have no talent, others paint who cannot draw the human figure, and you bear a title but are not a lady.
>
> However, I thank you for your insolence, for as there is so little human goodness in the earth today, I must be instructed by the liar, the fool, and the nonentity.[49]

Dahlberg placed only two more articles, short book reviews, in the *Freeman*, which was in serious financial trouble and about to fold. He developed an ulcer, which began to hemorrhage and led him to be hospitalized several times in 1953 and 1954. To improve his declining health and ailing spirits, he decided to redeem a pledge he had made to Rlene that they would one day settle permanently in Europe.[50] He sent the unfinished manuscript of his new book, *The Sorrows of Priapus,* to James Laughlin,[51] then immediately began seeking an inexpensive locale with a hospitable climate. One of his young admirers, the Scottish writer Alexander Trocchi,[52] suggested Mallorca, the Mediterranean island which had been lauded by Gertrude Stein in the 1920s and was now the home of Robert Graves. Buoyed with expectations, Dahlberg departed on a freighter for Palma, the capital, in February or March 1953. Rlene, who was obliged to finish the school year at the University of California, booked passage on another ship which was to sail in June.[53]

Ten years after he first set foot on this beautiful, semitropical island, Dahlberg wrote, in a rhapsodic article commissioned by *Holiday* magazine, "Islands have always tempted me":

> in 1953 I arrived in Palma de Mallorca, and thought I had discovered Prospero's Isle of Shakespeare's *The Tempest.* I was unreasonably sure that I could be contented there, or, at least, that I would not be stung constantly by the desire to go elsewhere.
>
> At that time, Palma was a sensual cafe town, not yet glutted with automobiles. The golden, Fifteenth Century sandstone edifices eased some fierce city wound in me: I was not punished all day long by grating cement and cruel iron. Every dirty, Arabic alley was a voluptuous experience. . . .
>
> I was ecstatic when I learned that I could go to a restaurant and get a beefsteak, with several vegetables and a bottle of wine, and all for about 14 pesetas—roughly 25¢.[54]

Dahlberg was not exaggerating at all. There were but a handful of automobiles on the island when he first arrived, and even today they seem intruders on the hilly, winding medieval streets. He could boast that he was not pestered by this avatar of the Wheel of Sheol until the 1960s, when U.S. Army engineers built a superhighway to give them access to a radar station built atop Puig Mayor, Mallorca's highest peak.[55]

But Dahlberg's initial experiences in the Balearics were in fact not as ecstatic as he declared in *Holiday*. He knew no one in Spain, and his only contact on the island was a friend of Trocchi's, Robert Creeley, then living in El Terreno, a suburb of Palma. It was Creeley who met Dahlberg when he disembarked. He immediately sensed the loneliness and fear of the older man, who asked few questions and quietly (at first) followed Creeley wherever he went. But Creeley, who was suffering from homesickness and his own sense of anonymity, was eager to cement a relationship with the first American writer he had met in months:

> So when Edward came, I was really impressed with him on the instant. He's obviously, as you know, a cranky, singular, and "loner" kind of man. But as we talked about senses of writing and whatnot, he became extremely attractive to my head. And he looked at my writing—I think primarily poems— he looked at a few lines . . . and was impressed that I seemed to have an almost compulsive need to say very little. He one time said, in fact, "Bob, why do you try so hard to say so little?" I think it's a good question.[56]

Unfortunately, Anne Creeley, who was supporting her husband at the time, took exception to Dahlberg's pontification and his blatantly hostile attitude toward women. When she questioned a quick, seemingly offhanded judgment of Creeley's work, he rebuked her—at first gently: "Young woman, I've been reading and writing for a long time, and I don't have to read all of the work to have a sense of what a writer is and it's literally present in any line." But Dahlberg and Mrs. Creeley were obviously natural enemies. By the end of the evening, after Dahlberg had been ranting about "pederasts," [57] she accused *him* of being a homosexual. Dahlberg then swelled with anger and shouted, "Young woman, when your bones are moldering dust, mine will be carried through the streets by the cheering multitudes!" Creeley thought this to be one of the great statements of all time.[58]

Dahlberg was henceforth forbidden entrance to the house, although Creeley, continuing to be his guide and constant companion, found Dahlberg "a pair of rooms, furnished in the traditional Spanish style, with a sun-fed balcony overlooking the sea." [59] Creeley had sided, at least tacitly, with Dahlberg in the argument and was eager to benefit from what the great writer had to teach. His identification with the older man grew daily:

> I wanted to talk to someone who had the intimate condition, as he obviously had, of being a very particular kind of American writer that I found myself hoping to be also—a loner, without the privilege or the habit of a social group, having to make up or *discover* a "language particular" all by oneself. . . . Edward told me, for example, that in his writing as a young man he would write on the trolleys in San Francisco, saying words over and over aloud, just to get the physical feel of them—words that he would be embarrassed to test out in silence just because he would become self-conscious. His is really an incredibly self-designed language—a language designed entirely with the responsibility of the writer. . . . It echoes and continues what I want to call "a beautifully calm and tested ring . . ." despite the rhetoric which is equally its pattern.
>
> I was shy in response to Edward, and really delighted in listening to him; and I think he sensed that I really needed him, because he called me "A lonely young man with no symptoms of worldliness." [60]

Dahlberg's "training" of Creeley was as impassioned as it was rigorous: "He began asking me in the classic, almost Poundian tradition, what I had read. Then he gave me a booklist, which, to my horror, I lost on the subsequent day, but I never dared tell him." It may have been this affectionate new relationship alone which compelled Dahlberg to remain on Mallorca, and Creeley did everything in his power to encourage him to stay.

It seemed logical that Robert Graves, who had been a legendary figure on Mallorca since his arrival in 1928, would be the best person to help the citified Dahlberg adjust to life on the still quite primitive island. Graves seemed well qualified for this task, since even native Mallorquíns, most of whom knew little of him as a writer, would speak affectionately of the tall, slender, and athletic Irishman, whose name they pronounced "Grá-bes," and who repeatedly defied the fascist government, preserving not only his adopted home town of Deyá but also the financial well-being of many of its residents. It did not take long, however, for the charming though pontifical Graves and the equally pontifical, though often less charming, Dahlberg to clash. Creeley witnessed the progress of their "friendship":

> At first the two men got on very well. For instance, they both had the same "take" on the function of Judas on the occasion of the Crucifixion. They felt that Judas contributed the most human vulnerability and "presence" in that he was guilty of betrayal—that he took the responsibility, so to speak, for the human dilemma and became a curious, paradoxical "saint" of that circumstance.[61]

Dahlberg had entertained this very concept in his essay, "The Bridegroom's Ache," in *Do These Bones Live*. His firm, virtually Calvinistic belief in the corruption of human nature necessarily insists that to be human is to be weak: Judas could not be "worthy" of our love were he not weak and tainted. Dahlberg could find much biblical evidence to legitimize his own character.

The strange American became a frequent visitor to the home of Graves and his wife, who were temporarily staying at Calle Guillermo Massot in the heart of Palma.[62] Graves was genuinely intrigued by his cranky new friend, but soon their egos began to clash. Creeley recalls:

> There was the morning that Edward arrived early, just to see what the apartment scene was, and found Graves and his wife just about to have breakfast, to which they invited him, but he'd just eaten. So Graves said, "Perhaps this will interest you," and gave Edward a copy of *Punch* in which Graves had an article. But Edward just slapped it on the table and walked out in a high dudgeon. He said, "It's bad enough to publish in such a magazine, but to expect another man to read it is absolutely insufferable!"[63]

It took only a few more days for the two men to loathe each other. "Graves would say things like, 'You mean to say you don't read Greek?' "[64] touching on one of Dahlberg's sorest points—his obvious, often embarrassing ineptitude with foreign languages. Dahlberg retaliated with even less subtle attacks. Graves had just published *The Nazarene Gospel Restored*,[65] and Dahlberg, aware that Graves had a collaborator, Joshua Podro, who did most of the research, began accusing Graves of having had most of his books written by someone else. At the time Graves had published well over one hundred books.[66]

Dahlberg also failed utterly to appreciate Graves's famous study of mythology, *The White Goddess*, which, Creeley thought, "was probably boring to Edward." In an unintentionally humorous letter to Herbert Read, Dahlberg condemned Graves's use of big words while falling victim to polysyllables himself: "Graves, a drab of a stylist, is unable to bring homage to the deities. . . . *The White Goddess* is a farrago of blowsy polysyllables which neither quenches the soul nor delights a learned palate. The best style combines frugal words with sublime ones, and can best be described as Ariadne taking her last rest in an earthenware coffin."[67] Dahlberg was, in fact vexed by Graves's willingness to write "venal" prose, which gave him enough income to allow him to write poetry. Graves became branded as an "author for hire" and an enemy of gentle letters who wrote for corrupt interests: "Edward was adamant in that attitude, and once he got to that point emotionally, he stuck to it," Creeley asserted.[68]

The last meeting between the two writers was anticlimactic, although it produced a famous anecdote on the island. Creeley and Dahlberg were sitting at the Bar Formentor, the traditional meeting place for many writers and artists in the ancient city of Palma. Creeley related:

> Graves happened by and sat down with us. Then, frankly, and absolutely in real fairness to Graves, he was trying to be placating, trying to get over the awkwardness that Edward had created by stomping out of his place. And he simply sat down and passed a few words, and Edward said simply, "Hullo," then sat like a little kid with a look of sullen withdrawal on his face. And I don't think he spoke to Graves.
> . . . Graves was talking for a moment to me, then he got up and offered his hand [to Edward], not as "Let's shake and be

friends," but sort of as a quick gesture . . . and Edward refused
it—he didn't respond, whereupon Graves said, in a really
brusque, irritated manner, "Keep it!" and just walked off.[69]

Over the years, Dahlberg magnified his grudges against Graves,
occasionally publishing "exposés" of his "plagiarism," as in this
epistolary essay to Herbert Read: *"The White Goddess* is the labour
of other authors: Robert Graves had played the role of Hermes, the
coney-catcher, and the books he has had in his wily fingers are in
Smith's Dictionary of Greek and Roman Biography and Mythology,
published in 1864, and Gerald Massey's *Natural Genesis,* published
in 1883." [70] Read, who was expected to respond to this undocu-
mented allegation, simply declined what he called "the Graves
gambit." [71] Graves himself leafed through a few pages of *Truth Is
More Sacred,* only to discard it, shouting: "Here is a book I cannot
read!" [72]

"It's a malediction to travel," Dahlberg once commented,
paraphrasing Samuel Johnson, "but the greatest evil is that
wherever you go, you take yourself with you." [73] He thus identified
his own difficulty on Mallorca, even though at the time he had
convinced himself, after less than two months on the island-haven,
that it was "a *cul de sac* in every respect. The people there either
died of alcoholism or left." As at Black Mountain College, he felt
oppressed by the "poor bleak foliage," [74] and he reported to his
wife that the natives were "lumpish" and mere "stumps of
Phoenicia." [75] Rlene was astonished when, just as she was about to
embark for Mallorca, Dahlberg cabled that he was on his way back
to the United States.[76]

Dahlberg was so emotionally distraught that when he reached
New York he immediately suffered another stomach hemorrhage.
Rlene joined him briefly, but it was several weeks before he had the
strength to follow her back to California, where she had decided to
remain at her job. There they rested and began another round of
visits. One of their hosts, Kenneth Rexroth, was not eager to
receive Dahlberg after "he came over the house and insulted
people, as he usually does." [77] But Rexroth was aware of
Dahlberg's genuine physical distress and recommended that he
visit the famous Dr. Emil Conason, whom Dahlberg had known
earlier, but who was Rexroth's physician and the best friend of

Henry Miller (who represented him unflatteringly as "Milton Kronski" in *Sexus*). Physically imposing (he weighed 350 pounds) and extravagantly generous to artists and writers, the jolly Conason was regarded by many of his clients as something of a "witch doctor" or miracle worker.[78] He also had an authentic reputation as a highly talented biochemist and physician. Nonprofessionals supported the rumor that he had invented many modern wonder drugs, although his widow explained: "Emil did not invent drugs as much as he invented methods of using drugs. It was similar to *Gestalt:* if it works here, it should work there." [79] Throughout his career, Conason made it a point to stay in contact with many of his colleagues in medicine and related fields. The most important of his collaborators and his lifelong friend was Professor Oscar Hechter, a biochemist and a member of the team of scientists who developed the birth control pill. Through Conason, Hechter became one of Dahlberg's amazing variety of acquaintances: "The relationship between Dahlberg and Emil was a very strange one. Dahlberg is a hypochondriac. He, after going around to various places in search of 'cures,' met Emil, who gave him a series of shots which made him feel better." Dahlberg came quickly to admire Conason and regard him almost as a father figure. And while he no doubt regarded many of Dahlberg's ailments as imaginary, the physician enjoyed long, often heated verbal debates with him—and, to everyone's surprise, sometimes emerged victorious: [80] "Emil was able to manage Dahlberg and tell him tactfully that he was full of shit. And you know, Dahlberg liked that—he liked being challenged and Emil was able to do so and apparently to help him." [81] Conason was, in fact, well equipped to duel with the man who regarded himself as America's foremost man of letters, for not only was he a "healer," but "an intuitive psychologist" and an omnivorous reader whom many people, like Dahlberg, came to need "in a strange, strange way." [82] Mrs. Conason also understood why Dahlberg constantly found excuses to turn up in the doctor's office:

> My husband had a strong personality. He could talk you out of your sickness when no one else had "cures." . . . Emil knew people and loved people, as he knew literature, science, and politics. . . .

Edward was always concerned about his health and was constantly visiting my husband's office, but Emil encouraged him when he was feeling very low and wasn't writing.[83]

Dahlberg, like his mother, had learned to seek refuge in illness. Although, like Lizzie, he tried to avoid surgery, he habitually fell sick when forced to confront disagreeable situations. Though he remained unusually vital almost to the end of his life, he compulsively ran from one doctor to another.

Life remained unsatisfying for Dahlberg throughout 1955, since his writing was sporadic and he published nothing. In numerous retreats from his much-vaunted "asceticism," he sought satisfaction by accumulating material possessions—rare books, expensive clothing, and a Morgan automobile which cost nearly $3,000—all paid for mostly by the remainder of his inheritance and Rlene's savings. The tireless foe of "the wheel of Sheol" was inordinately proud of this ungainly car, which was exotically built with a wooden frame and a leather belt to secure the engine cowling. When unknowing motorists would mistake it for the similar, though more common, MG automobile, Dahlberg would loudly correct them: "It's a Morgan Plus-4!" [84]

The joy of acquisition failed to sustain Dahlberg, however, and depression again settled in. In desperation, Rlene insisted that they try once again to find a congenial European country. At first, Dahlberg refused to consider returning to Mallorca; but he had been corresponding with a strange, vaguely schizophrenic writer named Richard Newman: Newman used the pen name Hillel Frimet and posed as a communist when he appeared in such magazines as *Black Mountain Review;* [85] but when he wrote under his own name, his politics were invariably conservative.[86] Frimet/ Newman, who was residing in Marlboro, New York, had corresponded with Dahlberg throughout 1955, writing him flattering letters, sending him poems, and suggesting that they start a private press together.[87] And when he moved to the tiny Danish island of Bornholm in the Adriatic Sea, Newman bombarded the Dahlbergs with rhapsodic letters and photographs of the place and beseeched them to join him.

Dahlberg was enchanted by his admirer's portrayal of an untouched, preindustrial retreat, which was sparsely populated by superb craftsmen and where a six- or eight-room house could be purchased for eight to twelve hundred dollars. He accepted an invitation from Newman and his wife to live with them in Svaneke, a hamlet on Bornholm. Since Rlene was teaching, her departure was delayed, but when she was finally able to join her husband, in April or March 1956, he informed her that he wasn't talking to the Newmans because they "hadn't treated him well." [88] He was as forlorn as when he had left America, and, as a result, work on his new book, *The Sorrows of Priapus,* had ceased.[89] Dahlberg recalled: "I liked Bornholm the first time I saw it, but like everything else, it was destroyed by the automobile. About once every seven years, you get a lovely summer, [but] if you arrive in the wrong year, the sun vanishes about every half minute. And it really irks you—you find yourself becoming quite irascible." [90]

With the arrival of his wife, Dahlberg's mood reversed itself, and he found himself enjoying better health than ever before in his life. He discovered that he could travel easily from one end of Bornholm to the other, on bicycle or on foot, on the virtually traffic-free roads. When his spirits had rallied, his ulcer attacks vanished in the restful climate and clean air. He had few opportunities to get into arguments—no one spoke English except the five Americans on the island, and he was speaking to only two of them, Rlene and a Negro painter, Harvey Cropper, plus his Swedish wife, Marika.[91]

The Dahlbergs rented a house quaintly named *Krusehuset* (Danish for "house of Kruse") from a woman who put them in touch with Fraiken Rasmussen who, Dahlberg was intrigued to learn, had reputedly been a "catamite to a German general" during World War I.[92] Dahlberg's persisting interest in sexuality (especially the aberrant forms) was awakened, just at the time James Laughlin agreed to publish *The Sorrows of Priapus.* Dahlberg and Rlene worked feverishly for the next six months assembling the manuscript.[93]

Laughlin assigned his senior editor, Robert MacGregor, to the onerous task of editing and correcting the book. MacGregor remembered spending many hours in libraries: "We had to check on all those mythological names. Some had been misspelled, others were wrongly attributed—it was a tremendous job." But in his labors, MacGregor had an indispensable ally: "Dahlberg didn't take my suggestions well, so I had to ask Rlene and she got many of them through." [94] By the time they moved to Bornholm, Rlene had become Dahlberg's full-time amanuensis, proofreader, and editor. Although she later insisted that none of the actual writing was hers, she suggested many of the source books that he read, especially those dealing with pre-Columbian history, early American explorations, and native American humor, were ones which she had studied with Walter Blair and other scholars. Often she reread the books Dahlberg had marked, typing out on small five-by-seven-inch sheets of stationery passages which he had underscored or marked with the letter *U* for "use." [95]

Either MacGregor or Laughlin, aware of the poor sales of *The Flea of Sodom,* decided upon an ingenious method of "selling" the still obscure Dahlberg. He knew that in Paris important artists such as Picasso had sometimes illustrated the books of relatively unknown writers like Apollinaire to attract buyers. Beautiful books often resulted. MacGregor decided to invite Ben Shahn, who, born in 1898, was of Dahlberg's generation. William Carlos Williams, who often socialized with Shahn at the Downtown Gallery in Manhattan, was enlisted to approach the artist. Reluctant at first, Shahn finally bent to pressure and agreed to do the illustrations for half the royalties. Since Shahn was much better known than Dahlberg, this was a most generous gesture, even though in France artists and writers had always "split down the middle" when they collaborated.[96]

Dahlberg, a persistent foe of modern art, was far from delighted by Shahn's contributions. For some time, he perversely referred to the forthcoming book as *"The Sorrows of Priapus,* by Ben Shahn, with subtitles by Edward Dahlberg." [97] He later wrote to Jonathan Williams:

> You might ask why Ben Shahn did the drawings for *The Sorrows of Priapus* . . . You can't get people to read, and so you prepare a snare for them, drawings or photography, hoping that after they have glanced for a delirious minute at the camera pictures or the artist's illustrations, they will then be tempted to peruse the book. . . . Stieglitz, a wonderful nature, is responsible for this, but then seers are often charlatans.

Dahlberg grew even less sanguine in his comments about Shahn's art, often likening it to "drawings on the walls of a jake." [99] When *The Sorrows* was reissued in 1972 by Harcourt Brace Jovanovich, it was without illustrations; but Dahlberg insisted on including in the introduction a question which he claimed to have put to his former collaborator: "Who is Ben Shahn and what cause had he either to be born or to inhabit this pustular globe?" [100] Fortunately, Shahn was no longer alive to hear of this singular piece of gratuitous nastiness.

After the brief summer in Bornholm, it became clear to Dahlberg that he could expect no more than three months of even moderately warm weather on this northerly island. While he had never been fond of tropical climates, the unrelenting gloom of a Scandinavian winter began to gnaw, and he wrote to virtually everyone he knew even vaguely, hoping to get an invitation to some place farther south. The first response that seemed at all promising came from Richard Aldington, then separated from his wife, Hilda Doolittle, and living in the French provincial hamlet of Montpellier.[101] Aldington had apparently not read Dahlberg's attack on him in the *Freeman:* "Most men hate what is not average, and there is a great deal of the ordinary in Richard Aldington's gifts." [102] Aldington sent Dahlberg a cordial note in which he complained of his loneliness; [103] Dahlberg apparently read this statement as an invitation and finally convinced himself that "Aldington had begged me to come down and see him." [104] Although the two men had met briefly in New Mexico in 1939, it seems most unlikely that Aldington either wanted or expected a visit from the man whom he had once described to Herbert Read as "a tragic example of the unhappy American." [105] Nonetheless, Dahlberg allowed his wife to go with Marika Cropper for a brief visit to Hven, a Swedish island even smaller than Bornholm, while he proceeded by train to Montpellier.[106] The pale and rather stout Aldington, whom Dahlberg had remembered as "a very vascular and handsome young man," did not open his doors to Dahlberg, who, apparently undaunted, allowed him to place him in another suite in the *pension* and take him for a good French meal.[107] Herbert Read soon heard of Aldington's discomfort: "I'll try to take him off you for a bit. Of course he is gifted and I like the fellow personally, but, damn it, everyone has to try to adapt to his age. I admit it's hard to do this without caving in to the yahoos, but Dahlberg doesn't try." [108]

While the two men were discussing their respective works-in-progress, Dahlberg invited James Laughlin, then vacationing in Europe, to meet Aldington in the hope that Laughlin would become interested in publishing a book Aldington had written on the Provençal poet, Frédéric Mistral. According to Dahlberg, trouble began when Aldington was angered by Laughlin's failure to appear. And though Aldington praised the manuscript of *The Sorrows of Priapus*,[109] he privately complained to Read: "The Priapus work is a disappointment. . . . I can't see any structure or line of thought in the book. . . . the trouble is all this unnatural history is cited as if it were still accepted fact." [110]

The two men were still superficially friendly when Rlene arrived at Montpellier, although signs of friction between them were unmistakable. Aldington insisted on "correcting" Dahlberg's fables with natural facts, and the next day a violent argument erupted, as Dahlberg recalled:

> Aldington said, "What about this insect, or flower, or plant? Can you describe it?" I said, "No." Then he said, "You must be a fraud," and then, "Edward, you're a failure!" and we had a very vitriolic disputation. . . . He decided to attack me after telling me that *The Sorrows of Priapus* is a wonderful book of poetry!

Aldington blamed the conflict on Dahlberg:

> Unluckily, E. D. has so much of the neurasthenic temperament of the neglected and unpublished writer that he lost his temper, abused me, was furious when I retaliated, and went off in a huff. . . . Unluckily, I either had to invent lies or blurt out the truth—that I don't know what he's talking about. Most deplorable. But from the moment he arrived here his purpose was plain—i.e. to engage me to praise his works in

print on a reciprocal basis, the long arm of coincidence engaged in log-rolling.[111]

Dahlberg and Rlene left Montpellier on October 8, bought an old Austin automobile, and drove leisurely to Malaga and Torremolinos. During this interval, a limited edition of *The Sorrows of Priapus* was being printed. Shahn insisted that the boxed, oversized book, limited to 150 copies and priced at fifty dollars each, be executed on expensive Arches paper, which was hand-produced in France. He also stipulated that it be printed by offset lithography at his favorite printing house, the Crafton Graphic Company. To meet these demands, the text had to be printed first, then the sheets carried by messenger to Crafton Graphic. This cumbersome process caused considerable spoilage. As an added complication, the signature sheets destined for the rear of the book had to be signed by Dahlberg, who was en route from Malaga to Seville at the time. An enormous package had to be airmailed to him at an indefinite address.[112]

Edward and Rlene, 1956. (Courtesy of Rlene Dahlberg.)

The signature pages went astray but eventually reached Dahlberg after he had left Spain and was staying in Ascona, a town in the Italian sector of Switzerland. His host there was R. F. C. Hull, the friend and translator of Carl Jung.[113] Herbert Read, worried that Dahlberg had been "languishing" in Seville, wrote that he would consider it a kindness if Hull would entertain his friend for a few days. Hull recalled: "Then the most incredible vehicle drew up, festooned with kitchen utensils and driven by Rlene. Dahlberg stopped for about one week with me, during which time he stated he was thinking of settling in Switzerland." Since Hull's son, Tristram, had published a small portion of *The Sorrows,* Dahlberg's reputation had preceded him. Like Aldington, Hull was less than enthusiastic about his houseguest:

> He's a very wearing person to be with. You can never say anything: if you're talking to him, you're arguing with him; if you're agreeing with him, it's for all the wrong reasons. . . . There's no conversation, it is an argument. You must listen to how awful every writer is. All of them are *ad hominem* attacks. The only writers he admires are safely dead.

After supper, Dahlberg would give readings from the still un-published *Sorrows:* "One day I praised it, and he screamed at me, for no reason, 'You don't understand a word of it!' " Hoping to appeal to Dahlberg's interest in mythology, Hull loaned him a copy of Jung's *The Symbols of Transformation.* The book was returned with numerous underscored passages.[114] Dahlberg later dismissed Jung with the contempt he had for most writers and all scientists of the twentieth century:

> I was only interested in Hölderlin. . . . [Hull] translated a little of Hölderlin. But if you want mythology, don't read Jung—it's a waste of time. Jung doesn't know anything about mythology or anything at all. He's an extremely shallow man and he's tainted with Freud.[115]

When Dahlberg concluded that Ascona was not the most promising place to nurture his talents, he and Rlene moved to

Paris, where they stayed for several months at the Hôtel de Lille, and then on to El Terreno late in the summer of 1957. They had decided to settle on Mallorca after all.[116]

NOTES

1. Letter: John Cech, July 13, 1973. Quoted is Cech's paraphrase of several of Dahlberg's letters to Olson.
2. Creeley sent tape-recorded responses to questions I mailed him. The cassette was accomapnied by a note, date Aug. 11, 1973.
3. See, for example, Fred Moramarco's *Edward Dahlberg*, in which *The Flea of Sodom* is dismissed as "enigmatic" and "unsatisfying" (p. 70).
4. Interview: E. D., Mar. 28, 1973.
5. The name Proletcult may be a take-off on Proletco, the Communist cafeteria located on Union Square during the 1930s (see Ch. IV).
6. Interview: E. D., Nov. 16, 1972.
7. Interview: E. D., Nov. 16, 1972.
8. Interview: E. D., Dec. 5, 1972.
9. *Confessions,* p. 266.
10. Dahlberg could not recall Golem's real identity.
11. Interview: E. D., Nov. 16, 1972.
12. "The Rational Tree," *Edward Dahlberg: American Ishmael of Letters,* ed. Harold Billings (Austin: Roger Beacham, 1968), p. 40.
13. Interview: Robert MacGregor, Sept. 4, 1973. MacGregor, who joined New Directions just as *The Flea of Sodom* was being published, later became chief editor.
14. Interview: Rlene Dahlberg, Sept. 6, 1973.
15. Interview: Joel Oppenheimer, Oct. 29, 1972.
16. Interview: Ephraim Doner, May 27, 1973.
17. 27 (Sept. 30, 1950), 108.
18. "Prophet or Pedant?" *Poetry,* 77 (January 1951), 237-38.
19. "How Do You Spell Fool?" *Poetry,* 77 (April 1951), rpt. *The Leafless American,* p. 46.
20. Ibid., pp. 42-43.
21. Interview: Rlene Dahlberg, June 28, 1973.
22. "Reviewer's Notebook," *Freeman,* 1 (July 2, 1951), 634. Read's comment appears in his Foreword to *The Flea of Sodom,* p. 9.
23. Interview: Rlene Dahlberg, June 28, 1973.
24. Letter: E. D. to Oscar Cargill, April 30, 1950.
25. Letter: Joseph A. Byrne (Assistant Secretary of the University), July 2, 1973.
26. Interview: Herbert Miller, April 3, 1972.

27. *Tomorrow,* 10 (March 1951), rpt. *The Leafless American,* p. 19.
28. Ibid., pp. 1-2.
29. "My friends, Stieglitz, Anderson, and Dreiser," *Tomorrow,* 10 (May 1951), 22-27.
30. *Freeman,* 1 (August 13, 1951), 728.
31. Letter: John Cech, July 13, 1973.
32. "Laurels for Borrowers," *Freeman,* 1 (Dec. 17, 1951), 187.
33. Interview: E. D., June 17, 1973.
34. Letter: John Cech, July 13, 1973. Cech notes that Olson claimed to have written Dahlberg several times, but that his letters were intercepted. Rlene stated unequivocally that "Edward wrote a letter of congratulation about [the birth of Olson's son], and referred to Olson as 'Leviathan.' . . . Apparently Olson didn't react to that too well and wrote back a rather short letter which Edward made me answer in a very nasty manner. . . . I did *not* intercept any letters." (Interview: Oct. 2, 1973.)
35. Interview: Rlene Dahlberg, April 13, 1973.
36. Interview: E. D., Jan. 7, 1973.
37. *Confessions,* p. 197.
38. Ibid., pp. 197-98. Dahlberg hoped to start a press called Untimely Press, after Bourne.
39. Letter: Oliver Carlson to E. D., Sept. 17, 1972.
40. "The Art of Concealment," *Freeman,* 2 (June 30, 1952), 670-71.
41. "Carpers on Lawrence," review of *D. H. Lawrence: Portrait of a Genius But . . .* by Richard Aldington, and *Journey with Genius,* by Witter Bynner, *Freeman,* 2 (July 28, 1952), 744.
42. Ibid., p. 743.
43. (Boston: Little, Brown, 1952).
44. Interview: Isabella Gardner, April 27, 1972.
45. "A Long Lotus Sleep," *Poetry,* 81 (February 1973), 313-19.
46. Interview: Isabella Gardner, April 27, 1972.
47. "Two Poems," *Poetry,* 83 (January 1954), 193-96.
48. "Lawrentian Analects," *Poetry,* 83 (March 1954), 347-49.
49. Letter: October 23, 1953.
50. Interview: Rlene Dahlberg, July 24, 1973.
51. Letter: E. D. to James Laughlin, Sept. 11, 1953, *Epitaphs,* pp. 128-29.
52. Dahlberg would often travel to Hoboken to visit Trocchi in the 1950s. Dahlberg is paid extensive tribute in Trocchi's book, *Cain's Book* (New York: Grove Press, 1960).
53. Interview: Rlene Dahlberg, July 24, 1973.
54. "Mallorcá: An Island Haven," *Holiday,* 37 (February 1965), 48.
55. Interview: Rlene Dahlberg, July 30, 1973.
56. Tape recording: Robert Creeley, Aug. 11, 1973.
57. Interview: Rlene Dahlberg, July 24, 1973.
58. Tape Recording: Robert Creeley, Aug. 11, 1973.
59. "Mallorca: An Island Paradise," p. 48.

60. Tape recording: Robert Creeley, Aug. 11, 1973.
61. Tape recording: Robert Creeley, Aug. 11, 1973.
62. Interview: Elaine Kerrigan, Aug. 2, 1973.
63. Tape recording: Robert Creeley, Aug. 11, 1973.
64. Interview: Robert Goulet, Aug. 9, 1973. Goulet, who knew both Dahlberg and Graves, is a French-Canadian author residing on Mallorca.
65. Garden City, N.Y.: Doubleday, 1953.
66. Interview: Robert Goulet, Aug. 9, 1973.
67. *Truth Is More Sacred,* p. 154.
68. Tape Recording: Robert Creeley, Aug. 11, 1973.
69. Tape Recording: Robert Creeley, Aug. 11, 1973.
70. *Truth Is More Sacred,* pp. 154-55.
71. Ibid., 158.
72. Interview: Ruthven Todd, Oct. 30, 1972.
73. Interview: E. D., Sept. 16, 1972.
74. Interview: E. D., May 22, 1972.
75. Interview: Rlene Dahlberg, July 24, 1973. Mallorquíns, who are often short people, are descended from many races, including ancient Iberians, Phoenicians, Romans, Catalans, and Jews.
77. Interview: Rlene Dahlberg, Aug. 2, 1973.
78. Interview: Kenneth Rexroth, Feb. 17, 1973.
79. Interviews: Rlene Dahlberg, Feb. 2, 1973; Mrs. Celia Conason, Mar. 15, 1973.
80. Interview: Mar. 15, 1973.
81. Interview: Michael Sands, April 19, 1972.
82. Interview: Oscar Hechter, April 18, 1973.
82. Ibid. Hechter added: "I've always liked Dahlberg. I'm not put off by his *mishigas.* . . . He's an educated 'Tevye,' and so am I."
83. Interview: Mrs. Celia Conason, Mar. 15, 1973.
84. Interview: Rlene Dahlberg, May 12, 1973.
85. Frimet appeared in *Black Mountain Review,* 7 (Autumn 1957).
86. Interview: Rlene Dahlberg, Feb. 2, 1973.
87. Letters: Richard Newman to E. D., May 6, 1955, Aug. 31, 1955, Nov. 3, 1955, and Nov. 19, 1955.
88. Interview: Rlene Dahlberg, July 20, 1973.
89. A small portion of *The Sorrows* had already been published in *Nimbus,* 2 (Winter 1954), a short-lived and very small magazine published in England by Tristram Hull.
90. Interview: E. D., Feb. 11, 1973.
91. Interview: Rlene Dahlberg, July 20, 1973.
92. Interview: Rlene Dahlberg, Feb. 6, 1973.
93. Interview: Rlene Dahlberg, Feb. 6, 1973.
94. Interview: Robert MacGregor, Sept. 4, 1973.
95. Interview: Rlene Dahlberg, April 13, 1972.
96. Interview: Robert MacGregor, Sept. 4, 1973.

97. Interview: Rlene Dahlberg, Feb. 2, 1973.
98. Letter: E. D. to Jonathan Williams, June 27, 1964, *The Edward Dahlberg Reader*, ed. Paul Carroll (New York: New Directions, 1967), pp. 327-28.
99. Interview: E. D., Jan. 22, 1973.
100. Interview: E. D., Jan. 22, 1973. *Sorrows*, p. xv.
101. Interview: Rlene Dahlberg, Sept. 3, 1973.
102. "Carpers on Lawrence," *Freeman*, 2 (July 28, 1952), 744.
103. Interview: Rlene Dahlberg, Sept. 3, 1973.
104. Interview: E. D., Sept. 3, 1973.
105. Letter: Richard Aldington to Herbert Read, June 27, 1956, "Richard Aldington's Letters to Herbert Read," ed., Davis S. Thatcher, *Malahat Review*, 15 (July 1970), 34.
106. Interview: Rlene Dahlberg, Sept. 3, 1973.
107. Interview: E. D., Jan. 14, 1973.
108. Letter: Richard Aldington to Herbert Read, Sept. 5, 1956, "Aldington's Letters to Read," p. 35.
109. Interview: E. D., Sept. 3, 1973. Laughlin would not comment.
110. Letter: Richard Aldington to Herbert Read, Oct. 8, 1956, "Aldington's Letters to Read," pp. 36-37. Dahlberg included an "Author's Note" in *The Sorrows:* "This is fable and not natural history" (n.p.).
111. Letter: Richard Aldington to Herbert Read Oct. 8, 1956.
112. Interview: Robert MacGregor, Sept. 4, 1973.
113. Hull was engaged for many years in translating the complete works of Jung for the Bollingen Foundation. He died in 1975.
114. Interview: R. F. C. Hull, Nov. 11, 1972.
115. Interview: E. D., Nov. 16, 1972.
116. Interview: Rlene Dahlberg, July 24, 1973.

The Way Up

The Dahlbergs rented rooms in a house in El Terreno while they looked for a *finca* to buy on Mallorca and awaited the publication of *The Sorrows of Priapus,* due in December 1957. Robert Mac-Gregor, who was by now not only Dahlberg's editor but his most enthusiastic advocate, had suggested that he again try writing autobiographical fiction. Casting about for a title with a good biblical ring, Rlene and Dahlberg hit upon "A Breath That Passeth Away," from "because I was flesh, and a breath that passeth away and cometh not again," from the Book of Psalms. But Paul Carroll suggested that the first part of the epigraph might be more memorable, and MacGregor agreed that "Because I Was Flesh" fully captured the Elizabethan quality of Dahlberg's prose: "[Edward] talked so well about his youth, and I thought he would get his feet back on the ground where he had been getting lost, I thought, in metaphysical ramblings. The more he got into it, the more excited he became. And [*Because I Was Flesh*] turned out to be his best book in my opinion." [1]

More immediate problems occupied Dahlberg's attention than producing a new book. He and his wife were lodged in the cheapest quarters available in Torremolinos, and while Rlene tried to protect his tender stomach by cooking all their meals, their food shopping was severely constricted by their lack of Spanish. Never before was Dahlberg so discomfited by what he had hitherto considered a minor embarrassment: his ineptitude with foreign languages. They moved to a converted chicken house, where they could enjoy the services of a one-armed boy named "Churi," who tried to do the shopping. Dahlberg decided one day that he wanted some very bland cheese and sent Churi out for *huesos blancos* (white bones); what he in fact wanted was *queso blando,* but Churi took the order literally. Dahlberg fulminated, "What in hell am I going to do with white bones?" The poor boy innocently suggested that El Señor make soup.[2]

On another occasion, a Spanish couple staying nearby became concerned about the tall American who seemed constantly to be complaining about his health. One morning they politely asked him in Spanish, "How do you feel?" Intending to reply, *"Un poco mejor"* ("a little better"), Dahlberg unfortunately blurted, *"Un poco mujer,"* which translates loosely as "slightly effeminate." Rlene recalls that a strange look came over the Spaniards' faces and they avoided her husband from then on.[3]

Circumstances seemed to improve when the Dahlbergs met a bilingual couple, the translator Anthony Kerrigan and his wife Elaine. Kerrigan, who had been raised in Cuba and spoke perfect Spanish, owned a *pension* in Palma once occupied by Gertrude Stein. They found comfortable quarters for the Dahlbergs, but suggested that Edward's frayed nerves might be soothed in a quieter and more isolated part of the island. After several weeks of searching, they decided on a little town in the North called Sóller and placed a down payment on an ancient, unelectrified nut-picker's cottage named *Ca'n Peretons* (Mallorquín for "House of the Little Walls"). They hired the local lawyer, Don Tomás Terán, to arrange the restoration of the dilapidated house. At the time, Don Tomas observed that the estate was a virtual *despoblado* (wilderness), with only eight ragged almond trees and two pathetic figs in the orchard.[4] But the house was spacious, surrounded by considerable land, and remarkably cheap, as were the costs for labor necessary to make it livable. Don Tomás was left in charge of the project while the Dahlbergs took up their quarters in Palma once again.

While they were experiencing their first damp and chilly Mallorcan winter in December 1957, the long-awaited *Sorrows* finally appeared. Dahlberg immediately flew into a rage when he discovered that Shahn's name appeared first, facing the copyright page, while his own name appeared above the book's title. More than usual, this tantrum was unwarranted, since Dahlberg's name is more conspicuous than Shahn's, and the book is plainly attributed to Dahlberg, "with drawings by Ben Shahn."

The title of this curious miscellany is a capsule of its theme: man, the most "salacious biped," is the only creature in the animal kingdom to be tortured by the demands of his pudenda: "What is copulation that man should be tickled into dotage?" (pp. 7-9). To buttress his thesis, Dahlberg turned, not to natural history, but to fable and mythology, thereby subtly implanting his strongest concern, the importance of legends to the human race. What emerged was an often beautiful prose poem, the most refined application to that time of his "baroque" style. Ostensibly to allow more space for Shahn's drawings, [5] but probably because the editors feared that readers might be put off by the superabundance of misanthropic and misogynistic passages in the book, Dahlberg had Rlene cut his manuscript by nearly half. The deleted portions were published separately eleven years later as *The Carnal Myth*. [6] This book, although it lacks the whimsicality of the earlier voice, speaks with the almost nihilistic voice that Dahlberg was developing during this period. Angry themes—the very ones the New Directions editors excluded—quickly emerge from behind general statements ("Ultimately, only style is important."). Men choose their wives foolishly: "They see a trull with nothing to recommend her but a pair of thighs and choice hunkers, and so smart to void their seed that they marry her at once" (p. 13). Any woman can destroy a man: if he marries an "untried" or virginal one, he is likely to end up with a frigid or barren wife; but a libidinous creature is even a weaker choice, since she will make a bad wife who will exhaust her husband (p. 20). Better to give up sexuality altogether, since it destroys man's most vital function—his interest in learning (p. 49).

The author's purported contempt for sex (Dahlberg truly showed few such reservations in practice) is nearly equaled by his misanthropy: "The brain is a poor reed shaken by every wind and its fruits are the sport of dust" (p. 62). Man is a martial animal, who "casts away peace for war, for Ilium, Helen, pelf, and copulation" (p. 31). Priapus, the phallic god, is the scoundrel who distracts men from the serious business of life and deludes them into thinking that women *want* them. But Dahlberg, now involved in his sixth marriage, predicted only betrayal for the man who imagines he has a woman's love. He is helpless against *any* female, "whose body is her wisest mind, against which man is raving dust." Xerxes was an "obedient" (i.e., fearful) husband and therefore a poor warrior (pp. 29-30).

Try as he might, Dahlberg could produce no example of a man who is free of the "two pests of mankind"—Mars and Venus (p. 24). Hence, there is little hope for the human race: "Aristotle thought happiness was energy," but men waste their force in copulation. Ironically, when they are old and are no longer tortured by their pudenda, they are beset by the horrors of old age: "At sixty one should relinquish pleasure; at fifty, prepare for abstinence, or else be ready, as Plato says, to educate his diseases." Dahlberg was in the midst of these critical years as he commented bitterly: "Those who despair of the race know that man cannot be seraphic until nature has altered his body." He adds a grisly footnote to this thought: "Maybe higher man will be a eunuch" (p. 22).

The terrors of old age color the final pages of *The Carnal Myth:* Dahlberg "regrets" his own solitude, yet claims to take responsibility for it. Perhaps everyone is as "alone" as he chooses to be, but the author now despises his isolation—there is plenty of it in the cemetery. Perhaps he is doomed to be a "dotard": "The philosopher increases his knowledge as he rots." The book reaches a crescendo of cynicism worthy of the King of Brobdingnag in *Gulliver's Travels.* Man is the "loneliest worm, and there is no spider or reptile so desolate as Aristotle's forlorn featherless biped" (p. 84):

> Man seldom relinquishes a single fault he condemns in
> others; for he is deaf to a rebuke. He covets what he does not

want; alas, the bread he casts upon the water is returned to him. Most of the time is given to improving his vices; he cannot bear to be taken for a simpleton in the game of malice. When the viper is unable to poison his victim he fetches his whole brood to pour out their venom with more success. When the fangs are not shown at once, we do not know where they are; the teeth of the polypus are between her feet. (p. 83)

Daily existence can supply man with little to sustain him. "One's origins matter most," declares the rootless and fatherless Dahlberg, who came to identify originality with self-love: "A poet ought not to trust himself, for he is a chameleon, assuming the complexion of his surroundings and has the slavish vices of his time" (p. 64). The notion that no one really "invents" anything at all unites *The Carnal Myth* with *The Sorrows of Priapus,* which begins with the assurance that "This is a fable and not natural history," which Dahlberg mostly paraphrased from numerous learned sources.

The Sorrows opens with an extravagant concept that Dahlberg learned through bitter experience: "Copulation is a dangerous pastime" (p. 2). He has chosen sex as his theme, since it is such a prodigious instinct, present even in castrated animals. After treating the reader to some particularly grisly sexual lore—"When the testicles of the boar are swollen he is at times so beside himself that he rubs them against a tree until he is castrated" (p. 11)— Dahlberg blends his misanthropic sentiments in *The Sorrows* with his indictment of sexuality. Although his language is often whimsical and ironical, his revulsion toward humanity and its bodily functions is clearly in earnest. Two of his great bugaboos, adultery and venereal disease, are clearly juxtaposed in a tight, epigrammatic paragraph:

Countless adulteries are committed without lust, and with no thought of the peril which attends this folly. Animals do not give each other the pox; when men attempt to lie with a beast it rejects the malady that is said to be the companion of the human genius. The adulterer is more senseless than the earthworm who keeps part of his tail in the hole he inhabits when copulating so he can disappear at once should he see an adversary. The tibulae hide in the hedges all day, and seek the delights of the female at dusk. (p. 12)

Dahlberg soon identifies the source of man's evil as his predatory nature: "He has extirpated most of the beasts which he no longer has as tutors." All quadrupeds are more gentle than humans, the fabulist observes, as he wittily surveys human anatomy and draws some metaphysical analogies: "The tongue is even less covered than the scrotum, and can hardly ever be called a secret part since few men have enough character to keep it in their mouths. It is difficult to know whether the tongue or the phallus is more harmful to men" (p. 27).

Although the strident confessional tone of *The Carnal Myth* is largely absent from *The Sorrows* section, several of Dahlberg's most painful personal problems gain a forum in the latter book. For instance, it is the author himself who distrusts people when he says, "Man is the most inconstant of companions," though he distances himself and abruptly generalizes his statement by making learned comments about the social habits of the pelican, the widgeon, and other birds of prey (p. 34). Man is not only the most easily deceived of animals, but the greediest of "feeders"—his voracious appetite gives him a bad stomach, which "is not good for wedlock, friendship, or philosophy" (pp. 42-46). Dahlberg's peptic ulcer was never far from his mind as he was writing this book.

After accumulating massive "evidence" that *Homo sapiens* is a "misshapen and forlorn" creature in the realm of being, Dahlberg moves on to the most important section of *The Sorrows of Priapus*. In "The Myth Gatherers," dedicated to William Carlos Williams as thanks for his having induced Shahn to illustrate the book, Dahlberg concentrates on the theme which had preoccupied him since 1951, when he first began his intensive study of pre-Columbian America and the early explorers of the New World. Although "Europeans came to the Americas for a new energy," they succumbed to the immensity of these continents: "It was sterile earth which brewed fatal ends." The early settlers quickly forgot their legends and traditions and, ironically, neglected the grandest "booty" this land had to offer, the legends and gospels of the Indians. Instead, they harvested "the pinion nut, tanned hides of the woolly cattle of the Platte, or virgin discovery, which, like learning, is tombstone destiny" (p. 62). Modern Americans, unlike the indomitable Spanish *caballeros*, have become vitiated and suffer more than any other culture from mankind's most loathsome disease—boredom. Dahlberg offers us enticing samples of the riches we might have inherited from the Indians:

> The American fable is a table of seasons, the moons, days, and annals of the pilgrimages of tribes. The Aztecs lamented their separation from *Tulan* so bountiful in maize, gourds, flowers and cacao. . . . One of the gifts of Montezuma to Hernando Cortes was two round emblems in gold and silver representing the sun and the moon, but the wagon or wheel was lost long before Tolteca and the Inca. (p. 66)

Unfortunately, only isolated pockets of such elevated culture existed. The continents were vast, and "much of the Americas was dead ground," as barren as northern Siberia (p 69). The store was dispersed and could sustain neither the natives nor their conquerors.

But Dahlberg felt we can still go back to dead civilizations for nourishment. He details some of the more exotic Indian customs which served to defeat boredom. Even warfare, if properly executed, could have a tonic effect: "The last free king of the Mexicans was Montezuma, who told Cortes, his conqueror, that he made war upon his neighbors to exercise the people, which is what Plato had in mind, because idle citizens are insane men" (p. 73). Dahlberg was fascinated by the mixture of barbarism, melancholy, and refinement which he perceived in Montezuma, but he was even more taken with cannibalism and the suggestion of sexual perversion it entails. Nearly fifteen pages are devoted to proving how eating human flesh is more sensible than the covert cannibalism of Western sexuality: "Cannibals are not interested in rapine or the Occidental disease called love, and do not find it essential to practice furtive polygamy, as a woman can be had for a knife or a hatchet" (p. 99).

Dahlberg stops short of recommending cannibalism as a cure for mankind's ills: sadly, though, he offers little hope at all. Defeated by "wit, the parent of malice and of letters" (p. 98), man is "the most vain of all animals on earth." He willingly embraces all the bizarre and foolish traits of animals but learns little else from them: "Men take their habits from animals, they lose their symbolic life apart from them. . . . Man is the tragic animal" (p. 103).

The Sorrows of Priapus ends on an elegiac note: "Our annals are weak, and we know not our rivers; we cannot understand today which is father Ra, the Egyptian sun, until we gather up yesterday, who is Osiris" (p. 106). Rivers, for Dahlberg, came to symbolize tradition and legends, and since Americans have not learned to explore their sources, this remains a "wild land, undomestic," (p.115). The book concludes with a solemn, if somewhat pompous and obscure warning reminiscent of Thoreau: "Be primordial or decay" (p. 119).

Aided by Shahn's drawings and almost unanimously favorable reviews, *The Sorrows* sold better than any of Dahlberg's previous books. Jack Jones, in a review misleadingly entitled "People Are No Good," commended the unity of purpose of the book, which "is beautifully made and has forty-two attractive drawings of Ben Shahn—who, like Mr. Dahlberg does not employ the figleaf to excess." Jones was one of the few reviewers disposed to appreciate the embittered irony of the book, as Richard Aldington did not:

> [Dahlberg's] advice is accompanied by a liberal amount of odd or uproarious information upon human and mythological venery. It becomes clear that Mr. Dahlberg is inveighing not so much against incontinence or even epicurianism, as against sex empiricism in the absence of faith or value.[7]

Far less flattering to Dahlberg was a review by Robert Duncan, who tried to pigeonhole him as "a son of D. H. Lawrence." Although *The Sorrows* is "brilliant and elaborate," the author has the morality of a "high-brow Walter Winchell." He is "perverted" in the most deplorable sense since he is hostile to nature itself: "Dahlberg ransacks classical literature for invective and verification of his disgust for the body and mind of man, sensitive as Old Nick himself to man's possible disgrace, and outraged by the suggestion of beauty . . . or Eros."[8] Herbert Read rushed immediately to Dahlberg's defense by trumpeting the glories of the book's style: "The obvious comparisons are with those masters of the English music, Sir Thomas Browne and Robert Burton. But Dahlberg has also the geographical imagination of a Milton and the moral fervor of a Montaigne." Dahlberg, says Read, is hardly puritanical, as some reviewers had insisted: "Rather, he would purify sex from its lewd abuses. . . . *The Sorrows of Priapus,* like *Leaves of Grass,* or *Moby Dick,* is an authentic and rare contribution to the formation or elucidation of an American myth." [9]

Dahlberg's joy in having finally published a successful book could not hold against his chronic inability to endure his own happiness. His decision to settle on Mallorca was not sitting well with him, and he vented his anger on the lawyer, Don Tomás, whom he accused of inefficiency and "extortion." Local people took very obvious exception to his noisy condemnations of a respected elder of the town.[10] To distract Dahlberg from his problems with the house in Sóller, Anthony Kerrigan and Rlene decided, in the spring of 1958, to take Dahlberg on a tour of the ancient cathedral towns of southern France and northern Spain. Dahlberg and Kerrigan were especially eager to visit Salamanca, the home of Miguel de Unamuno, whose works Kerrigan was translating, and Avila, identified with St. Teresa, "the little Jewess of Avila," of whom Dahlberg, Kerrigan, and Emma Goldman had several times written.[11] The trip they planned was circular: the threesome took a boat from Palma to Barcelona, then traveled in a rented car to Seo de Urgel, the major Spanish town near Andora. They then drove across Andora and the treacherous Envelira Pass, up through Toulouse, and then to Paris.

The multiple irritations of traveling and being confined to a small automobile rapidly took their toll on Dahlberg. The inevitable cataclysm finally occurred at a dinner with Georges Duthuit, the son-in-law of Henri Matisse and art critic to whom Read had once introduced Dahlberg.[12] Unfortunately, the fact that Duthuit had been an editor of *transition* magazine in the 1930s grated on Dahlberg. Kerrigan recalled their "Wonderful French meal, out in the open, under the trees, the petals falling all over us. It was a day everybody was in love with something, whether it was the trees, or women, or the food":

Then a handsome woman, who had been in the Resistance, came over to the table and [Duthuit] stood up. He saluted, bowed, spoke a few phrases, and then returned to our table. And Edward said, "You see? I'm sitting here, and you got up and you spoke to that woman!" Duthuit, who was a giant of a man (there was no question of his being afraid of Edward), replied, "She was in the Resistance and is an old friend. We have been through many things together." But Edward replied, "That has nothing to do with it! I was telling you that Joyce was a transvestite, and you didn't listen to me! You were talking to that woman! And I said *transition* was a worthless rag. . . ." And he pretended that he did not know that this man had been an editor of *transition*, which may have been more rudeness than anything. Then Edward began smashing the table and carrying on. It made no sense at all.[13]

Dahlberg relaxed somewhat as the pace of the journey quickened. The three took the coastal route from Paris to La Rochelle, Bordeaux, east to Toulouse and Fois, then briefly west again to the coast and Biarritz, then over to St.-Jean-O-Pied de Port, a tiny border town near a small pass over the Pyrenees. Dahlberg then settled into an uncharacteristic state of contentment as the trip progressed through Pamplona, Burgos, and Valladolid.[14] At this time, Kerrigan was moved to write of "Edward Dahlberg/ with whom I'd as lief pray, or wail or sorrow,/ in these, or other, cathedral towns." [15] But tranquility was not to prevail, for Dahlberg's volcanic temper erupted again during dinner. The Dahlbergs and Kerrigan had settled down to a leisurely meal in Segovia; but as their orders were being taken, Dahlberg reminded Kerrigan that they both had stomach ulcers and should not eat spicy food. But Kerrigan insisted on ordering *paella* instead of boiled chicken, Dahlberg's choice. Before anyone knew what had happened, Dahlberg had flown into a rage, attempted to overturn the table, and then strode out of the restaurant. Kerrigan and Rlene took time finishing their meal, then went outside to look for Edward, who appeared strikingly diminished as he stood, still fuming, framed by one of the towering arches of a Roman aqueduct.[16] Undaunted, the party continued on to Avila and Madrid (where they had an auto accident), and finally, thoroughly weary, east along the Valencia Road to Valencia. The trip ended on the ferryboat back to Mallorca.[17]

An exceedingly hot summer had descended prematurely on Palma when the Dahlbergs returned there during the first week of June 1958. They made the winding journey across the mountains to Sóller, only to be disappointed: the Spanish workmen were proceeding at what seemed to Dahlberg an inordinately leisurely pace. It would be at least another full year before *Ca'n Peretons* could be occupied. He also learned, belatedly, that central heating was almost unknown on the island and that electric lines had not yet been strung near the house. They would have to rely on bottled butane for heating, lighting, and refrigeration.

Rather than risk having Dahlberg's impatience disrupt or even terminate the work, Rlene insisted that they spend the following winter in New York. They booked passage on a freighter, but the passage was so rough that Dahlberg had to be hospitalized briefly in New York for a hemorrhaging ulcer. After his release, he took a room at the Marlton Hotel at 5 West Eighth Street, then placed a deposit on a small tenement apartment near the Hudson River at 88 Horatio Street. Rlene meanwhile visited Santa Monica.[18]

The celebrity Dahlberg had acquired during his absence from the United States was not entirely of the sort he would have expected or desired. While staying at the Marlton, he was taken aback that many of his callers were, as he labeled them, "pederasts"—young men who interpreted what they read in *The Sorrows* as his preoccupation with the phallus. Dahlberg protested, "I wrote *about* the worship of the Phallus. I was *not* recommending it!" [19]

Rlene returned from California to take a job teaching English at Grover Cleveland High School in lower Manhattan. She and her husband were now living in the walk-up on Horatio Street, and, during the hours that Rlene was at work, Dahlberg had abundant time to read, write, and continue receiving visitors. One of the earliest and most persistent of these was Irving Rosenthal, a young writer who was consciously imitating Dahlberg's highly inflected style. Rosenthal had assumed the editorship of the soon-to-be suppressed *Chicago Review,* which became *Big Table.* He recalled:

> I looked Edward up in September of 1958, on my third visit to New York, to collect mss. for the *Chicago Review.* I was 27 and genuinely turned on by his writing. . . .

Then and later I made sure that Edward met all the best writers that I knew, because I thought he and they were spiritually akin. Also I thought he would give them a sense of literary tradition, and I thought they would appreciate his waywardness. I didn't see him as a fusty antique cribber. I put him in *Big Table 1* along with Burroughs, Kerouac, and Corso. . . .

That first issue of *Big Table* was seized by the Post Office, made Burroughs famous, and gave Edward a new audience. It used to tickle me that occasionally, in reviews of *Big Table 1,* or of the notorious Autumn 1958 issue of the *Chicago Review,* which brought the house down on me, Edward was listed as one of the new Beat writers who were destroying the English language.[20]

Rosenthal published two excerpts from material deleted from *The Sorrows of Priapus,* but his editorial eye was on the steadily growing and profoundly beautiful autobiographical memoir to which Dahlberg had turned almost all his attention. To the young man's amazement, the notoriously stubborn author gave him virtually a free hand in editing the manuscript and in selecting those portions which he thought would be suitable for publication in *Big Table.* Thus, Rosenthal became the first of four editors to labor over the massive manuscripts of *Because I Was Flesh.*[21] He wrote, "I was glad to be trusted that much by Edward, and especially by Rlene, his usual editor."[22]

Despite the extensive cutting and rearranging done by Rosenthal, the portions of *Because I Was Flesh* published in *Big Table 2* were only sketches of the final product. The early version began with maudlin abruptness: "My mother and I were luckless souls. She strove fiercely for her angels and was wretched most of her days in the earth. She fought because, as Pascal writes, of the automatic necessity to finish one's life no matter what it may be."[23] However, the final version of the autobiography—which had now swelled to an epic—opens most appropriately with a lyric incantation:

Kansas City is a vast inland city, and its marvelous river, the Missouri, heats the senses; the maple, alder, elm and cherry trees with which the town abounds are songs of desire,

and only the almonds of ancient Palestine can awaken the
hungry pores more deeply.[24]

In the latter version, the geographical setting of Dahlberg's youth
is lavishly re-created, only after which the two principals in the
drama are skillfully interpolated:

> My mother and I were luckless souls. She strove fiercely for
> her angels, and was wretched most of her days in the earth.
> Moreover, if she failed, who hasn't? If she prayed for what she
> thought was her good, and none heeded her, that had to be
> too. (p. 2)

Dahlberg's regular appearance in *Big Table* brought him to the
attention of numerous younger writers. Rosenthal arranged meetings between Dahlberg and Allen Ginsberg, who was fascinated by
the older man's use of classical allusions, "the aptness and
adeptness he had in making a mosaic of texts. I remember how
startling and how random it was." Ginsberg's interest quickened
even further once he discovered the subject of Dahlberg's "epic":

> This was at the time that *Kaddish* had just appeared, and a
> piece of *Because I Was Flesh* had appeared in *Big Table* on a
> very similar theme—both of us recollecting our mothers. I
> hadn't realized that he was working on that and I was really
> astonished at the humanity of his description of Kansas City
> and the barbershop. It reminded me of Neal Cassady's stories
> of his barbershop childhood too, which is published in *The
> First Third.* . . .
> I was also interested that Dahlberg had the same nostalgic
> recollection of orphan childhood that we all had, so I was very
> attracted to his new book and it was a humane breakthrough
> for him to break away from purely literary material back to
> the American particulars.[25]

A close friendship never developed between the kingpin of the Beat
generation and Dahlberg, the solemn purveyor of the past. The
latter recalled:

I don't dislike Allen Ginsberg, but once, when he came to see me with his catamite, the catamite looked at my books on the shelves. He screamed, "Books! Books! Books!" And then he began to scream that he hates books—he's terrified of them! [26]

A truly hilarious encounter took place between Ginsberg and Dahlberg when these two utterly different men met accidentally one day at the intersection of Eighth Street and Fifth Avenue. Ginsberg, who invited Dahlberg for lunch at Schrafft's (of all places), related:

> We had this funny conversation upstairs, in the balcony. . . . I was really curious what his opinion of *Kaddish* was; I didn't really think he'd care for it too much, but I did think he'd like its sincerity. He *did* have one very specific criticism of it, which was that the mention of my mother's asshole was "inappropriate" or "obscene" and aesthetically unnecessary. . . .
>
> But the conversation was pleasant—it wasn't accusatory; it was concerned with just what was aesthetically interesting, what was aesthetically right, what was aesthetically lasting. The phrase I used was "what was appropriate for eternal letters."
>
> But I was a little freaked out by his disapproval of *Kaddish*. [27]

But despite their different idioms, both writers were consciously (even self-consciously) "vatic" and preoccupied with the opinions of posterity. Ginsberg, however, understood that his long poem was written in one weekend and in one sitting, while Dahlberg's writing was invariably premeditated and ritualized:

> Since my principle was the first thought is the best thought, or spontaneous origination, then by aesthetic principle, I couldn't really censor it or doctor it up. . . . But that seemed to be what [Dahlberg] was proposing, so I realized that a basic aesthetic difference existed between his approach, as well as the approach of some of the other people who were interested

in the "spontaneous mind." But there *was* a common depth, because he really could deal with the same material as I did.

Ginsberg emphasized that his meetings with Dahlberg "had some influence on me in the direction of condensation, in 'cranky-succinct elegance,' in sentence style." [28] Later, Dahlberg was to declare that he had "no idea" why the Beats were interested in him, [29] though he obviously welcomed their attention as well as that of other young writers. When Elias Wilentz, founder of the Eighth Street Bookshop, assembled his anthology, *The Beat Scene,* he made no mistake in including two photographs of Edward Dahlberg engaged in animated conversations with various members of the Greenwich Village "underground." [30]

Dahlberg accepted numerous invitations to parties and informal gatherings and readings during 1958 and 1959. He met Jonathan Williams, an alumnus of Black Mountain College and owner of a small press called The Jargon Society in Penland, North Carolina. Williams grew passionately fond of Dahlberg's bravura writing style and later printed (in capital letters) some of his scoldings as postcards:

BY GOD, JONATHAN, YOU KNOW EVERYBODY. AND THAT IS WHY YOU ARE IN TROUBLE ALWAYS. IF YOU WISH TO COMPOSE A TRUTHFUL POEM YOU WILL HAVE TO ACQUIRE A FINE AND SOLID SODALITY OF ENEMIES. . . . INVOLUNTARILY I LIVE LIKE AN EREMITE. WHOM CAN I TALK TO BESIDES A WISE BOOK? HAVE NO DOUBT ABOUT IT, I ENJOY CHATTERING AS MUCH AS THE NEXT FOOL, BUT WHEN I WISH TO ASCEND THE CORDILLERAS WHO IS THERE TO ACCOMPANY ME? EACH MAN MUST GO ALONE TO HIS WRITING, TO HIS ADAGES, AND TO HIS GRAVE.

They were finally thrown together at a party at the Downtown Gallery:

We ended up that afternoon eating at a delicatessen and going to see some ladies that Irving Rosenthal knew who ran the First Zen Institute of Atlantic City, New Jersey. Edward got very furious at them, "those icy, cold-hearted females."

They were putting him down and he came back in his usual, furious way.[31]

The friendship grew to the point where a decade later, Williams felt impelled to organize a collection of essays, poems, and tributes as a *Festschrift*, "For Edward Dahlberg." [32] Ironically, this volume of encomia virtually ended their friendship:

> As I recall his answer when I asked him if he liked it at all: "Oh, yes, it has quite larded my fame." Thanks a lot, Edward. . . . "Never chide a friend," says our author. His whole life has been spent inexorably abusing everyone in sight. It's very sad, but I've had enough of it. Olson felt that way, Herbert Read did. I'm very slow, being a southerner.[33]

Joel Oppenheimer, a former classmate of Williams's at Black Mountain, [34] had read *The Flea of Sodom* and *Do These Bones Live* in a poetry workshop run by Charles Olson in the early 1950s. Oppenheimer, who was immediately taken with "Dahlberg's nutty ferocity with the language," exclaimed that in his circle, *"The Sorrows of Priapus* and *The Flea of Sodom* were the type of thing hip young students and intellectuals would pick up." Oppenheimer introduced Dahlberg at the old Cedar Tavern on University Place near Eighth Street, which, before it was demolished in the late 1950s, was the most popular watering hole for Greenwich Village artists and writers. Though a nondrinker himself, Dahlberg was no stranger at the bar:

> Edward walked up to me one night in the "Cedars" and said, "Joel, why are you standing here drinking?" I said, "Well, getting high, heh, heh, heh."
> He then continued, "Joel, I have read your poems. I find them to have admirable substance for a man so young. I feel that with proper labor and attention to your art, you could conceivably compose a line worth something to the world. But you must not spend your time carousing! Ben Jonson studied Greek and Latin!"

I said, "Edward! Ben Jonson got drunk every night of his life in the Mermaid Tavern!"

He shouted, "Ben Jonson never drank!" and stomped out.[35]

At times, Dahlberg found himself the butt of ridicule among the lusty young writers. Gilbert Sorrentino recalled one poignant winter evening around 1958:

> Edward was really remarkable that night. He could have "wasted" us all. We had met him in the Cedar bar this particular night when he was very lonely. Nobody had any money, as usual. Then we went to my home. I was living in Brooklyn, and it was a long trip, one and a half hours by train and bus. Fee Dawson was with us and Max Finstein. We were all very young and knew everything, so we were patronizing him.
>
> I remember that Edward delivered a long harangue about writers who drink never being able to do anything because alcohol destroys your brain. I was putting him down, but later we learned that Edward didn't approve of *any* writer who drank, so I suppose it made sense to him. . . .
>
> All there was to eat was soup—bean soup. He ate his bean soup, then he had to eat a couple of tablespoons full of a jelly-like liquid like Maalox. We realized that we had given him something that was going to be death to his stomach. But he was really terrific—he didn't say anything about it. He ate and later praised the food.
>
> Then he began to talk about the old days. Max and I asked him if he knew an old song, "Hello Central, Give me No-Man's Land." I don't know where we got this title, and we didn't even know if the title was real, but Edward began to sing it in a wonderful old-timey music hall tenor. We laughed to hide our shame at having thought to bait him.[36]

Despite his loneliness and financial worries, Dahlberg worked fitfully on his autobiographical fiction. Sections of *Because I Was Flesh* continued to appear in *Big Table*, which had been judged "serious literature" and cleared of obscenity by the same judge,

Julius J. Hoffman, who ten years later presided at the Chicago Seven trial. By the time the last issue was hastily assembled, Dahlberg's contribution was full of digressions and showed little evidence of thoughtful editing. Only three paragraphs from this issue were eventually incorporated into the final text of *Because I Was Flesh*.[37] Financial troubles then caused this remarkable little magazine to fold.

When Rlene returned from Santa Monica in February 1959, she learned that Stanley Burnshaw, who had been making numerous editorial suggestions about the manuscript of *Because I Was Flesh*, had arranged for Dahlberg to receive a much-needed fee for giving a lecture at New York University. She suggested, "Why don't you speak on something that you can say 'Yea' to, instead of attacking? Why don't you go back to Melville?"[38] With characteristic perversity, however, he prepared a bitter attack which was aimed directly at Melville and indirectly at Olson and Rlene. At this time he had not seen or spoken to Olson since 1954, when they had quarreled over a sardonic "portrait" of Olson that Dahlberg had written to Creeley.[39]

The lecture was reworked and printed in the *Literary Review* under the title, "Moby-Dick: An Hamitic Dream."[40] As ever an ardent advocate of Melville's, Rlene undertook her customary editorial duties with great reluctance now. Melville had always been a crucial figure in her relationship with her husband; it was Melville's writings that had brought them together and Rlene fully expected Edward to don the Melvillean mantle, though not by displacing him with this vitriolic, often pointless attack. With a slap at Olson, Dahlberg dismisses *Moby Dick* as "a verbose tractarian fable,"[41] after he opens the essay by announcing: "I have changed my mind about Herman Melville, for I once loved this Cyclops whose father is Oceanus."[42]

Some of Dahlberg's indictments, couched in a less spiteful essay, would seem just. He emphasizes and reemphasizes the book's ponderous length. He suggests that "Melville seems to have taken revenge against the characters in his book as a reprisal for his own solitude" (p. 120), though Dahlberg seems here to be projecting his own dilemma onto the man he is attacking. Similarly, he begs the question that "none can misdoubt Melville's misogyny" by adding the fanciful and unelaborated theorem that "The hatred of women is the pederastic nausea that comes from the mention of the womb" (p. 133). This statement would seem to reveal more about Dahlberg's compulsive interest in homosexuality than it does about Melville.

Dahlberg, the advocate of convoluted and self-conscious prose, then criticizes *Moby-Dick* as "a rabble of words which could not have been excreted without much travail. Moreover, does one go to a novel to apprentice oneself to a mariner?" [43] He eventually recommends that the reader abandon Melville altogether and turn his attention more profitably to such authors as Rabelais, Purchas, Seneca, and St. Paul. Melville, he alleges, was unable to comprehend St. Paul, since "Melville himself was the prey of corrosive acedy. The work of the moth and rust had deprived him of energy, without which morality is a basilisk." [44]

Even if one can submit to the notion that the "weakness" in Melville's work derives from his "velleity" and his latent homosexuality, Dahlberg's pointless (if typical) attacks on homosexuals do not aid the argument: "There is now a pederastic hagiography composed of people who prefer the bad to the good, who like excrements instead of pond-apples, and who choose men rather than women to be their paramours" (p. 142). Extravagant, too, is the statement that Melville committed mental sodomy "with a beast of the deep" (p. 139). Though Dahlberg may be aping Melville's own dark humor in this assertion, he doggedly overlooks the "wicked" comedy of Melville's mariners: "Whose gorge is not qualmish as he witnesses Stubb eating his 'spermacetti supper' as thousands on thousands of sharks are swarming around the dead whale roped to the Pequod?" (p. 132). Dahlberg counters Melville's "crudity" with sentimental bombast on the fair sex: "Woman is still the imperial booty of the races, and men will sack towns, capture cities to furnish their courtesans with money to purchase cosmetics and soap, or rape the Sabine virgins when they cannot obtain wives otherwise" (pp. 134-35). He is steadfast in his central assertion that Melville "failed" in his art because his misogyny blocked him from understanding passion: "A good sentence or emotion in *Moby-Dick* will come as dear as the cost of dove's dung at the time of the famine in Samaria" (p. 131).

The Dahlbergs quarreled bitterly and for years over this essay and Dahlberg's repudiation of Melville. The turning point in their marriage had been reached in 1958, but despite their differences they sailed together for Mallorca on June 4. Dahlberg had been invited by the School of Continuing Education at New York University to teach literature courses in the fall, [45] so they were not overly disappointed when they found *Ca'n Peretons* still not ready and had to lodge at the Hotel El Guía in Sóller.[46] They absorbed themselves in selecting furniture, "all antique, tables from Aragon, Catalan [sic], Extremadura, and Madrid, Castile, all your Spanish earth." [47]

It also seemed a sensible time to begin acquiring some friends in the Sóller Valley, since the trip across the "Coll," the treacherous mountain pass to Palma, was one that Dahlberg detested. In a letter to William Carlos Williams, Dahlberg speaks of having met two brothers, "One ninety-one and the other eighty-five, retired English businessmen who had more sense and judgment than the bogus youths of the present day":

> They had lived in India, South Africa; the older had spent seventeen years in Russia and has met Tolstoi in Moscow. What a celestial privilege. He has the most genial face, with faculties altogether vibrant and clear. . . .
>
> Thirty-three years ago the older brother had bought a simple peasant house for less than five hundred dollars, which included a marvellous orchard of lemon and orange trees and a profusion of flowers that could have drawn envy from Adam before being lubricious or discontented.[48]

This letter was written in 1958; by 1959, the older brother, named Don Carlos Rober, had been widowed, and the younger man, incongruously nicknamed "Dolly," was due to inherit his riches. Carlos had acquired a young Irish nurse named Julia Lawlor, who daily visited his house, one of the most beautiful in the Valley of Biniaraitx, a medieval hamlet in the hills above Sóller. Don Carlos, whom Dahlberg called "Charlie," was inordinately fond of buckwheat pancakes, which were unavailable on Mallorca, so the Dahlbergs made a point of bringing him an ample supply of mix every time they came from the United States.

Not long after she assumed custody of Don Carlos, Miss Lawlor astonished and shocked the entire Sóller community by becoming engaged to this man fifty-seven years her senior. She was to inherit his property in return for nursing him to the end of his days.

Rlene quickly became friendly with the effervescent young woman with her ribald Irish humor, and the two often seized the opportunity to escape their respective charges by drinking at the Bar Molino in the outskirts of Sóller. Eventually, Rlene brought Miss Lawlor to meet her husband, who was also charmed by the earthy young lady.[49]

Dahlberg was eager to meet Julia Lawlor again when he and Rlene returned to Mallorca in the summer of 1960 to assume permanent residence in their house. By this time, Don Carlos's relatives, who resented Miss Lawlor's being the sole heir to the old man's property, had taken legal action against her, thwarted the wedding plans, and evicted her from the house. She gladly accepted the refuge offered by the Dahlbergs.

It did not take long for Dahlberg to earn a reputation in the vicinity of Sóller as "the crazy American." Since he was always "forgetting" to pay bills, he quickly alienated the druggist, whose services he constantly required, as well as the doctor and the mechanic who serviced Miss Lawlor's aging Austin automobile. Don Tomás became an enemy after Dahlberg wrongly imagined he had paid the lawyer for the previous year's services. Dahlberg took to calling him a thief and a liar and following him around town shouting insults after him. "That was the end of our dealings with Don Tomás." [50]

Dahlberg finally succeeded in isolating himself from his Sóllerense neighbors in a most exotic way. This was possibly only because he thoroughly failed to comprehend the nature of Mallorquín civilization. Fearful of intruders, he contracted with a local builder to construct thirteen-foot-high stone walls around his property and have broken glass imbedded around the top of them. A massive iron gate, decorated with a spear motif, was placed at the entrance. Dahlberg insisted that the walls be of "authentic" Moorish stone, though it is unlikely that the builder bothered to find enough (if any) such stones for this enormous project. Quite predictably, Dahlberg exploded when the contractor presented his bill, which was for more than the renovation of the entire house, but the charges were for antique stones and workmen's wages, which had nearly tripled in the previous few years.[51]

The Mallorquíns fiercely resented this grotesque wall with its jagged fringe of broken glass. Nothing else like it existed anywhere on the island. Robert Goulet, a French-Canadian author residing in Fornalutx (another hamlet above Sóller), noted that the Sóllerenses considered Dahlberg's wall a personal attack on themselves, an indictment implying "You will come and steal my things." Goulet explained that Arabic custom, handed down from antiquity and incorporated in Article 14 of the Spanish Constitution, makes it certain that "a Mallorquín will not enter and will not steal. This is something that is sacred to them." [52] Even today, Mallorquíns are impeccably honest and the island is virtually crime-free save for petty larceny perpetrated mostly by tourists. So offended were Dahlberg's neighbors that they attempted one night to destroy the glass and haul down the walls. But Rlene, well aware of her husband's talent for driving guests away, wondered ironically if the wall hadn't really been intended to keep people *in*. [53] Dahlberg's gardener, Gori, a native Sóllerense, suggested that El Señor install a watchtower with machine guns at each of the four corners of his enclave. He made Dahlberg half believe that when it rained *Ca'n Peretons* would become the biggest *estanque* (irrigation reservoir) in Sóller. [54] A knotty complication arose when it was discovered that the wall had illegally blocked an ancient right-of-way, which was used only once or twice a year when the *torrentes* (Moorish-built drainage ditches) overflowed. Again his neighbors were up in arms, and Dahlberg had to settle their claim. [55] The costly settlement involved building another road around the wall up to the main thoroughfare.

Dahlberg soon found that he was no longer welcome at his favorite outdoor tavern the Club Náutico at the Playa de Sóller. Eventually, nobody on the hospitable island would even greet him on the street. [56] He was no doubt mindful of his ostracism when he wrote to Allen Tate from Sóller: "My good publisher, James Laughlin, does not want me to live in the States; he fears that every time I meet a simpleton I shall have one reader less." [57] For many years, Dahlberg planned some literary "revenge" on his "arid" neighbors, but only in 1976, with the publication of his very slight satire, *The Olive of Minerva,* [58] did he succeed. Sóller becomes "No Hay Nada" ("There Is Nothing," the postman's daily reply to Dahlberg's frequent requests for mail); Gori retains his own name; the doctor becomes "El Médico Muchas Pesetas"; while Don

Tomás is repulsively depicted as Don Barolomé, "gorbellied, squab, with patches of Tyrian purple on both chaps":

> Bartolomé blew out his breath of the jakes, and two Major-cans hastily departed. In great amaze Don Bartolomé smelled himself, then bit his foul beblubbered lips, and wondered why one odor is worse than another, and if a man gave out an evil scent, was he immoral or helpless. (p. 10)

Don Pablo Williams and Dolly Patch are the hardly disguised Rober brothers, but the most wicked portrait in this confusing book (which spares no one, including "Abel"—Dahlberg himself) is that of "the newly arrived alleged virgin, Lais O'Shea"—Julia Lawlor, who by 1976 had become the seventh Mrs. Dahlberg:

> Unlike Janus's door, Lais is never shut. She has a most hospitable vulva. Take care, lest she be infected as the woman of the Moabites.... She's the water closet deity of love, Astarte, the fornicatress. If you stink, you're her paramour. A wheel because it rolls might also arouse her. Though she's not wed, she's already provided Pablo with the bitter aloes of cuckoldry. (p. 106)

Despite his problems in the community, Dahlberg settled into temporary satisfaction with his enclave and the lush orchard that had grown at *Ca'n Peretons* (the name, "house of the little walls," seemed rather inappropriate now). He had two women to attend him, and his publication prospects were brighter than ever before in his life. Lawrence Ferlinghetti, seeing *Bottom Dogs* as "an important landmark in realist proletarian naturalism which runs through American literature from James T. Farrell to Jack Kerouac . . . a pre-Beat ON THE ROAD," [59] agreed to reissue the book under the imprint of his City Lights Books. To save Dahlberg from being "embarrassed" by his earlier style, he was allowed to write an introduction to his first novel, denouncing its "rough bleak idiom":

> Why write savage, loveless books with the vulgar obscenities of the street arab. We have been so determined to destroy the Puritan lechers and all the sexual mania of the social

reformers that we find it essential to spew forth every vice in human skin and in words dirtier than Job's muckheap. (p. v.)

Aware that Dahlberg's stock was on the rise, James Laughlin offered to print a second edition of *Do These Bones Live.* A young protégé of Ben Shahn's, James Kearns, was engaged to illustrate the book in order to boost its sales. Dahlberg seized the opportunity of replacing the embarrassing "Do" in the title with "Can"; but the book became an unexpectedly onerous task for Robert MacGregor and Rlene after Dahlberg insisted on numerous minor revisions in phraseology through the text. These "improvements" did little to enhance the orginal book, [60] and for the most part, the two texts are identical.

A number of periodicals were opening their pages to Dahlberg. Early versions of chapters 4 or 5 of *Because I Was Flesh* appeared in *Sewannee Review.*[61] *Yugen,* the small avant-garde magazine edited by LeRoi Jones, accepted a strident essay called "On Passions and Asceticism," in which Dahlberg excoriated sensuality and human nature even more harshly than in *The Sorrows:* "More towns and cities are destroyed by sexual disorders than by plagues, famine, and disease. Unless men follow some discipline they are demented from birth until their demise." One of Dahlberg's standard themes ("It takes many years to learn nothing"), a mainstay of his forthcoming autobiography, also appeared in the essay: "Vice is constant and ripens with old age; old mulled sins are the worst, and he who has never shed the leaves of his youth is always stupid." [62]

By September 6, 1960, [63] when the Dahlbergs returned with Julia Lawlor to the Horatio Street apartment for presumably the last time, Miss Lawlor had assumed most of the wifely and domestic duties in the household, while Rlene devoted herself almost exclusively to her husband's correspondence, bookkeeping, and editorial work on *Because I Was Flesh.* She shared this last chore with Stanley Burnshaw [64] and with James Laughlin, who, though convinced that the book was a masterpiece, had made no final commitment to publish it. It was Laughlin who tenaciously streamlined the book and excised many of Dahlberg's favorite, though extraneous, satirical pieces, such as "The Tailor's Daughter," which was later included in *The Confessions of Edward*

Dahlberg.[65] Although this piece is one of Dahlberg's most hilarious travesties, it is a trivial, wholly fictional incident, [66] which is inconsistent with the tone of *Because I Was Flesh.* The young, vagrant Dahlberg is courting "Mary," the daughter of a Los Angeles tailor, who tried, to no avail, to discourage the articulate though penniless young scholar. The would-be Oscar Wilde archly defends himself:

> "Where did you find this urchin?" the tailor demanded of his daughter. "Are you a ragpicker? He says he lives by himself. What frightful company he keeps. I'm not a pitiless man, but how much sympathy can one have without dying of it?"
>
> "Sir," I protested, "I'm in the lost and found department, since no one has ever claimed me. Hear me, I belong to the prophetic hosts of outcast Ishmaels."

The tailor investigates Dahlberg's tangible assets:

> "What have you to offer my Mary?"
>
> "Nothing, sir."
>
> "Is that a bargain or an inheritance? Are you laughing at me? Who can afford to possess Nothing?"
>
> "The Truth," I replied. . . .
>
> The Tailor's chaps glowed. "As patient as I am, I am compelled to repeat: What are your prospects?"
>
> "My present condition may be better than my future which might be worse. Even a pessimistic outlook decays."
>
> The tailor groaned. "I need a headache powder," he pleaded. "Mary, an aspirin."

In the end, Dahlberg vanquishes the tailor but loses the daughter: "Tailor," I cried, "you've won your small triumph, but there are no victories. My desolation is potable as muscadine" *(Confessions,* pp. 95-99).

Another section, intended to satirize Dahlberg's neighbors in Wellfleet, Massachusetts (see Chapter V), was also deleted. While it would have been a distraction in *Because I Was Flesh,* by itself it is a delightful spoof of cat lovers and predacious old maids:

"Cats are really philosophers," she goes on. "I have heard the ancient Chinese told time by looking into their eyes. One veterinary, of more repute than my spiritualist or Plato, told me she had a venereal disease. I assured him she had been altered, but he said a cat can get the pox from—I beg to apologize for my English—snuffing up the anus of a stray who has no shelter but an alley, or from eating garbage in our hygienic gutters, and even—O Lord, heal my mouth—syphilis if I take her out for the air. Dolly does pass water often, and I suspect she has heart trouble, or is suffering from the stone."

When this crumpled udder takes Dolly for a walk she prays she'll meet a man who does his own cooking and darns his socks and who'll stop to caress her companion. Should nothing come of this, wearing the same deceased dress and withered felt hat she visits her faith healer. (p. 71)

Dahlberg, meanwhile, busied himself with his last semester of teaching at New York University. Professor Warren Bower, head of the School of Continuing Education, remembered that Dahlberg was a "thorny" individual, although a fascinating one. For once, Dahlberg was not informed that he would be happier elsewhere— he was invited to continue offering his course, "Reading for Pleasure," but he abandoned it.[67]

Truth Is More Sacred, an exchange of letters between Dahlberg and Sir Herbert Read, was published almost unnoticed by Horizon Press in April 1961, even though the publishers, anticipating controversy over this strange and highly contentious series of epistolary essays, advertised it as "an event of the highest order." But Dahlberg had not expected a rash of blistering reviews, mostly directed at himself. The most virulent of these was written by Dahlberg's old enemy, Granville Hicks, who blasted Dahlberg for his "violence of temper not often matched in the history of criticism." Hicks praised Sir Herbert for his patience, as well as his gentle, discriminating, and persuasive rebuttals of Dahlberg's attacks. Dahlberg's intolerance of his contemporaries is ascribed to jealousy, "as if Joyce, Lawrence, James, Eliot, and Pound had done him some harm. And perhaps they have, just by being what they are, which is so much more than he could ever be." [68] Hicks, who had not seen Dahlberg for twenty-five years, was not aware that the former curmudgeon of the Communist party now considered himself the greatest prose stylist of this century—a boast which he was constantly reiterating to friends. Certainly, no writer, including the "gentle Sir Herbert" (as Dahlberg referred to him), could hope to win an argument with a man self-elevated to such a position. For it is all too apparent that, as in "Moby-Dick: An Hamitic Dream," Dahlberg was not discussing literature in *Truth Is More Sacred*, but merely defending his own ego as he ground out unfounded charges of plagiarism against Graves (p. 155), "ignorance" and "pornography" against Joyce (p. 34), "scatology" against Kafka (p. 47), "servility" against Pound (p. 126), and against the bulk of the literature of the New World as "inhuman."

Read's responses grew increasingly more exasperated as he labored without success to win his opponent back to "objectivity." His frustration gave way to bewilderment as he paused to wonder why, indeed, he was enmeshed in this wearing controversy: "What is my role in this exchange of letters? To be *advocatus diaboli*, and to find some few virtues, some extenuating circumstances, to throw into the scales you have so heavily weighted with your wrath?" (p. 57).

Read's amicability and generosity are almost legendary among those who had been his friends. "He was the most gentle man I have ever known," wrote Graham Greene in a recent article.[69] Ben Raeburn, who suggested the title "Truth Is More Sacred" (from Plato's "Truth is more sacred than friendship"), recalled that Sir Herbert valued his knighthood because "it has only one virtue: it makes it mandatory for all your acquaintances to call you by your first name." [70] His benevolence, however, often damaged the effectiveness of his arguments in *Truth Is More Sacred*, since he was saddled with the uncomfortable task of defending many writers who had been his close friends. While eloquent, his apologies seem politically motivated and often facile. Invariably, he blamed our "barbarous" civilization for many "defects" in modern writing which Dahlberg attributed to the writers themselves.

The controversy strained, but did not terminate, the friendship between Read and Dahlberg, who wrote to Stanley Burnshaw:

It was my duty, and is, to sweep the dung out of the Augean stables of literature, and that is what I did. What did Read do? Instead of saying even a word or two what Graves was, or in place of not bothering altogether, he praised him! Why? The answer is simple; Read is a very timorous man, and he has a reputation to protect, lectures at sundry colleges, a position as one of the directors of Routledge although they will not allow him to select one book a year that he believes is worth a reader's good and honest eyes.[71]

Dahlberg later claimed he "broke off relations with Herbert Read, until Laughlin at New Directions told me that Herbert was sorely grieved, and that I should write to him, which I did, and continued to do until his last, few tormenting days." [72] But clearly, Read set himself a hopeless task in trying to contend with Dahlberg, whose dominant passion, according to Ben Raeburn, was his "raging desire for fame. ... If you were to say to him, 'Edward, you're the best writer since Homer,' do you think he'd ask you why you thought so?" [73]

It should be added that few people who knew both men have comprehended the friendship between them. One of Read's sons wrote:

Why did my father put up with Dahlberg for so long? I don't know; it must be something to do with ... my father's personality. There are a number of friendships that came to grief, but not a lot. And I think he was generally patient and generous towards those whose talent, whether major or minor, he respected, even where the style of expression of this talent differed from his own personal tendencies.[74]

George Woodcock, Read's biographer, commented:

I find it hard to say anything about Dahlberg, since I have not Herbert's gift of patience, and the reading of Dahlberg which I did while I was preparing my book left me with the sense of a being ponderously and malevolently active yet essentially heavy and dull—something like a rogue elephant. I suppose he is a kind of caviar—if one can mix metaphors so atrociously—but I prefer my caviar pure Caspian.[75]

Although a semblance of goodwill was restored between Read and Dahlberg, the latter nursed his grudges and exacted incredibly vicious revenge. In the autumn of 1967, Read's younger son, Piers Paul, took a course under Dahlberg at Columbia University's School of Creative Writing. Sir Herbert was by that time dying of cancer. Young Read wrote:

My misgivings about Dahlberg as a teacher were amply fulfilled. He had a bullying manner and a total intolerance of any writing but his own. He had read my first novel, GAME IN HEAVEN WITH TUSSY MARX, which had already been published by this time and rejected it as worthless in front of the class. I think by this time he was offended because I had not called him. This was a case of misplaced diffidence on my part: I had not wished to push myself into a friendship with my professor just because he was a friend of my father's, but he took this as coldness. We more or less made up the quarrel—my wife and I had a pleasant dinner at his apartment—and it was more because of his manner and attitude that I "passively resisted" his lessons. He was not, however, a man to be ignored and he continued to bully me—saying, at one time, in front of the class, that I was responsible for my father's cancer because I had been married in Strassbourg!—until such a time that I so dreaded the classes that I ceased going to them.[76]

Dahlberg eventually assigned a grade of F to the young man after he led a successful campaign to have Dahlberg fired.[77] Piers Paul emphasized that one of his father's chief worries while he was dying in the summer of 1968 "was that my mother and the rest of his family should somehow prevent him from seeing Dahlberg who was then due in England. He died before Dahlberg arrived." Dahlberg reacted with only mild interest when notified of his old friend's passing.[78]

At the end of 1962, James Laughlin was still holding the manuscripts of Dahlberg's autobiography when he finally made a firm commitment to publish *Because I Was Flesh,* "first volume," [79] as Dahlberg described it, since he was projecting several volumes of his life story. The National Institute of Arts and Letters was sufficiently impressed with the published portions of the book to grant him $4,000 to continue his work. Laughlin was no less enthusiastic. He undertook much of the editing himself, a job which consumed much of his time for nearly two years.[80]

Beginning in 1961, Dahlberg managed to remain on Mallorca almost steadily for three years while the work on his masterpiece proceeded. He accumulated, from the time of its inception until its completion, 1,216 pages of "draft material and notes." [81] From 1962 until 1964, when unbound galleys were printed, he hardly ever examined revisions or editorial comments on his manuscripts. Since Laughlin was well aware of Dahlberg's intractability, he corresponded weekly with Rlene about details concerning wording and punctuation and minor problems of reorganization.[82] Rlene was fearful that Dahlberg would accuse her, as he often did, of claiming authorship of his books. Thus, she limited her editorial work to "juggling" certain passages in order to preserve the chronological sequence in the autobiography. She also learned to write transition sentences in Dahlberg's style after she noticed that many of the paragraphs did not flow together. But she insists that she never wrote or rewrote any of his essential lines.[83] Occasional suggestions were referred to Dahlberg, who was usually irate over what he thought was New Directions' conspiracy to "dismember" his book. But Laughlin was able to make his will prevail by gently reminding the author that he had given Rlene and the other editors considerable latitude in making corrections.[84] Dahlberg's impatience was caused in part by his anxiety to have the book published in the spring of 1963, before his sixty-third birthday.[85] Unfortunately, he still failed, after having seen nine books of his published, to appreciate how publishing schedules almost always go awry.

Dahlberg's paranoia added to his impatience. He suspected that Laughlin "has had all sorts of people ransacking the memoir, and each one has a new suggestion." [86] Laughlin had in fact shown the manuscript to Hayden Carruth, who had made numerous minor suggestions, [87] and to Stanley Burnshaw, [88] about whom Dahlberg

complained for no obvious reason. But Laughlin's tactful suggestions were eventually accepted; the editor pointed out that in
many places Dahlberg's story did not "follow" correctly—his
chronology was illogical, or mysterious characters made their
debuts at inappropriate moments. Dahlberg confused pronouns so
that the reader could not keep track of Lizzie's many suitors, who
would also crop up at unlikely and illogical points in the story.
Laughlin suggested the elimination of several "admirers" to relieve
redundancies in the plot.[89] Dahlberg was finally quite amenable to
his editors' suggestions, although he complained perfunctorily to
Allen Tate:

> I am having my woes with my good publisher, James
> Laughlin, who insists the punctuation should be altered in
> some places, and that the reader is not sure of the identities of
> the mother's suitors. She lived to be about 73, and in that
> thwarted and tragic part of her life she had about five to six
> men who were interested in her. How anybody could confuse
> them or imagine that the first or the second was the last, I
> don't know.

Dahlberg quickly added, however, that "There is no controversy
between Laughlin and myself; he is doing his utmost to make a
book perfect."[90] It is an amazing fact about Dahlberg that he
never actually gave any of his editors much trouble. Edwin Seaver,
for example, was permitted to excise enormous passages from
Epitaphs for Our Times and *The Confessions of Edward Dahlberg*.
Similarly, Ben Raeburn of Horizon Press and Walter Arnold,
Dahlberg's editor at E. P. Dutton & Company, both found him
uncommonly amenable to their suggestions.[91]

Dahlberg's impatience with Laughlin was aggravated by his
growing disenchantment with his island paradise. Rlene, who was
holding down three jobs in the United States,[92] visited Mallorca
only intermittently; and Dahlberg, who had never learned to drive,
was dependent on Julia and her troublesome Austin for transporta-
tion. He was welcome virtually nowhere in the area. His few
tentative attempts at learning Spanish had come to naught, and
his English-speaking neighbors shunned him. His own desolation

was projected onto his surroundings in a pathetic letter begging Josephine Herbst and her friend, Jean Garrigue, to visit him in Sóller:

> There are no people except ourselves, and we are disappearing; we are in a peopleless wilderness, and Hagar could not have been more solitary or thirsty for the angelic fountains of perception than we are. Would to heaven, not caring a mite for that region, that I could say there is one human being in Soller who has reached beyond mammon, comfort, or greedy ambition. There are the usual arts and letters tramps in Soller; I know a couple of translators in Palma [the Kerrigans] who should translate themselves into some other shape.[94]

Garrigue and Herbst never arrived, nor did James Laughlin, who had promised repeatedly to visit the house "a half a kilometer después de la Bar Frontera."[94] Laughlin had the chore of giving Dahlberg the news that neither Routledge nor Faber & Faber could be convinced to bring out an English edition of *Because I Was Flesh*. Attacking what he considered T. S. Eliot's stranglehold on Faber (Eliot was a senior editor there), Dahlberg inveighed: "I would not change one word to please Eliot or his anthill scribbler, Pound."[95]

Boredom and anxiety on Mallorca had taken their toll on Dahlberg by the spring of 1963. He wrote to Josephine Herbst on May 24: "I had a stomach hemorrhage, and high blood pressure, which affected my eyesight. I had five blood transfusions, and can now read a little, but am feeble and useless."[96] At this same time, however, he unexpectedly enjoyed the largest financial windfall of his life. Rlene was dispatched to her parents' home in Michigan to gather and organize his papers and notes,[97] after Dahlberg learned that the University of Texas had offered to buy his literary archives. He received for his papers $20,000 (minus a commission to the agent), which was, ironically, more than three times what he had ever earned from his published works.

The year 1964 was promising to be the most auspicious year in Dahlberg's life when Rlene arrived back on Mallorca late in February.[98] An advance edition of *Because I Was Flesh* was circulated in paperback that same month, and the hardbound edition followed on March 16, 1964. Methuen & Company, a smaller press than Dahlberg had hoped for, agreed to produce the book in England, but a second printing of the American edition was demanded almost immediately after the first quickly sold out. Dahlberg enjoyed still another boon when Allen Tate arranged the publication of a collection of Dahlberg's essays, *Alms for Oblivion.*[99] Nearly in the sixty-fifth year of his life, Dahlberg finally had belated recognition and money to indulge his lifelong penchant for wandering.

NOTES

1. Interview: Robert MacGregor, Sept. 4, 1973.
2. Interview: Rlene Dahlberg, July 24, 1973.
3. Interview: Rlene Dahlberg, July 24, 1973.
4. Interview: Rlene Dahlberg, April 13, 1973.
5. Interview: E. D., Feb. 15, 1974.
6. (New York: Weybright & Talley, 1968).
7. *The Nation* (Jan. 11, 1958), 37.
8. "Against Nature," *Poetry,* 87 (April 1958), 55-58.
9. *Sewannee Review,* 66 (Spring 1958), 315-18.
10. Interview: Rlene Dahlberg, July 24, 1973.
11. Interview: Anthony Kerrigan, July 30, 1972.
12. Dahlberg makes no mention of any trouble in a letter, dated September 20, 1958, to William Carlos Williams: "I am told by a dear friend in Paris, who is married to Henri Matisse's daughter, that France today is ruled by the gendarme and the concierge" *(Epitaphs,* p. 182).
13. Interview: Anthony Kerrigan, July 16, 1973.
14. Interview: Rlene Dahlberg, Sept. 8, 1973.
15. "South of France—North of Spain, April-May, 1958," *At the Front Door of the Atlantic* (Dublin: Dolmen Press, 1969), p. 25.
16. Interviews: Anthony Kerrigan, July 29, 1972; Elaine Kerrigan, July 29, 1973.
17. Interview: Rlene Dahlberg, Sept, 1973.
18. Interviews: Rlene Dahlberg, Sept. 8, 1973; E. D., Aug. 17, 1972.
19. Interview: E. D., Nov. 5, 1972.
20. Letter: Irving Rosenthal, Nov. 15, 1972.
21. The other three were Stanley Burnshaw, James Laughlin, and Rlene Dahlberg.
22. Letter: Irving Rosenthal, Nov. 15, 1972. Rosenthal had by this time turned over the editorship of *Big Table* to Paul Carroll.
23. *Big Table 2* (Summer 1959), 71.

24. *Because I Was Flesh* (New York: New Directions, 1964), p. 1.
25. Interview: Allen Ginsberg, Oct. 7, 1972.
26. Interview: E. D., Dec. 29, 1972.
27. Interview: Allen Ginsberg, Oct. 7, 1972.
28. Interview: Allen Ginsberg, Oct. 7, 1972.
29. Interview: E. D., Aug. 17, 1972.
30. Interview: Jonathan Williams, Feb. 24, 1974.
31. Interview: Jonathan Williams, Feb. 24, 1974.
32. *TriQuarterly,* 19 (Fall 1970).
33. Letter: Jonathan Williams, Feb. 24, 1973.
34. Neither Oppenheimer nor Williams was at the college during Dahlberg's brief tenure there.
35. Interview: Joel Oppenheimer, Aug. 29, 1972.
36. Interview: Gilbert Sorrentino, Sept. 27, 1972.
37. *Big Table 5* (1960), 23-30.
38. Interview: Rlene Dahlberg, Jan. 13, 1973.
39. Letter: John Cech, July 13, 1973.
40. (Autumn 1960), 87-118.
41. "Moby-Dick: An Hamitic Dream," *Alms for Oblivion,* p. 119.
42. Ibid., p. 120. Dahlberg often referred to Olson as a "Cyclops."
43. *Literary Review,* 4 (Autumn 1960), 99-100. This passage was deleted from the version published in *Alms for Oblivion.*
44. *Alms for Oblivion,* p. 137.
45. Letter: Joseph A. Byrnes, Assistant Secretary of the University, July 2, 1973.
46. Interview: Rlene Dahlberg, July 24, 1973.
47. Letter to Josephine Herbst, Aug. 18, 1960, *Epitaphs,* p. 158.
48. Letter: July 1, 1958, *Epitaphs,* p. 202.
49. Interview: Rlene Dahlberg, Aug. 9, 1973.
50. Interviews: Rlene Dahlberg, Aug. 9, 1973; Robert Goulet, Aug. 9, 1973.
51. Interview: Rlene Dahlberg, July 24, 1973.
52. Interview: Robert Goulet, Aug. 9, 1973.
53. Interview: Rlene Dahlberg, July 24, 1974.
54. Interview: Gregorio ("Gori") Duran, Aug. 12, 1973.
55. Letter: E. D. to Allen Tate, Oct. 8, 1962, *Epitaphs,* p. 243.
56. Interview: Robert Goulet, Aug. 9, 1973.
57. October 8, 1962. *Epitaphs,* p. 239.
58. (New York: Thomas Y. Crowell, 1976).
59. Letter: Lawrence Ferlinghetti, Aug. 15, 1972.
60. Interview: Robert MacGregor, Sept. 4, 1973.
61. 68 (Autumn 1960), 548-64.
62. *Yugen 6* (1960), 48.
63. Letter: E. D. to Josephine Herbst, Aug. 18, 1960, *Epitaphs,* p. 160.
64. Letter: Stanley Burnshaw, June 1, 1972.
65. Interview: Rlene Dahlberg, May 22, 1972. Interview: E. D., Dec. 31, 1972.
66. Interview: E. D., Dec. 31, 1972.

67. Interviews: Warren Bower, July 16, 1973, and Sept. 28, 1973; E. D., Sept. 30, 1973.
68. "Speaking of Books," *Saturday Review* (April 18, 1961), 47.
69. "Herbert Read, a Memoir," *Art News*, 73 (February 1974), 20.
70. Interview: Ben Raeburn, July 13, 1972. Mr. Raeburn is editor in chief at Horizon Press.
71. Letter: Nov. 1, 1961, *Epitaphs*, p. 276.
72. Quoted in Moramarco, p. 98.
73. Interview: Ben Raeburn, July 13, 1972.
74. Letter: Benedict Read, Sept. 25, 1972.
75. Letter: George Woodcock, Nov. 3, 1972.
76. Letter: Piers Paul Read, Dec. 15, 1972.
77. Interview: Frank MacShane, Mar. 29, 1972. Dean MacShane, who heads the School of Creative Writing at Columbia, originally hired Dahlberg.
78. Letter: Piers Paul Read, Dec. 15, 1972. Interview: Julia (Lawlor) Dahlberg, Oct. 10, 1973.
79. Letter: E. D. to Josephine Herbst, April 23, 1961, *Epitaphs*, p. 165.
80. Telephone interview: James Laughlin, Aug. 2, 1972.
81. Warren Roberts, *A Creative Century: Catalogue of an Exhibition of Twentieth Century Manuscripts at the University of Texas* (Austin: University of Texas Undergraduate Library, 1964), p. 17.
82. Interview: Rlene Dahlberg, July 24, 1973. Letter: James Laughlin to Rlene Dahlberg, Sept. 26, 1962.
83. Interview: Rlene Dahlberg, Feb. 9, 1974. Letter: James Laughlin to Rlene Dahlberg, Sept. 26, 1962.
84. Letters: James Laughlin to E. D., Sept. 17, 1962, and Oct. 17, 1962.
85. Letter: E. D. to Josephine Herbst, Dec. 19, 1962, *Epitaphs*, p. 166.
86. Letter: E. D. to Allen Tate, Oct. 8, 1962, *Epitaphs*, p. 242.
87. Letter: James Laughlin to Rlene Dahlberg, Sept. 26, 1962.
88. Letters: Stanley Burnshaw, June 1, 1972; James Laughlin to Rlene Dahlberg, Sept. 26, 1962.
89. Letter: James Laughlin to E. D., Oct. 2, 1962.
90. Letter: E. D. to Allen Tate, Oct. 8, 1962, *Epitaphs*, p. 242.
91. Interviews: Edwin Seaver, July 12, 1972; Ben Raeburn, July 13, 1973; and Walter Arnold, July 14, 1972.
92. Interview: Rlene Dahlberg, Oct. 10, 1973.
93. Letter: E. D. to Josephine Herbst, Dec. 19, 1962.
94. Letter: E. D. to Josephine Herbst, Dec. 19, 1962.
95. Letters: James Laughlin to E. D., Sept. 26, 1962; E. D. to Josephine Herbst, Dec. 19, 1962, *Epitaphs*, p. 166.
96. *Epitaphs*, pp. 168-69.
97. Letter: E. D. to Allen Tate, Oct. 8, 1962, *Epitaphs*, p. 243.
98. Letter: E. D. to Allen Tate, Feb. 3, 1964, *Epitaphs*, p. 248.
99. Letter: E. D. to Allen Tate, Feb. 24, 1964, *Epitaphs*, p. 250.

8.

Consummation

Few reviewers, not even those who were by 1964 Dahlberg's sworn enemies, shared Charles Olson's embittered opinion that *Because I Was Flesh* was a "filthy book." [1] In fact, Dahlberg received unqualified praise which he had never expected during his lifetime—the dustjacket, for example, contained tributes from Louis Untermeyer, Allen Tate, Josephine Herbst, Harry T. Moore, and Robert Creeley. The reviewers did not overlook Dahlberg's continuing preoccupation with the seamy aspects of life in this "hairy, smelly book," [2] which, through a creative miracle never before achieved by Dahlberg, transformed a "squalid quack and chinscraper" into the redemptive figure in her son's life. [3] Dahlberg redeemed *himself* as a writer, not only by producing one of the most lyric autobiographies in history, but by finally achieving a degree of modesty (absent in *Bottom Dogs,* for example) which enabled him to admit that his mother's life was more interesting than his own. Of course, this claim is debatable.

Certainly, the most abrasive elements that often marred Dahlberg's style ("I completely rewrite; I don't risk a page or a line without consulting the masters" [4]), and especially the overuse of quotations, are never obtrusive in this highly polished book. Although the heavy editing of the book contributed greatly to its perfection, the language and insights were Dahlberg's own. Those of his editors who volunteered comments (especially Irving Rosenthal and Rlene Dahlberg) insisted that their work was secondary to the final achievement. Indeed, similar efforts were lavished on the work of such writers as Mark Twain, Thomas Wolfe, and Malcolm Lowry.

The book itself, neither autobiography nor fiction, is impossible to classify. Dahlberg actually had no intention of writing a straightforward biography of himself, simply because he was committed to the notion that "the difference between art and fact is enormous. . . . Fact has to be altered and heightened by art: STYLE AND IDEAS ARE INDIVISIBLE." [5] Armed with such a philosophy, he was at liberty to reconstruct, rearrange, delete or invent the facts of his "life" according to the demands of his art without formal consideration of what other people might regard as the "facts." Thus he felt justified in telescoping or omitting fallow or embarrassing periods of his life while intensifying and expanding dynamic episodes. For example, it suited his purpose to mention only one of his wives (Winifred), who, though she is not named, is not the one (Rlene) to whom he dedicated the book.

Over the thirty-five years that intervened between the writing of *Bottom Dogs* and *Because I Was Flesh*, Dahlberg had become convinced that "mythology"—the fusing of artfully selected factual and historical material with noble language and poetic invention— was the only authentic manner of presenting a narrative: journalism and "realistic" fiction were equally worthless. He felt especially compelled to recast the oft-repeated facts of his own childhood and early manhood. Thus, when Luiga Miller (who dramatized *Because I Was Flesh* as *Mia Madre Lizzie*) suggested that his purpose in writing *Because I Was Flesh* was as a "purification" of *Bottom Dogs*, Dahlberg barked in response, "No! It is a *denunciation* of *Bottom Dogs!*" [6]

Indeed, the almost identical "factual" material common to Dahlberg's early naturalistic novel and his later masterpiece does not prevent them from being almost as different as two books can be. Arno Karlen correctly observed that the writing in both books is "artificial": *"Bottom Dogs* is a young writer's self-conscious attempt to capture regionalisms and slang popular thirty and forty years ago," while the later writing proves that Dahlberg's prose "has taken a course exactly contrary to that of his time." [7] Of course, even while he was producing his proletarian fiction and essays, Dahlberg was haunted by the elegance of his Ivy League education and the splendor and culture he had seen in Europe in the late 1920s: "Remember, I disavowed my alleged 'education' and fell into uncouth jargon." [8] In later life, he never mentioned his early work without deploring it: "Never use *Bottom Dogs* as your model. . . . I attacked the book because I felt it was my duty to younger people who wanted to be writers never to be duped by me. . . . I put sick figures of speech in *From Flushing to Calvary*, which I have never reread." Though Dahlberg had a fleeting interest in "local-color writing" during the 1950s, he felt it could not produce authenticity: "True, poverty is an inverted benison, but you *cannot* use ignominious prose to describe a squalid plight." [9] He insisted further that, for any writer, "the books are the life: don't go to the life for the books. Commonly the life of the writer teaches you nothing, as in the cases of Ruskin and Shakespeare." [10] Unlike the works of Ruskin and Shakespeare, however, Dahlberg's writing was all, in one way or another, autobiographical. But despite his selective garnering of facts, Dahlberg managed, through a highly personal tone, to reveal more of himself and his mother in *Because I Was Flesh* than in any of his earlier work.

The epigram "Nobody can endure his own happiness" summarizes the predicament of this mother, who seems, in *Because I Was Flesh*, to miss no opportunity to sabotage herself. (p. 55). We immediately learn that although Lizzie "never desired to be miserable," she was born under a bad star. Even so, it is painful for Dahlberg to ennumerate her faults, which roll forth in biblical phrases: "Would to God that my mother had not been a leaf scattered everywhere as the wind listeth. Would to heaven that I could compose a different account of her flesh. Should I seem to mock that *mater dolorosa* of rags and grief, know that all my laughter lies in her grave. *Mea culpa* is the cry of all bones" (p. 4). Though Lizzie is unquestionably the focus of this novel, the reader immediately senses that Dahlberg is exploring his own character while examining his mother's: "My mother was utterly separated from the whole race of mankind save when she was concupiscent.

This woman suffered immensely from solitude—and what eases the lonely so much as sexual pleasure?" (p. 5). Her life is blighted in her youth by a selfish brother, who callously evicts her from their household; like Dahlberg, Lizzie becomes an orphan, and, in his mind, a reluctant prostitute: "My uncle Herman, anxious to be rid of his sister, but still moved by some niggish filial feeling, came to New York to see whether he could peddle her flesh. He found a stocky fur operator [Simonowitz] who was eager to wed her. This man's only virtue is that he had no conspicuous vices" (p. 7).

In Dahlberg's mind, his mother had no choice in how she conducted her life. As always, the deterministic author insisted that "A man's character is his fate." Thus, after being attracted by a handsome "dude" near her home, Lizzie, "wholly deprived by a lubber [her husband] in bed, could not resist Saul the Barber" (p. 8). A victim of her own weakness, she unhesitatingly abandons her two sons [Morris and Michael] and flees to Boston, where she bears Edward in a charity hospital: "She gave me her father's name to hide the fact that I was as illegitimate as the pismire, the moth, or a prince" (p. 8). Dahlberg does not mention (though he in fact knew) that Saul had by this time returned to his legal wife. No mention is made of Gottdank's being legally married or of his abandoning Lizzie.

Desperate for money, she sails steerage to London where she expects to inherit a large sum from a deceased relative. Apparently she never thinks to cable the executor of the estate, for when she arrives in London, she finds that the fortune has been left to the church. Now penniless, she must scrub floors to get return passage money. In New York again, Saul suddenly materializes, and the three travel to Texas, where the tiny Polish immigrant, after learning the barber's trade, is wholly in her element: "Lizzie liked being with the public and listening to the easy drawl about the swapping of a mare or shipments of stallions, geldings, and cows to Topeka, Sedalia or St. Joseph" (p. 9). But though she mixes easily with men in business, her early experience has caused her to be contemptuous of men—especially Saul, who is able to rob her and cheat her without effort. Lizzie seems to energize herself with her hatred for Saul, while convincing herself that she will never find a man (though she goes through the motions of courtship), and that the domestic tranquility that eludes her may be gained in some manner through her illegitimate child, the only being she cares for. And so, she binds him to her and painstakingly fosters what will become his lifelong dependence on her. The child, as if intuiting what this relationship will cost him, winces and grows sick. He is unable to look at his frumpy and prematurely aged mother as they walk home every night from her barbershop. By the time the fictional Dahlberg is four years old, he cringes as she recites every night her litany of grudges against *"verdammter Saul."* This stranger becomes a monster haunting Edward's childhood. As a means of retreating from the sadness and anger which surround him, he develops psychosomatic illnesses: "He learned anatomy by being sick" (p. 49).

Lizzie, who is strongly attracted to shady dealings of all kinds, supplements her tonsorial income by practicing quack medicine and by pimping for her farm-girl barbers, "as wild as Semiramis." From them she learns a legal form of prostitution—breach-of-promise suits ("heart balm") instituted against unwitting bachelors and farmhands. Her child quickly imbibes the cynicism of both parents, even though he does not learn until much later that Gottdank is his father. He is aware only that Saul "blows into town" long enough to fleece Lizzie, who passively allows his exploitation so that she may later complain that fate is persecuting her. Neither Dahlberg (the fictional persona in the story) nor Dahlberg himself seems at all aware that Lizzie set herself up. Both mother and son prefer to believe that their lives are blighted. Like Byron's Manfred, Dahlberg became convinced that "Nobody can endure his own happiness" (p. 32), and the narrator emulates his mother's behavior by becoming hypersensitive to insult, hostile to the opposite sex, and generally neurotic. With few reserves herself, Lizzie is unable to deal with his bizarre behavior:

> All that Lizzie could understand was that the child of her profligacy vomited and that he would grow up ugly. Sometimes she would whip him in an endeavor to force him to take food; but the act of eating, and thinking about what his teeth did, made him irreparably ill. Who can consider the carcasses he puts into his mouth? (p. 41)

On the surface, Lizzie seems highly solicitous but in truth her own self-interests inform her actions. As life threatens to overwhelm her, she can conceive of redemption only through marriage to a wealthy man. The thought of "loving" a man, however, seems alien to her, since she cannot imagine a relationship that is not exploitative. Thus she continues to submit to Gottdank's humiliations: "Saul cared only for low-class women. . . . [He] wanted money to hire pleasure, and Lizzie gave him that as well as her body" (pp. 42-43).

Lizzie's longing for a normal, middle-class existence is false, since she sabotages every sincere marriage proposal. Her best friend is the two-timing Emma Moneysmith, from whom she tries to learn the art of swindling men. But in one instance she chooses the wrong victim, a baker named Harry Cohen, who, after vaguely promising matrimony, tricks her into buying him a livery stable, which he insures (in his name) against fire and then burns. Lizzie seems to invite such disasters, since she "could withstand almost anything except the promise or assurance of a windfall. No matter how absurd the scheme, she was ready to believe in it, and this looked like a sound business investment" (p. 55). In other words, Lizzie thrived on being miserable.

Dahlberg represented himself at nine as already the "prey of Eros" as he listens, with mixed fascination and disgust, to his mother copulating in the room next to his. Preoccupation with carnality will haunt him for the rest of his life: "The greed for voluptuous sensation is a disease. Who invented the torments of the testicles? Had he the nature for it, he would have renounced the lunacy called sensuality. Pleasure is the tickling of the maggots that ravin upon the bones" (p. 57).

The boy also becomes faintly aware of "culture," which his mother, with her smattering of "refined" German, admires but does not understand. But this, like any other pleasure, young Dahlberg associates with sickness and death. While he is reading of the murder of Emma Moneysmith, killed by a cowboy whose money belt she was trying to rob, he comes upon the obituary and picture of Leo Tolstoy. For no reason he can comprehend, "the boy was so pierced by the death of this savant, of whom he had never heard before, that he wondered and asked: 'Who was Leo Tolstoi?' " (p. 59). The kinship Dahlberg felt for the Russian was mostly with the Tolstoy of *The Kreuzer Sonata,* possibly the most misogynic novel ever written.

Lizzie's business is precarious, and her one marriage (to Popkin) fails, but *Because I Was Flesh* portrays her greatest burden as her "adhesive child," who "was the burden of Tyre to himself. He had all the disgusts of his environment without any of the health of the place" (p. 61). Into his unsatisfying (but, we sense, rather secure) world intrudes Henry Smith, a Kentucky riverboat captain who entertains the mother but loathes the boy. The child, who is desperate for a father, clings to Smith, who responds by convincing Lizzie to have him ejected from the house. Too late she learns that the blustery captain is but another parasite, exceedingly stingy (though he earns a fabulous two hundred and fifty dollars a month) and that she is doomed to support him. Edward, not quite twelve years old, is shipped off to the grisly Jewish Orphan Asylum.

At the home, number 92 (as Dahlberg refers to his fictional persona throughout the orphanage chapters), finds himself subjected to the deprivations and humiliations characteristic of prisons: mail is censored; movements are restricted; and tin cups and plates are used while the boys and girls eat at what they call "convict tables" (p. 68).

Dahlberg's treatment of the orphanage, which he felt had blighted his life, has been dealt with extensively in Chapter I of this book.[11] In *Because I Was Flesh,* he selected memories which reinforced his impression of the home as a brutal work camp whose employees and inmates deliberately singled him out for persecution. Certainly this mama's boy, shielded from any broad human contact, was an easy mark. When number 92 arrives, tall, gawky, and painfully shy, the tough, runty orphans can scarcely contain their sadistic glee.

But number 92 has no appetite for the struggle for survival into which he is plunged. Pining for his mother, he vomits and faints. He writes to her as often as regulations allow, begging her to take him back to the streets of Cleveland: "He was no stoic and wept, because he had no choice, and at the age of eleven one of the few illusions that he still had was that one could do what one wanted to do" (p. 70).

Only after his release from the asylum does number 92 feel entitled to resume the name Edward Dahlberg, although the sense of anonymity he has acquired during his years of abandonment continues to plague him. As if the semifictional Dahlberg is straining for an identity, he begins narrating his autobiography in the first person, where formerly he had done so in the third. Upon returning home, the young man finds that his six-year absence from Kansas City has made him far more sensitive to the squalor of his mother's trade and her attachment to the loathsome Henry Smith, who continues to bleed her:

> I could no longer bear to watch my mother fawn upon an old codger in smelly, bepissed overalls, and I cringed when she announced: "Star Lady Barbershop, you're next, sir." What would I have given not to eructate, piss, gender, grunt and hiccough: yet, according to Aristophanes, Zeus urinates. (p. 93)

Still, young Dahlberg remains the heir of his mother's predatory nature. He covets knowledge, but mainly to impress women. Only later does he conclude that all women are "tarts," incapable of being "serious and reflective": "How often have I lost unusual raptures because I was polite and taken for a weakling; I can be so excessively civil that I am able to persuade a light woman that she is really a prude" (p. 103). "Carl Waller," Farrell's parody of Dahlberg, could easily have made this pompous statement (see Chapter IV).

Eager to shed his virginity, but so hostile to women that he shuns the polite young women of Kansas City, young· Dahlberg visits a prostitute, who gives him an even greater feeling of inner vacancy than before. Indeed, the stigma of prostitution still hangs upon his mother with her now useless, bedridden lover. Smith no longer persecutes Dahlberg (who is now a fully grown man), but his presence still irks the son who covets all his mother's attention. He finds consolation in imagining that Lizzie is Mary Magdalene, a "virtuous prostitute," who is sacrificing herself for this obscene, gluttonous sinner. But after Lizzie finally throws Smith out—and Dahlberg can finally enjoy her all to himself—he finds himself hastily fleeing her endless tales of woe. With money borrowed from her, he boards a train to Omaha.

Dahlberg recognizes, although faintly, that his flight is for self-preservation: "I was fleeing her to find my life." But geographical distance does not resolve his dependence on this most powerful character in his life: "Wherever I was, I endeavored to perceive her nose, mouth and eyes, maimed by the driest of gods, hopelessness." Shy and unable to make conversation, he quickly fails as a traveling salesman: "I thought I smelled because I was separated from everybody." But his true problem again confronts him—his aversion to gainful (or at least rough) employment:

> I had no trade; I was no vintner, miller, harness maker, fuller, or tailor. Already plagued by ennui, I had no desire to perform futile or bestial work. What could I do that would not sink my faculties? Could I shed Adam's guilt by simply toiling, though the products I made were loathsome and immoral? (pp. 115-16)

Though still in his adolescence, Dahlberg simply gives up. He sells his wristwatch and accepts a twelve-dollar gift sent by Lizzie, but by this time he is a confirmed hobo, wracked by self-pity. He leaves a hotel bill unpaid and jumps freight trains to Green River, Wyoming; Ogden, Utah; and the Mojave Desert. Ragged and filthy, he arrives in Needles, California, certain he has hit rock bottom:

> What had I gained from my misfortunes? I crept into coal cars, and snow, hail and rain were my roof. . . . My suit was a sickness; the moth sighed in my shirt and trousers. I was threadbare, hungered when I ate and imprisoned when I was free. . . . Was I wandering on a peopleless comet without herbs, grass or ocean? How much punishment can the body take without corrupting the spirit? (p. 119)

Like Christ, Dahlberg emerges from the desert, but not before framing a precept: "The worst misery is not an empty belly, but a vacant mind: the fell pain of not seeing" (pp. .122-23).

To restore his vision, Dahlberg, "clad in moth-eaten penury," journeys to the greatest metropolis he has ever visited—Los Angeles. His first impression is that the city "is a sewer of Sodom, though it once had been a grove at Lebanon." As his loneliness again threatens to overwhelm him, he projects his sorrow onto his surroundings:

Some afternoons I visited that plaguy plot of cement surrounding a few scurrile patches of grass called Pershing Square. Almost every American park is a lewd tryptich composed of a cannon, a sign reading KEEP OFF THE GRASS and a homosexual. Cruddled pederasts and sulphured hermaphrodites slouched on the benches, waiting to ambush an urchin who had just come to town by freight train from Columbus or Detroit. (p. 125)

Dahlberg's fear of homosexual assault is coupled with his terror of losing his seductive prowess—already he is growing bald. His confidence is buoyed, however, by a chance meeting with another veteran of the orphan asylum, Lao Tsu Ben (Max Lewis), with whom he developes an idolatrous friendship. Tsu Ben responds solicitously: "I was the most original fool he had ever encountered. A crazy waif of the Muses, I was one of his most remarkable pastimes" (p. 128). Dahlberg is as attentive to his mentor as an impassioned lover:

He took the greatest care in shaving his handsome, peaked face and dusting powder on his pimpled cheeks; were I in the room while he was making his toilet, I always managed somehow to step on his shoes which he had just shined, or to jostle him so that he cut his chin. Had he not found me so droll, he would have gotten rid of me forthwith. (p. 128)

Dahlberg's life is transformed by the impact of Tsu Ben upon him, but not even this formidable intellectual can overcome his disciple's horror of sexuality. Although Dahlberg does not seem to understand that his friend is a most sadistic lover, often a near-rapist who treats women as utensils to gratify his lust, he instinctively shrinks when the older man offers him his cast-off lovers. Dahlberg's alibi is that he fears syphilis.

Superficially, Dahlberg seems to glory in Tsu Ben's brutality toward females. With wit and bravado he brags of his tutor's adultery: "Lao Tsu Ben was a gourmet in feminine flesh. He would not couple with a woman whose husband had a corrupt breath . . . nor did he relish a bedmate who hiccoughed, eructated or sneezed—unless she was moved to do so while he was lying with her" (p. 135). But Dahlberg's subliminal instincts again tell him that his friend is on the wrong track: dissipation, especially sexual excess, is destroying him. He is wracked by disease and obsessed with old age and poverty at the age of twenty-four. Dahlberg notes, not without satisfaction, that Lao Tsu Ben, in his older and wealthier days, became a misanthrope and recluse, "While I remained a beggar, with windmills in my brain, going to and fro in the lazar house of literature for a few pennies a page" (pp. 137-41). Just as Tsu Ben's decay is the logical outcome of his dissipation, so Dahlberg's lofty aspirations bring him Don Quixote's fate.

The narrator benefits from one opportune piece of advice from Tsu Ben—that he ripen his talents at the University of California. He arrives in Berkeley feeling much superior to the "intellectuals" at this "academic dump":

> I soon found that the work and the talk in the classes at Berkeley were tiresome and bootless. I had chosen one course in botany, and the lectures were given by such a drab that the notes I had jotted down on paper I gave to the goats, who devoured them. Any love of natural history was spoiled for me for at least a generation: I would never have believed that I would some day go to the works of Buffon, Humboldt and Darwin with such joy. (pp. 142-43)

Intent on ignoring his courses, Dahlberg concentrates on libidinal pursuits. Hardly free of his virginity, he is as bumbling a lover as Don Quixote. His first attempted conquest is an "erotic morsel" named Angelica, who is the lover of a graduate student. Dahlberg, however, chooses to ignore this aspect of his Dulcinea's life: "Some days I haunted the library waiting for this maiden. I could not think of her otherwise, for every woman who is loved is a virgin, and her chestnut tresses and slender exhalations were holy to me" (p. 145). So fearful is he of rejection that he fails to make an affirmative move. She disappears with an "ignoramus" who owns a big automobile, whereupon Dahlberg (who by this time has gained some celebrity on campus by publishing his essay, "The Sick, The Pessimist and the Philosopher"), courts Portia Kewling (Kate Carla). But Portia, who is four years older than Dahlberg, prefers the role of mother to that of mistress. He speaks frankly to her of his fantasies, such as that about a fifteen-year-old girl "who took a great fancy to my eccentric haircut," and of his intellectual and literary ambitions. She eventually tires of him, but Dahlberg imagines that he has frustrated her sexually: "Portia began to avoid me—probably because I had not taken her when she forbade me to" (p. 149).

By this time, the narrator Dahlberg seems entirely submerged in fantasy. He continues neglecting his coursework while he resumes stalking Angelica. Seemingly imitating Lao Tsu Ben (or perhaps the lovers of his mother), he "possesses" her by virtually raping her in the Berkeley Hills: "She repelled me with all the vehemence of her body. My hands were surd and numb, and though she was in my embrace, the globe had soured in my flesh. It was an amative battle" (p. 151). Dahlberg would have us believe that the girl comes to enjoy sexual brutality, but his conquest leads him to pain: "Spite of my many days with her, I cannot recollect a single pleasure" (p. 152). Disappointed in Angelica, there is nothing to keep him in California, so he decides to transfer to Columbia University. At this moment, Dahlberg represents himself as having lived twenty-two years without the experience of satisfaction.

On the way to New York, he stops over in Kansas City to see Lizzie, now fifty years old and trying to preserve her youth with cheap henna hair dye. More than ever, her appearance humiliates him as he views her through the eyes of a disappointed lover:

When I regarded the loose, dangling throat and the skin of her face that was beginning to yellow, or looked at a straggling shoelace, I thought no other son was as unfortunate as I. . . . When I considered my mother's privy sheets and illicit pillowcases I abhorred them, though I myself was weaker than grass. (p. 155)

Almost at once, the son begins to shrink from Lizzie's tales of misery—of her operations; her failing health; her "flaccid dropping belly"; and, of course, her persecution by men. As he watches her trying to seduce her cadaverous lovers, his speech takes on suicidal overtones as he nearly understands that his mother is not the perennial victim she claims to be but a predatory and selfish woman:

> My life was a heavy affliction to me at this time; the chasm between my mother and me had widened. I blamed her for everything; whom else could I find fault with except my sole protector? Why had she not provided me with a family? . . . My grievous childhood stuck in my gizzard, and I recalled how Captain Henry Smith had persuaded my mother to send me to an orphanage. (pp. 163-64)

Dahlberg nearly accepts her facile excuses, though he is still eager to punish her: " 'even a worm has a parent, but nobody begat me. I am nothing, and I came out of nowhere,' and I was filled with gall, and layers of grief lay over it" (p. 169). This tirade is suddenly stifled as Dahlberg suddenly endures the cruelest revelation of his life. Crossing the room, he notices a yellowed picture of Saul, "showing the teeth of the fox that spoils the vine." He immediately recognizes this odious man as his father. Renewing his attack, Dahlberg laces his mother with invective that would wither Moses:

> It is Saul! Who else could my father be? I know it is Saul. My blood is ruined; a thousand lusts boil in his skin and in his tumored brain. But where is he? You must know. He is my father. Tell me, I must know . . . or live and die unborn . . . for I will wail all the hours of my flesh if I am unfilled by a father!

Lizzie remains silent. The battle is concluded (p. 170).

Probably because he invented Lizzie's amorous adventures, Dahlberg did not depict his mother's dotard lovers with disgust. Instead, he seized the opportunity to display his skill at writing burlesque. The most outrageous suitor is Tobias Emeritch—a real person, though his actions in the book are Dahlberg's fabrications.[12] Emeritch is one of the most memorable of Dahlberg's characters, combining qualities of Dickens's Uriah Heep with those of Thomas Peacock's Glowry, the "lover of shadows" in *Nightmare Abbey*. He is both a hypochondriac and a devotee of Arthur Schopenhauer: "Whenever I have a little spare time I read him." Lizzie wonders he is dejected all the time! To enliven conversations, which almost always die around him, he complains about his rheumatism. His discourses on the prices of horseradish and sour cream reveal a mind marinated in banalities:

> I wonder what a quart of sour cream brings, or if a barrel of smoked whitefish has gone up since last June? If you are in the market for coleslaw, I could do something for you, or should you be interested in pickles—dill or sweet, wrinkled ones, it makes no difference to me . . . I'm a retired manufacturer of pickles, myself.

Lizzie counters this bathos with a sense of humor we have never seen in her before in Dahlberg's works. Recalling an earlier suitor, who "had a ketchup factory in the West Bottoms and that he had a similar kind of bent-in pot of a head and that his nose resembled a potato," Lizzie puts some saucy questions to Emeritch: "Are you in the ketchup trade also? Are you positive, sir, that you don't have an uncle or a distant cousin who's a wholesaler in sauces, relishes or cucumbers?" Tobias misses her sarcasm and blithely launches another digression.

After dismissing Emeritch, mostly because he is an undertaker who stirs her ever present fears of death, Lizzie makes no more sincere attempts at securing a mate. Only one candidate remains: "Maybe—and she shook her head mournfully—her son would return from New York where he was teaching. Was he not a buffer between her and every cruel mischance? Her own flesh and blood would shield her from old age."

We are not surprised, at this time, to find Dahlberg thinking along very similar lines. Heroically, he forms a resolution: "My mother must not be taken by surprise: I will watch over her with the spear and javelin of the mind" (p. 187).

A somber tone descends as Lizzie's death approaches. Dahlberg explains the final ignominy of her death without conviction: "My mother was born unfortunate, and she was pursued by that evil genius, ill luck" (p. 233). Her life had indeed been wretched, although Dahlberg seems to realize that no one will easily believe that bad luck was alone responsible. More for his own benefit than for Lizzie's, it would seem, some form of redemption must be contrived to clear her record, even if only in the imagination of her son. To consummate her life, she must find a man worthy of herself, and she does, in a remarkable dream. Just before his mother's death, the son is visited in his sleep by "Jesus the Paraclete": "The sensual, auburn curls of Saul crowned his head, but the face was dominated by the long Nazarene nose of my mother." Dahlberg askes this specter, his twin, "Art thou Jesus?" and the answer comes, "I am Yeshu of Nazareth." Believing it holds the clue to his own confused identity, he questions the doppelgänger about its parentage. The ghost, unsure about this information, replies: "My real mother must have been Miriam Megaddela Neshaya, Mary Magdalen, the women's hairdresser, because I loved her more than anyone on earth." Jesus's mother, Mary Magdalene, rather than Mary the Virgin, according to Dahlberg, was a barber like Lizzie! As Mary the Prostitute ascends the throne of Queen of Heaven, the devil Saul is exorcised by Lizzie-Mary:

> These words were nails in my eyes and they pained me so bitterly that I could not see the voluptuous ringlets of Saul. Did Miriam Megaddela, the lady barber who had dressed Yeshu's locks also shave and manicure customers in Memphis, Louisville, New Orleans, and Dallas? . . . Who was sitting in her chair—the Nazarene or I? (pp. 217-18)

As the dream fantasy continues, Dahlberg comes to understand that Yeshu, like himself, is an illegitimate waif, so solitary in this world that he cannot count even the twelve disciples as his friends: like Dahlberg, Jesus is unable to maintain close relationships. Jesus is also perplexed over his father's identity: "Was your mother Miriam the adultress? Did she lie with Joseph's groomsman?" So painful has his life been that Jesus inhabits the world of dreams rather than reality: "the only magic I ever practiced was the sorcery of the dream. When a man slumbers, he can perform miracles" (pp. 217-19).

The slumbering Dahlberg, now secure in his complete identification with Christ, is transported to the site of his mother's barbershop as Jesus chants its address, "16 East 8," ". . . for both the address and the name Jehovah are made up of seven characters." Miraculously, Lizzie suddenly appears as Mary Magdalene, while Dahlberg, whose identity merges with that of Jesus, finally succeeds in displacing Saul from his mother's affections: " 'Yeshu! Yeshu!' I cried, clinging to the curls of Saul, but before I could open my eyes, I saw that my lips were on my mother's long, Galilean nose, and I whispered in her ear, 'Miriam Megaddela Neshaya, the lady barber, oh my mother!' "

Having undergone this ritualistic "marriage" to his mother, Dahlberg awakens, "but the vision of Miriam was still before my eyes, and in my ears I heard the refrain of 16 East 8. . . ." Rlene Dahlberg remembered being so shocked by the incestuous quality of this passage that she asked her husband, "Do you know what you wrote in that last chapter, Edward?" Quickly, he retorted: "I know what I wrote!" [13]

Lizzie dies her pitiful lonely death, but in the book she is purified, delivered from the squalor and disappointment which had characterized her life, both by her suffering and by her union with the only male who ever truly loved her—her son. And Dahlberg, seeming to realize that he has clung fast to this woman who maimed him, apostrophizes his dead mother:

> When the image of her comes up on a sudden—just as my bad demons do—and I see again her dyed henna hair, the eyes dwarfed by the electric lights in the Star Lady Barbershop, and the dear broken wing of her mouth, and when I regard her wild tatters, I know that not even Solomon in his lilied raimant was so glorious as my mother in her rags. *Selah.* (pp. 233-34)

With *Because I Was Flesh,* Dahlberg had finally told his story in a manner satisfying both to him and to the public. But now that his publishing prospects were good, he had little fresh material to offer. Domestic turmoil interfered with his writing; after their return from Europe in 1966 Rlene found herself an apartment on Avenue B, near where she was teaching high school on the Lower East Side of New York, and she located Dahlberg and Julia Lawlor nearby on Rivington Street. *Ca'n Peretons* was left in charge of Irving Rosenthal, who finished his novel, *Sheeper,* there.[14]

The Rivington Street apartment, though inexpensive, proved to be a dramatic contrast with the peaceful cottage in Sóller, which Dahlberg had left for good. On Rivington Street, Lizzie had first met Dahlberg's father before the turn of the century. It would seem Dahlberg's life had come full circle: in his sixties he returned to his youth in his writings and in his residence and to his mother with whom in death he carried on his love-hate affair. He was living with a young woman with highly developed maternal instincts—Julia Lawlor was a fine cook, a skilled seamstress, as well as a trained nurse who could responsibly administer the drugs that he came to depend on more and more for the rest of his life.

Although Dahlberg had again made New York City his permanent home, he did not relinquish his life as an "urban nomad." [15] A grant from the Rockefeller Foundation brought him to the attention of the University of Missouri, located in his hometown of Kansas City. Although his appointment as writer in residence was for the spring semester of 1965,[16] Dahlberg found that he was less able than ever to adhere to the routines of the classroom, and he resigned after a few weeks and returned to New York, where Rlene was finishing assembling a book of his aphorisms, *Reasons of the Heart,* which was published in 1965 by Horizon Press. Culled from his correspondence and from his earlier works, the maxims illustrate themes which are woven throughout Dahlberg's writing. In a chapter entitled "On Writers and Writing," the gallows humor comes forth: "A painter can hang his pictures, but a writer can only hang himself." "On Love and Friendship" finds the author as cynical as ever about human relationships: "We are uneasy with an affectionate man, for we are positive he wants something of us, particularly our love" (p. 16). His distrust of sexuality is outlined under "On Lust": "What man's head would do is always defeated by his scrotum"; "Disease came into the world when man looked upon the skin of woman" (pp. 23-26). According to Dahlberg, "The only intelligence that a woman has is her body, and when she thinks with that she knows more than Aristotle" (p. 30). Yet, women think far too energetically: "No matter what a man may do he cannot force his wife to be honest, because she is a clandestine animal" (p. 34). The book, however, lacks the energy of his earlier writing and sags under the weight of the author's growing contempt for humanity: "The supreme happiness of the ordinary man is an easy bowel movement" (p. 74).

*   *   *

"Everyone completes his life when he quenches his appetite. After that, he resumes his life as an ambulatory cadaver." —Edward Dahlberg, September 16, 1972.

*   *   *

Though he planned two more volumes of his autobiography, Dahlberg's best material had gone into *Because I Was Flesh*. Now in the middle of his seventh decade, he became more and more sensitive to criticism and Dahlberg could find no editor willing to spend the enormous effort required to reduce his manuscripts and weather his increasingly explosive rages. Rlene alone continued as his part-time editor until *Cipango's Hinder Door,* a collection of verse, was published in 1966.[17] On June 9, 1967, the Dahlbergs obtained a quick Mexican divorce, and on June 13 he married Julia. ("The thirteenth hour of the thirteenth day of June '67—three thirteens in a row, that's me!" Julia wryly quipped.[18])

With his seventh and last wife, Dahlberg honeymooned in Dublin, Julia's city of birth, while Dahlberg's publications began to appear with unprecedented frequency. *Epitaphs of Our Times,* which collected many of Dahlberg's letters from 1937 to 1962, appeared in 1967, as did the *Edward Dahlberg Reader,*[19] a retrospective miscellany selected from Dahlberg's letters and published works, and *The Leafless American,* another miscellany. Though *The Confessions of Edward Dahlberg* received a review by Hilton Kramer on page one of the *New York Times* Sunday Book Section,[20] Dahlberg suspected his force had been dissipated. Patched together largely from material cut from *Because I Was Flesh,* the *Confessions* lacked the strong narrative line and tight editing of the earlier book. While diehard Dahlbergites rushed to praise the *Confessions* (which is less an Augustinian self-revelation than a series of farces and character assassinations), it remained unread by the public at large and, like most of Dahlberg's publications from 1967 on, was remaindered.

Edward and Julia, 1969. (Courtesy of Bernard Gotfryd.)

Nonetheless, Dahlberg did not consent to live out his life as "an ambulatory cadaver"—even if his prose was moribund, his appetites were not. Improved finances plus the constant and devoted attentions of Julia kept his illnesses at bay and gave him the opportunity to make new friends he desperately craved. On an earlier trip to Ireland, he made the acquaintance of the Hon. Garech Browne, heir to the Guinness fortune, and Dahlberg found himself spending numerous hours with the cultivated and urbane young man and his circle at Luggala, Browne's Dublin estate. Though Browne collected many anecdotes about Dahlberg, none amused or perplexed him more than when he heard Dahlberg intimate to a Jesuit priest that he had always been attracted to religion and wanted to be buried a Catholic. The good father, knowing Dahlberg's reputation, offered to do the job free of charge.[21]

The most important friend of Dahlberg's declining years, however, was Coburn Britton, with whom Dahlberg allowed himself perhaps the closest relationship of his life. A man of independent means, Britton had subsidized Horizon Press (where *Reasons of the Heart* had been published), and later founded an elegant magazine named *Prose,* dedicated to the propagation of beautiful English, of which, he thought, Dahlberg's was often a model. *Prose* gave Dahlberg (who appeared in all but one issue) the forum he needed as well as additional income. Britton, whom Dahlberg came to speak of as his "son" (after having renounced his two sons by Winifred), paid frequent visits to the older man and dedicated himself to seeing that the power of Dahlberg's "baroque" prose be felt in modern literature. Britton wrote:

Given words, lots of them, one can say, be, more of what one cares to say or be. And, generally speaking, one has a greater opportunity to do that if one has a broad vocabulary, supple and formed. E.g., I care not a whit for Edward Dahlberg's stoicism, but I care for his passionate use of the tongue which, if you will dwell on *this,* belies that stoicism. Now that is where his largeness lies. And what I mean by "Baroque" (an epicene epithet) is just that sort of encompassing, formed grandness which language will achieve if it is to go beyond mere thought, mere intellect—in fact its own limitations. There is not much of that prose about.[22]

It is indeed too easy to be put off by Dahlberg's sourness, or to dismiss him as a kind of crank, a romantic beyond romanticism, who thunders and then retreats like Job from the world which refuses to correspond to his fine rhetoric and hidebound idealism. His tendency to view people in the static manner of old-fashioned medicine, seeing "humours," traits, and even phrenology as immutable possessions of people, has all too often repelled younger writers. On the other hand, the very eccentricity of the writing (like that of e. e. cummings) spawns imitators attracted by his pyrotechnics but lacking his talents. Few college English teachers fail to turn up a few bundles of "good, warm, wise and laxative" prose (to paraphrase Herbert Miller) stuffed with Dahlbergisms.

Dahlberg, at times, regarded himself as a genius in a vacuum: "I am my environment," he declared. But as Boyle and Hook discovered, the nearer they got to a complete vacuum, the more difficult it became to achieve one. Nevertheless, the problem with Dahlberg, which we do not encounter with Pound, Joyce, Eliot, and other modern writers, is that Dahlberg's writing is often so intensely isolated and psychogenic that he cannot be related to the literary currents of his time. Pugnacious and agitated like Hazlitt (one of Dahlberg's favorites), he writes in a staccato style of his violent disappointment with women. Like Wilde, he has no coherent system of philosophy: his wit, which surfaces less often than Wilde's, is savage and alienated, with women serving as the frequent scapegoats for his bitterness. Paul Carroll makes an effort to place the "Job of American letters" in the American Puritan tradition:

What strikes the unmistakably indigenous note about Dahlberg's dialogue with the body is that he never celebrates or documents the ecstasies or even the animal delights of the flesh. .... he works at the core of one of the most persistent traditions in American writing—a tradition which he was among the first to define. I allude to the tradition of the morning after the Fall into sexual consciousness: the body, now the adversary, is viewed with suspicion, anger, contempt; violence against the female or against oneself often erupts; the cultivation of an exacerbated state of frustration usually begins. *Omne animale post coitu triste:* this melancholy dogma informs the American classics.[23]

It is not easy, however, to find a being as totally lost and spent as Dahlberg in the history of American literature. In order to link him with a "tradition," one might be forced to turn to Huysmans, whose character Des Esseintes (in *Against the Grain*) rejects nature completely and retreats into a curiously detached limbo like that of Dahlberg. Huysmans, however, finally found consolation in Anglo-Catholicism, while Dahlberg remained far from any faith.

Other writers, such as Holbrook Jackson (in *The Anatomy of Bibliomania*), Ronald Firbank, and Djuna Barnes, have, like Dahlberg, constructed strangely archaic prose styles, but the first three were mostly striving for some comic effect. None of them, like Dahlberg, fought so strenuously to move forward by plunging into the past. None ever let his method overwhelm him to the point where readers were discouraged.

Yet Dahlberg, at his best, is a stunningly appealing writer whose influence can be seen in many younger writers. Irving Rosenthal, one of Dahlberg's most steadfast admirers, flamboyantly outlined his debt to Dahlberg, in *Sheeper,* much of which was written at Dahlberg's home on Mallorca:

> Read Edward Dahlberg but pay no attention to anything he says. He is so critical and cantankerous, so grum, small, and jealous, that if you took him at all seriously, he would drive you as batty as he is. The quotations he burdens his work with are never to the point, and, as he is incapable of placing two sentences in logical order, such a thing as a quiet, scholarly paragraph, let alone essay or chapter is outside his reach. But he is *the* poet of sentence design. . . . [I have] thrown myself at his feet, for he is a great pure writer in the sense he will sacrifice any meaning however important he may have made it out to be for any flourish or conceit, and he would sell his soul to the devil and mine too for the power to write one

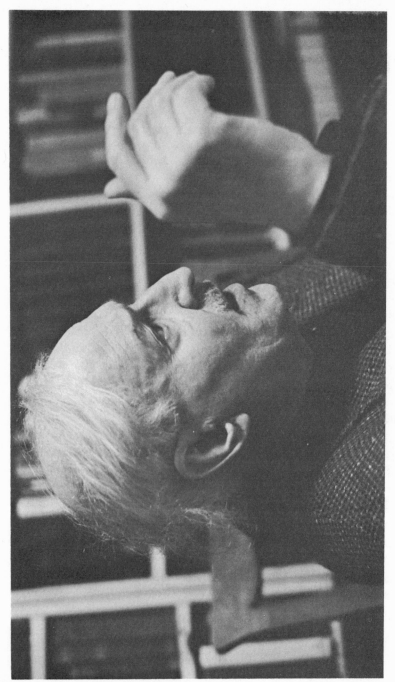

West 75th Street, 1969. (Courtesy of Bernard Gotfryd.)

unalterably beautiful sentence. Read him for vocabulary, too, though he never coins words, his motto being "Rob graves, don't make babies." [24]

Another admitted disciple, Alexander Trocchi, clearly reflects Dahlberg's tone of writing as well as his syntax in *Cain's Book* (whose title he took from *The Sorrows of Priapus:* "Cain was a profligate and all malcontents are licentious."): "Whatever I write is written deep into my own ignorance. And I find myself cultivating a certain crudity of expression, judging it to be essential to meaning, in an age vital to the efficacy of the language." [25] Perhaps the finest young writer working in the same aphoristic style as Dahlberg is William O'Rourke, born in Kansas City, who was one of Dahlberg's closest companions during the 1970s. O'Rourke's prose shows only a trace of archaism, while he retains the sensual character and often biblical lushness of the best of the older writer's work. O'Rourke praised his friend and teacher in an obituary that complimented Dahlberg both in form and in substance:

> A good many people had been waiting for him to die. A small cottage industry has developed in the literary world of telling outrageous Dahlberg tales: of offense taken and given, of majestic rudeness, and sidereal insult. The good stories, alas, are often not interred with the bones. . . . What can you say about a 77-year-old author who has died? . . . That Edward Dahlberg was a Man of Letters, not of the World. That he was quite crazy at times, from a combination of drugs and bodily ills. And, that he was always kind to me, even kind enough to suggest that I had plagiarized *Because I Was Flesh.* [26]

On the whole, however, Dahlberg's isolation and loneliness have followed him beyond the grave. The very eccentricity which brought him fame has made it difficult or forbidding for younger writers to learn from him. Other writers continue to heighten and mythologize their everyday experiences, but none so far has attempted to do so with the grandiloquent panache of Dahlberg.

As life became easier for Dahlberg—he was elected to the National Institute of Arts and Letters and received grants from the

Rockefeller Foundation and PEN International—his discomfort with his physical surroundings again grew intolerable. Several sojourns in Europe did not ease his agitation, until finally, in 1970, he accepted the suggestion of an admirer to buy a home in Sarasota, on Florida's western coast. Within a few weeks, the admirer was not speaking to Dahlberg and he was complaining to Coburn Britton of the "putrescent gulf" filled with "saprogenic fishes." He was soon gaunt and pale from several acute ulcer attacks and many bouts of anger, during one of which he brandished a nickel-plated pistol. In March 1972, the Dahlbergs subleased a small apartment from a college professor, and later found themselves a narrow, coffinlike apartment on East Ninety-first Street in New York City. Visitors were surprised to find Dahlberg, in his sparsely furnished quarters, almost invariably sitting in bed, with the air conditioner running both summer and winter: he desperately feared air pollution. Many came away with the impression that he was alone with his books wildly scattered on every surface and his giant television set. Julia was generally restricted to the tiny bedroom, with the 150 unopened cartons of books which Dahlberg had accumulated and moved across the Atlantic many times over the years. He had grown so wildly possessive of his wife that those few men allowed to meet her dared not look at her for fear of being accused of having "wanton desires." Visitors could enjoy an excellent meal when Julia was allowed to be present, but more often the fare was delicatessen roast chicken and pickles. Julia frequently fled her husband's verbal and physical abuse, but she could never leave him permanently.

By 1974, Dahlberg's few remaining friends in New York had either stopped seeing him or had terminated their relationships with violent quarrels. Nagging telephone calls and ever increasing demands caused even Coburn Britton to restrict his friendship with Dahlberg. Only Nick Ellison, Dahlberg's editor at Thomas Y. Crowell, continued to see him with any regularity, though Dahlberg understood that this relationship was mostly a business one. Consigned to the absolute loneliness to which he had finally doomed himself, and certain that he would never obtain a new lease on his apartment (neighbors were complaining about Dahlberg's noisy, often multiday tantrums), he and Julia left New

York for good and moved to Santa Barbara, California. By 1976, Dahlberg's energy was sapped by his age, his inner conflict, and the long-standing grudges he had nursed so fiercely. He looked stricken and old, and those, like his old friend and advocate, Harold Billings, who maintained telephone contact with him, noticed only fatigue and exasperation in his once rich voice. He even abandoned his chaotic notetaking and writing. Television became both his pastime and his obsession: his last writing efforts were madcap and pathetic attempts to parody TV commercials.

Dahlberg was taken to the hospital nine times during the last two years of his life—seven times with slight strokes, once for a hernia operation, and once for a stomach hemorrhage. At times he could not get himself into bed, and when Julia could not lift him she was often obliged to call passersby or the police to assist her. During his worst days, she was forced to bathe him in bed, shave him, and brush his teeth, but he would not permit her to hire any outside help.[27]

As 1977 approached, Dahlberg seemingly reversed himself on one major sore point in his life. He seriously considered traveling to Cleveland for the JOH/Bellefaire reunion, July 2 to July 4. Emil Palmer wrote: "Just think of it, Edward during his entire lifetime had very little feeling toward the 'Home,' but many times when a person realizes that his life is nearing the end, [he] decides to make peace with himself and his former inmates." [28] On page 22 of the bulletin of this reunion is one of the last photographs taken of Dahlberg, with a quotation thought to be typical of his work:

> At 20 you know nothing about women, but you don't realize it; at 40 you know nothing about women, but imagine you are not as ignorant as you were; at 60 you have no knowledge of women and can be enchanted for no more than two to three days. After that it is ennui, two bored people . . . together. . . .

On February 17, 1977 Dahlberg took a nasty fall, after which he began complaining of pains in his side. Lung congestion followed, but he refused hospitalization even though he needed oxygen every day. Doctors warned that Julia would soon follow him to the sickbed if she were forced to care for him alone, but he seemed determined to die at home: he trusted no one but Julia.[29]

Lizzie had died in February, "the month known as Shebat in
Hebrew, which is a time of tears and lamentations,"[30] and
Dahlberg had always been terrified of that month. Ironically, he
was feeling unusually chipper, singing some of his parodies of TV
commercials, when he went to bed on the evening of Saturday,
February 26. But on the morning of the twenty-seventh (a
Sunday—the day of the week Dahlberg most despised), Julia could
not awaken him. An electric blanket had kept his body warm, so
she did not immediately suspect that he had died, but Dahlberg
had quietly suffocated from lung congestion during the night. He
was buried at 2:30 on February 28 at Santa Barbara Cemetery. A
rabbi officiated, not a Catholic priest.[31] O'Rourke later supplied a
fitting epitaph, which does not appear on Dahlberg's gravestone:
"For whatever Dear Readers there are now, or are to come,
Edward Dahlberg wrote 18 books and one masterpiece that will
endure; at the end of his long life he had less than six people he
would have called friend."[32]

NOTES

1. Quoted in letter: John Cech, Oct. 9, 1974.
2. R. W. Flint, "Dahlberg's Wisdom," *New York Review of Books,* 1 (March 19, 1964), 4.
3. Daniel Aaron, "Out of a Dark Wood," *Hudson Review,* 17 (Summer 1964), 315.
4. Interview: E. D., Jan. 14, 1973.
5. Interviews: E. D., Dec. 31, 1972, and Jan. 11, 1973. Emphasis mine.
6. Interview: E. D., Sept. 7, 1973. Luiga Miller included certain elements of the earlier novel in her dramatization of *Because I Was Flesh,* entitled *Mia Madre Lizzie.* Dahlberg was displeased with the production and prevented its opening.
7. "The Wages of Risk," rev. of *Bottom Dogs* (1961) and *Because I Was Flesh, Nation,* 198 (Mar. 30, 1964), 331-33.
8. Interview: E. D., Oct. 17, 1973.
9. Interview: E. D., Oct. 17, 1973.
10. Interview: E. D., Nov. 5, 1972.
11. The orphanage section, by far the most remarkable episode in *Because I Was Flesh,* is rendered with remarkable economy. It occupies fewer than seventy-five pages, while the corresponding episode in *Bottom Dogs* is eighty-three pages in length and far less gripping.

12. Interview: E. D., Jan. 31, 1973.
13. Interview: Rlene Dahlberg, May 22, 1972.
14. Letter: Irving Rosenthal, Nov. 15, 1972. Interview: Rlene Dahlberg, Sept. 9, 1973.
15. Interview: E. D., Sept. 14, 1973.
16. University of Missouri at Kansas City *Bulletin*, 30 (Mar. 29, 1966), 6.
17. (Austin: University of Texas Press, 1966.)
18. (New York: Braziller, 1967.) These letters have been cited throughout this study.
19. Ed. Paul Carroll (New York: New Directions, 1967).
20. Jan. 31, 1971, Section 7.
21. Interview: Garech Browne, Nov. 1, 1972.
22. Letter: Coburn Britton, Aug. 2, 1972.
23. *The Edward Dahlberg Reader*, pp. xx-xxi.
24. (New York: Grove Press, 1967), pp. 122-23.
25. *San Francisco Review of Books*, III (March, 1978), 24.
26. (New York: Thomas Y. Crowell, 1974), p. 101.
27. Letter: Julia Dahlberg, Mar. 7, 1977.
28. Letter: Emil Palmer, June 23, 1977.
29. Letter: Julia Dahlberg, Mar. 7, 1977.
30. Quoted in Harold Billings, Introduction, *Bottom Dogs, From Flushing to Calvary, Those Who Perish*, p. xix.
31. Letter: Julia Dahlberg, Mar. 7, 1977.
32. "Edward Dahlberg: 1900-1977 (On the Occasion of the First Anniversary of His Death)," *San Francisco Review of Books*, III (March, 1978), 24.

Dahlberg and DeFanti, Fire Island, 1973. (Courtesy of Julia Dahlberg.)

Index